999
—
24

MW01098322

Rich Johnson's
Guide to
Wilderness
Survival

Jared,
I hope you enjoy this book.
Stay Safe!
Rich

Rich Johnson's Guide to Wilderness Survival

How to Avoid Trouble and How to Live Through the Trouble You Can't Avoid

McGraw Hill

New York   Chicago   San Francisco   Lisbon   London   Madrid   Mexico City
Milan   New Delhi   San Juan   Seoul   Singapore   Sydney   Toronto

The McGraw·Hill Companies

Library of Congress Cataloging-in-Publication Data

Johnson, Richard, 1947 Aug. 6-
    Rich Johnson's guide to wilderness survival : how to avoid trouble and how to live
through the trouble you can't avoid / Rich Johnson.
        p.   cm.
    Includes index.
    ISBN 0-07-158833-7
    1. Wilderness survival—Handbooks, manuals, etc.   2. Outdoor recreation—
Handbooks, manuals, etc.

    GV200.5.J67   2008
    613.6'9—dc22   2008006923

Copyright © 2009 by Richard Johnson. All rights reserved. Printed in the United States of America. Except as permitted under the United States Copyright Act of 1976, no part of this publication may be reproduced or distributed in any form or by any means, or stored in a database or retrieval system, without the prior written permission of the publisher.

1 2 3 4 5 6 7 8 9 10 11 12 13 14 15 16 17 18 19 20 21   DOC/DOC   0 9 8

ISBN 978-0-07-158833-1
MHID   0-07-158833-7

Interior design by Think Design Group LLC

McGraw-Hill books are available at special quantity discounts to use as premiums and sales promotions or for use in corporate training programs. To contact a representative, please visit the Contact Us pages at www.mhprofessional.com.

The information contained in this book is intended to provide helpful and informative material on the subject addressed. It is not intended to serve as a replacement for professional medical advice. A health care professional should be consulted regarding your specific situation. Neither McGraw-Hill nor the author shall have any responsibility for any adverse effects that arise directly or indirectly as a result of the information provided in this book.

This book is printed on acid-free paper.

For my wife, Becky, who was courageous enough to go with me to the cave and faithful enough to stick it out when lizards were on the menu. She's the girl of my dreams   always has been, always will be. And to our children. Sharlene and Eric were babies when we went into the wilderness. Ryan and Shane came along later to complete the team. Above everything else, our family makes life worth living.

Contents

Preface

It was February. Our breath hung in the air, a lifeless cloud of moisture that only moments before was inside the warmth of our lungs. All the trees looked dead, their gray, decaying leaves frozen to the ground. The stream was solid enough to walk on, and the stone walls of the cave we moved into were bitter as the inside of a freezer.

We had come to the wilds of southern Utah's slickrock country to live for a year. The ancient Anasazi had once dwelt among these same canyons. Our daughter Sharlene was three years old, and our son Eric was just a year. Later in life, when Eric explained to friends how he learned to walk while living in a cave, he took some flak for making up such a story. But it was all true.

The kids were too young to understand what was happening or to protest if they didn't like the idea. But my wife, Becky, was the real hero in our true-life adventure, supporting my desire to spend a year living in the wilderness in preparation for a career of writing about and teaching primitive living and outdoor survival skills. It was my job to keep us all alive and well during that year of isolated research.

This was no camping trip—it was a time to experience a more primitive lifestyle. We took no sleeping bags, no tent, no camp stove, no lantern, no axe, no saw, and no expedition gear. All we had were the clothes on our backs, and none of that was anything special. We each had a wool blanket, and Becky and I each took a knife. The rest—handmade traps, stone and bone tools, and such—we made from what we found in nature. Much of the time, we lived in an abandoned mine shack, but we also built a wikiup and spent some time testing caves both large and small, a mine shaft, and other expedient shelters.

We carried only a little food—wheat to be ground between stones in ancient style, rice, and a few other staples. Local ranchers who didn't quite understand what we were up to took pity on us and provided other foods as the year progressed. We were fine with that and gladly accepted their generosity—we weren't there, after all, to see if we could find enough food to survive, nor to prove our primitive prowess. We were there to research all that the region offered, and we didn't intend to starve ourselves or our children in the process. We were four consumers and one provider, starting with nearly nothing in a desolate spot. It was challenging, even with the contributed provisions. It was a year of learning not only about outdoor survival, but also about what's important and what isn't. It changed our lives forever.

In this book, I'll tell some stories from our adventure in the wilderness and from other interesting and/or tragic experiences—both ours and other people's. Mostly, I'm going to tell you how to avoid trouble, because prevention is always better than the cure. But you also need to know how to survive in the wilds when everything runs amok. Because if you spend enough time outdoors, the day will come when things will run amok. Guaranteed.

Maybe it'll happen when the canoe rolls over, or you are caught in a sudden storm, or you turn around and nothing looks familiar. When the realization sinks in that you are in trouble, it's likely that you will succumb to a certain level of fear. Your gut will turn over in a curious way, and your mind will race. If you could look at yourself in a mirror at such a time, you would see the face of fear, maybe even panic. And this is when things can go to pot in a hurry.

Read this book, then get yourself prepared for whatever may come. Because as sure as the sun rises in the east, something is coming, and you might as well know how to handle it when it does.

Acknowledgments

This book was long in the birthing process and was influenced by countless individuals along the way. I look back several decades to a botanist who patiently introduced me to wild edible and medicinal plants and taught me how to recognize one from another in each season of the year. That education resulted in some interesting meals at our table, and the experience spawned a passion for learning about primitive hunter-gatherers and how they utilized the natural resources that were available wherever they lived. I greatly value the records kept by visitors to primitive societies all over the world relating how those peoples combine wisdom and knowledge of their environment to thrive in what most "civilized" folks consider unsurvivable conditions.

My agents at Parkeast Literary Agency, Donna Eastman and Gloria Koehler, deserve a standing O for their tireless work in helping me prepare this book for presentation to the publisher. They not only shouldered the heavy load of editing, advising, and marketing, but they were also tremendous cheerleaders, working to keep my spirits high throughout the process.

To Bob Holtzman, acquisitions editor at McGraw-Hill, I offer my heartfelt thanks for his faith in this project, as well as his keen insights and solid expertise in shaping the book into the form it now takes. And to all the others on the McGraw-Hill team who applied their skill to bring this book into existence, I express my grateful appreciation.

Most of all, I thank Becky, the love of my life, for her endless faith and patience as we worked through this project together. Who could have known when we moved into a cave in southern Utah many years ago with two tiny babies that this book would ever come to pass? Even without an assurance that anything would come of our wilderness experience, she stood firmly at my side. Now that we're back in civilization, she keeps me from losing sight of what truly matters in life.

Introduction

A simple one-day hike into the Grand Canyon turned into a twenty-day survival ordeal for a young woman who decided to follow the trail to the bottom of the canyon to visit an Indian village that is a popular attraction for tourists. Park rangers said the survivor missed a turn in the trail and ended up in a side canyon 15 miles away.

Just outside of Salt Lake City, a cross-country skier went for a brief schuss in the hills and canyons near his home. A sudden snowstorm blanketed the area with a heavy layer of fresh snow, and the young man became disoriented in the blizzard conditions. That night, he died of hypothermia. When he was found, the recovery team said that if he had topped just one more ridge he would have been able to see the city lights.

In the Palomar Mountains, a forty-four-year-old man headed into the backcountry in search of his lost godson and became lost himself. Five days later, the man was rescued, 18 pounds lighter after surviving on acorns and freezing through the nights in a rain-soaked parka. The nine-year-old boy who was the original object of the search had become separated from his brothers during a day hike in the Palomar Mountain State Park. His body was recovered after a five-day search.

If someone were to ask you how most survival situations happen, would you say that the highest percentage of people who get into trouble are adventurers on expeditions to exotic and dangerous places? Or would you say that most survival incidents happen during day hikes or short outings in familiar surroundings? If you chose door number two, you would be correct.

Most survival situations arise out of a simple outing in relatively safe surroundings that feel comfortable and nonthreatening to the participants. The perception of a safe and easy outing leads to what is known as *day-hike mentality*, a condition in which people fail to prepare to survive the night (or several nights) in the wilderness because they don't think they'll need to. The rationale is as follows: "Hey, I'm only going on a short hike"—or bike ride or canoe trip (pick your poison)—"and I'll be back in a couple of hours, so why go to all the trouble to pack a bunch of gear with me?"

Day-hike mentality is a killer. And for those who don't actually die as a result of this sort of thinking, day-hike mentality can lead to a lot of misery and anxiety, both on the part of the survivor and for friends and loved ones who have to sit and fret and hope and pray and wonder about the outcome.

Every survival incident comes as a surprise to those involved, and each situation is unique. The survivors have their own set of issues to deal with, whether they are physical, psychological, emotional, or medical. Weather conditions, elevation, latitude, topography, and local plant and animal life all play a role in defining the mix of elements that must be factored into the equation. And then there's the question of equipment, available natural resources, and the experience level and skill of the people caught up in the situation. All of these things have an impact on the outcome—who lives, who dies, and how much privation and suffering there will be.

This book will prepare you to handle outdoor survival situations effectively and minimize adversity. The key to success is to learn the broad concepts and then adapt them to your individual needs. Although I've made every effort to present the best information available on the subject matter covered in this book, the elements of a survival situation are constantly in a state of flux, and you must learn to use what works and discard what doesn't. Be flexible and learn to think both inside and outside the box. But most of all, prepare yourself with knowledge, experience, skill, and the right equipment to get you through the challenges.

Even short outings in the wilderness have the potential to turn into survival incidents that may involve a medical emergency. Whether it's hypothermia, dehydration, drowning, malnutrition, heat stroke, a venomous snake bite, a lightning strike, or a cougar attack that leaves you bloody and wounded, whatever threatens your survival is related to a physiological issue that you are trying either to prevent or resolve. And that brings me to this.

Disclaimer: I'm not a doctor. I don't even play one on TV. Discussion of any medical procedures contained in this book is for information purposes only. Medical procedures change from time to time, and the responsibility rests with you to obtain the latest information about emergency medical diagnosis and treatment and then use your best judgment about how to proceed. The information provided here should not be used to diagnose or treat any medical problem. A licensed physician should be consulted for diagnosis and treatment of all medical conditions.

To be safe and confident in the outdoors, fill your head with the best information, fill your hands with skill, and fill your life with experience. Let knowledge be your guide and common sense your pattern. Do all of that, and wilderness survival will become instinctive.

Rich Johnson's Guide to
Wilderness Survival

Survival Strategy

In the middle of the night on the first of November, I left Sitka, Alaska, in a sixty-one-year-old wooden fishing boat, heading down the Inside Passage on a voyage that was supposed to last a week. Everyone the skipper and I spoke to before casting off expressed concern that this was too late in the season for such a trip. Wild storms can rage at this time of year, boats can sink, and men can lose their lives.

On the second day, the radio warned of hurricane-force winds, so we sought shelter in a deep cove on Baranof Island and listened to the wind scream through the trees as the boat bucked against its tethers. Two days later, the winds subsided and we set out again. But it's a long way from Sitka to Port Angeles, Washington, and one week stretched into two as we fought our way south and east against mountainous waves and relentless gales.

Psychologically, I was OK until I heard the skipper curse beneath his breath that the waves were too big, the wind too strong, as we took green water over the pilothouse, and the boat plunged what seemed to be straight for the bottom. He had thirty years' experience in Alaska and had weathered ferocious storms before, so I figured that if he was cursing now, we must certainly be in trouble. Then, as he worked the wheel, he turned to me, smiled, and said, "No problem."

I might have believed him, except that my tiny bunk, squeezed into the forepeak, developed a leak. Here we were in a wooden boat older than I was, it was leaking, and we were in a "perfect storm" over a bottom that was thousands of feet deep. Was I concerned? Well, let me put it this way, while the captain slept peacefully during my watch, I carried on a continuous conversation with God, promising that if He got me out of this mess alive, I would be a good boy all the rest of my life. Damn right, I mean, dang right, I was scared.

After two weeks in what at first appeared to be a watery grave eager to swallow me, I became a more capable crew and actually enjoyed the experience. The risk became a heroic adventure. I went to the gates of hell, rang the bell, and came back—and found out it wasn't so bad after all.

It's all in your head: The psychology of survival

Each of us has a different definition of what is acceptable risk. I know people whose mantra is "If you're not living on the edge, you're taking up too much space." To them, base jumping through blinding fog in the black of night would be a great rush. There are others for whom an overnight camping trip in Yellowstone would raise sweat in their palms because it is bear country. They're content to stay home, watch it all on National Geographic TV, and leave the dangerous living to someone else.

But most of us enjoy levels of adventure that fall somewhere between those two examples. We like to get out and see what nature has to offer. We're OK with the idea that what happens in the great outdoors is somewhat beyond our control. We respect the power of nature and take steps to stay out of serious harm's way but prepare ourselves to handle emergency situations when they arise.

However, if the situation gets too dicey, it's natural that our anxiety level rises and we feel uneasy or concerned about what is happening. This is actually a good thing. That warning voice in the back of our minds is a survival mechanism that helps keep us out of trouble if we pay attention to it. But at the same time, we must learn to keep anxiety under control. We can't let it run loose through our brains or we'll end up in a lot more trouble.

If we don't take control of our emotions, we quickly move from mild anxiety to gut-wrenching fear and then to a sense of panic or to a para-lyzing hopelessness. If we get that far, we lose our ability to cope with the situation and we begin making bad decisions that lead to disaster. If we're alone, our chances of survival diminish in proportion to the rise in anxiety unless we rein in our emotions, get control of our fear, and work out a logical survival plan. If we're in a group, we overcome our own fears by following a strong leader whose emotions are still intact—the calm captain who has been through this before and knows everything will be all right.

To a large degree, the ability to survive depends upon our state of mind. Of course, there are physical elements that come into play (the need for shelter, fire, water, food, etc.), but the ability to provide those things for yourself is severely hampered if you suffer a psychological breakdown. If you hit bottom emotionally and experience hopeless-ness, the decision to turn left or right and even the ability to take your next step forward is halted by mind-numbing fear that leaves you stand-ing motionless and unable to proceed. This type of mental paralysis is fed by fear and is unrelated to the realities of the physical world around you.

Many people are afraid of being alone in the dark. The reality is that being alone in the dark is not necessarily dangerous all by itself. However, if being alone in the dark causes you to go mindlessly screaming off into the woods as if you were being chased by a guy wearing a hockey mask and carrying a bloody hatchet, then being alone in the dark is indeed dangerous.

You see my point—I hope—that it is your reaction to your fears that causes the greatest potential hazard. If you calmly scratch out a campsite and go to sleep until morning, being alone in the dark poses no threat to your survival. But if you go paralytically numb like a kid who stands in the middle of the floor and dances because he knows he's not going to make it to the bathroom in time, or if you panic and go running down the trail as if your hair were on fire, you allow the anxiety to win, to your detriment.

How do you overcome your fears? There are only two answers. One is a lobotomy, and the other is practice. If you don't want to undergo brain removal, your best bet is to gradually, but safely, desensitize yourself by exposing yourself to conditions that create fear. Repeated exposure to risky situations progressively lowers the anxiety level until what once caused fear and trembling eventually brings exhilaration and a big grin. Along the way, positive self-talk helps: "Yes, it's dark and I'm alone, but that won't hurt me. I'll just make camp, go to sleep, and start again in the morning."

How to Overcome Anxiety

There is truth to the notion that in a survival situation it's what's between your ears that determines whether you live or die. Often, the failure to survive comes down to making one bad decision, one error in judgment, or losing your ability to cope emotionally and mentally with the stress of circumstances that cause you to feel threatened.

People who suddenly realize how far they are from civilization, how lost they are, and how serious the situation is can begin to break down. Uncontrolled fear is the enemy that keeps you from doing the things you must do to stay alive. Faced with a seemingly threatening situation, people sometimes panic. When panic sets in, they either do the wrong thing or do nothing at all. Often, the reason for this is because they never faced these circumstances in the past and don't know what to do. It's a matter of ignorance or inexperience, combined with fear.

The best way to prevent fear and panic from striking you is through gaining personal experience in survival situations. Nothing beats time on the ground and a hands-on approach, combined with as much book learnin' as you can muster. Outdoor survival classes are a help because they put you in survival environments where you can learn to face new challenges while still being relatively safe. The more you know, the less you fear. The less you fear, the more calm you remain.

If you are calm, it is possible that others in the group will tend to be influenced to be calm as well. If you present a confident and steady demeanor, others are likely to feel more confident.

You can see panic coming before it raises its ugly head among members of your group. Look at their eyes. Those who are starting to slide into an emotional quagmire will be wide-eyed and shifting their glances left and right, as if looking for an escape from the situation. When you see that, hear their quavering voice, or even see them break down and lose it altogether, here are some ways to help keep them calm:

▶ Maintain control of your voice. No shouting, no blaming. When you speak, use a calm and confident tone, and talk positively about the outcome of the situation. The way you talk and behave has a huge impact on others in the party. Be sure everything you say reflects your positive attitude.

▶ Promote unity of purpose by working together as a group to come up with a plan. The more you can involve everyone, the more focused they will be on a positive outcome.

▶ Openly talk about the inventory of everything that is in your favor—all your supplies, both the ones you brought with you and the ones provided by nature.

▶ Organize the work by setting priorities in line with the needs of the particular situation. (We talk about how to set priorities later in this chapter and will revisit the topic throughout the book.)

▶ True leadership is granted, not demanded. Lead by example. Get up and start doing the most important tasks and ask for—don't demand—help from others. Be clear (but not dictatorial) about the way you want the tasks to be done.

▶ Give consideration to the ideas of others who are willing to help but want to suggest other ways of doing the work. Recognize that no one has all the answers, and others in the group may have had valuable experience that can be beneficial in this situation.

▶ Express gratitude for the input of others and, where appropriate, try to use their suggestions. This instills in them a sense of importance and teamwork.

Getting to the most important tasks at hand is crucial. Here are five things you must do to maintain survival focus and positive mental outlook, both for yourself and for others in your group:

▶ Attend to any serious injuries. (Chapters 7 and 10 cover the basics for handling common medical emergencies.)

▶ Get a fire going. A campfire makes you feel like you have a lifeline. When venturing into the backcountry, always take survival supplies that include fire-starting materials. (See Chapter 3 for a complete discussion of fire-building techniques.)

▶ Establish a campsite and build a shelter. This task takes a while but accomplishes three important things: physically, it protects the body from the elements; psychologically, it establishes a zone of protection against hazards both real and perceived; and it puts everyone to work on a community project that helps build unity and cooperation. (Chapter 2 outlines the many options for homemade and store-bought shelters.)

▶ Signal to attract searchers. Make use of reflective surfaces. In clearings or on hilltops, use logs and rocks to form visual symbols to attract rescue. Keep signal fires burning—a smoky fire by day and a bright blaze by night. Utilize audible signals when you think searchers are near. (For an in-depth discussion of signaling techniques, both visible and audible, see Chapter 6.)

▶ Find a water source and organize food-gathering efforts. But work at a pace that conserves energy and doesn't cause sweating. (Chapters 4 and 5 provide information on how to find water and food in the wild and outline procedures for insuring they are safe for consumption.)

After you've done all that, your chances of survival are best if you stay put and await rescue. On a day-to-day basis, continually upgrade your living conditions. Improving the shelter not only increases protection against the elements but also gives strong psychological reassurance. Keep a fire going at all times—smoke by day and a bright blaze by night, for signaling purposes. A fire at night is not only one of the best ways to signal rescuers after dark, but it also wards off fear of the darkness and lends psychological comfort. Actively promote rescue through the use of every type of signal device and technique you can think of. This helps keep hope alive. Prepare at least one hot meal per day, if possible, because it helps survivors feel like life is bearable. Try to live as cleanly as possible; hygiene is important to prevent disease and helps maintain a sense of personal dignity. Remain optimistic and speak only in positive terms to others in the party.

As calmly as possible, handle the most important problem first, then move on to the next most important. Train anxiety to become your servant, not your master—a bodyguard with a reliable voice that issues warnings to help you survive. Learn to listen to this bodyguard, heed the warnings, consider all your options, then remain in control and take appropriate action.

Develop a Survivor's Attitude

Forty-nine-year-old Theo spent three days lost in the Michigan woods. The weather was nasty, and the rain soon soaked him. At night, his clothes froze. Theo was not a smoker, so he carried no matches or lighter to start a fire. He had no supplies with him, and his only food was rabbits that he caught and killed by hand and ate raw.

Two young women were lost for four days in the rugged wilderness area of Yellowstone National Park. They found some small bird eggs in a nest and ate them. "The eggs were warm, so they weren't too bad," one of the girls commented. There were grasshoppers and ants in the area, and the girls said they considered eating them, but they were rescued before they had the chance.

Seventy-nine-year-old Francis was lost for four days on the rugged slopes of a 4,000-foot mountain in Oregon. She kept herself going by eating wild berries, sleeping on a bed made of ferns, and using survival techniques she learned years ago. When she was rescued, she apologized for the huckleberry stains on her hands and shooed away photographers as she was carried to safety.

I know what you're thinking. This is about surviving in the backcountry by finding and eating wild foods. But we're not talking about food—we're talking about survival. And survival is really about overcoming the odds, reaching down deep inside ourselves, and going beyond what is normally required of us. It's about *attitude*. These stories are about people who adjusted their attitudes and overcame their fears and food prejudices and managed to live for several days in conditions of hardship. They all had an attitude about surviving, and it was that attitude that pulled them through.

It is no secret that 90 percent of survival is psychological, which means that only 10 percent is about the rest of it. This is easily proven by the countless stories of people who stunned the experts by living through situations that defied all the rules of logic. People survive extremes of heat, cold, dehydration, starvation, and all forms of misery for only one reason: they are unwilling to accept defeat.

On the other hand, there are countless other stories of people who gave up and died when they should have survived. Without sufficient will to live, they just didn't rise to a fighting stance, look adversity in the eye, and defiantly spit. They gave up.

Survival is an individual thing. The old saying holds true—whether you think you can or think you can't, you're probably right. On the extreme negative side, there is a condition of psychological dysfunction in which people become exceedingly depressed and simply give up, or they may fall victim to full-blown panic. They cease to function in pursuit of their own survival.

So it isn't always the food, water, shelter, warmth, or any of the other physical aspects of survival that make the difference. Sometimes it's the attitude.

The question is, what is the proper survival attitude? The simplest answer is that it's a fighting attitude. If you're not willing to fight for yourself, you might not survive. Somewhere, down deep inside, you must find a controlled level of hostility toward the situation, a burning anger, a righteous indignation. Identify the enemy, no matter what it is, and you will fight for your life against every threat. Never give up. Never!

No matter how you choose to define the attitude, control it. It's a defiance, not a wild rage. Clench your fist, grit your teeth, and hiss, "I ain't going down!" Then let that attitude motivate you to appropriate action. No matter what happens, you must always believe that you are going to survive.

Your attitude needs to involve four spheres of influence: yourself, the situation, others in the group, and your possessions.

▶ **About yourself:** Your attitude must be one of confidence. It's normal to feel a certain level of apprehension or even fear. Courage is nothing more than pressing on in spite of fear and continuing to work toward a positive solution. Do not allow your fears to go to the point that you think you're not going to survive. You are in control of your own thoughts, and if you need to shout out loud to yourself that you're going to make it, go ahead. In fact, the steady sound of your own voice speaking with firm resolve may help calm you. Use only positive affirmations when having these little discussions with yourself. Say things like, "OK, I know I can get a fire started." Don't use negatives in any form, such as, "If I don't get a fire started, I'm going to freeze." The brain and the body respond without prejudice to both positive and negative mental inputs, so focus on only the positive.

▶ **Regarding the situation:** You must deal with reality. Develop a clear and realistic assessment of the situation—where you are, what the weather is doing, your physical condition (illness or injuries), and the condition of everyone in the group. Make a mental note of every asset—someone back home who might initiate a search when you are overdue, every item of equipment (right down to your shoelaces), your survival knowledge, and the skills of every person in the group.

▶ **Concerning others:** Your attitude must be one of cooperation and compassion. Some may react negatively to the situation. Deal with them in a manner that inspires confidence and a willingness to pitch in and help solve survival problems. The most unlikely individual may rise to a leadership role. Be prepared that this individual might not be you. This is no time for office politics—be a good leader or a good follower, whichever position you find yourself in. But always bring a positive influence to the group. If you think you know something that the leader needs to consider, take him or her aside and discuss it calmly and in private so there is no appearance of mutiny.

▶ **Finally, about your possessions:** Your attitude must be one of careful and protective use of every resource so as not to lose, waste, or ruin anything. In a group survival situation, there is no such thing as a personal possession, because your knife or your compass might be the instrument that is used to save the whole group. That doesn't mean you freely give your knife to some club-fisted oaf so he can ruin it. Retain physical possession, but the benefit belongs to the group.

Survival is all about attitude. Whether you're a seventy-nine-year-old woman who is lost in the mountains, a group of hunting buddies trapped by a severe storm, or a young family that is suddenly stranded in the backcountry by a landslide that closes the trail, staying alive is a process that begins in the brain. Once your attitude is right, you will be more successful as you work through each challenge.

ASSESSING THE SITUATION

Every outdoor survival situation is based on some form of crisis that involves a potential threat to life. The problem may revolve around peril to yourself or other people. It may be immediately serious or it could escalate gradually to a critical stage. Each situation seems to offer a unique set of variables, presenting challenges in a different order or intensity or direction. Yet, if we take a broad view of survival situations in general, it is possible to see common threads that tie all such predicaments together and give us clues about how to handle them.

Evaluating the Situation

The first step in managing any type of crisis situation is the evaluation phase. Stop and analyze every aspect of the circumstances before proceeding with a logical and effective plan of action. The analysis phase doesn't necessarily need to be a long, drawn-out process—the first time I had a parachute malfunction, I learned how quickly a full analysis can be made and a survival plan implemented—but it does need to be continual. From the moment you enter a survival incident until you are rescued, continually assess the situation and manage your activities to suit your needs at the moment. Depending upon the complexity of the situation and the number of people involved, the evaluation should include such factors as:

▶ **State of well-being:** Is anybody dead, critically injured, ill? Is anyone displaying symptoms of psychological breakdown?
▶ **Immediate physical threats:** foul weather, wreckage, hazardous materials, predatory animals with an attitude, etc.
▶ **Long-term physical challenges:** shelter, water, food, fire, medical needs

The list goes on and on. Knowing these things gives you the ability to determine what needs to be done first and what can wait until later. Naturally, the more immediate the threat or the need, the higher that item goes on the priority list. For example, let's suppose you're lost in the mountains. The day is warm and dry, you have a daypack with some food and water, and you're not sick or injured. But you noticed a mountain lion hanging back on your trail following you, flicking his tail from side to side and staring intently in your direction. Now he's licking his lips. In this case, how high up on the priority list do you place food or water? Or is something else more important—a secure shelter, a weapon, knowledge of how to act in the face of a stalking cougar?

Another situation on another day might demand that you find or make shelter immediately or face the onset of hypothermia. Another day and another place may demand that you locate water to drink or perish from dehydration. Each predicament brings its own set of priorities, and it's your job to evaluate the situation before you set those priorities in proper order.

Determining Your Assets

Once you evaluate the situation, the next step is to determine all your assets. What do you have with you that can be useful for survival? What circumstances are in your favor? Consider the following:

▶ Everything on your body, in your pack, in your vehicle, or in your camp (wherever you happen to be) is part of your supply of potentially beneficial items. Take inventory. Think about all the possible uses of these items. (Chapter 9 provides valuable information regarding camping equipment and survival gear that can be purchased or made from objects in nature.)

▶ Look around and see what nature provides that adds to this inventory. Brush, tree limbs, boulders, an overhanging ledge—all those things can be used for shelter. A stream, a snowbank, a lake or pond—for a water supply. Dry wood, fibrous bark, dead grasses, dry moss—fuel for a fire or insulation or padding. You get the idea.

▶ Location: Are you lost or merely isolated? Does anyone else know where you are and when to expect you back? Are they likely to begin a search? (See Chapter 8 for a complete discussion of navigation techniques.)

The more complete the list of things in your favor, the better. Identifying all the things you have to work with lifts your spirits and stimulates creative thinking about ways to improve your situation.

Developing a Plan of Action

Next comes the formulation of a plan of action. Depending upon your circumstances, the best plan of action might be to lie low, conserve your energy and resources, and try to improve your camp while provoking a rescue through signaling efforts. On the other hand, the plan may call for an active approach to self-rescue. But one thing is certain—you can't come up with a logical plan of action until you do a thorough and honest evaluation of the situation and take inventory of what you have to work with.

Don't try to fool yourself into thinking the situation is less serious than it really is. You're not John Wayne, and this isn't Hollywood. People really bleed, and they really die, and somebody else is going to get the girl. Be realistic about your abilities and inabilities, and don't underestimate the terrain or the weather or the distance to civilization.

On the other hand, don't fall into the trap of believing the situation is hopeless—it never is. Look around and listen up. If you don't see the fat lady and you don't hear her singing, it ain't over. (If you do see and hear her, it probably is over and you're already dead. Take the rest of the day off.)

Assuming you're still alive, here's what you must do:

▶ Figure out how to attract attention. Sound, sight, and smell are your friends. Think of ways to make noise that carry a long distance, how to create visual evidence of your presence, and how to stink up the air so someone knows you're there and need help.

▶ If you are staying in one place and awaiting rescue (a good idea), busy yourself with camp improvement projects that don't drain away your energy. Preserve your food and water supply by pacing yourself and working in that part of the day (or night) that is most comfortable.

▶ If you decide to leave camp and try for self-rescue, leave a note to rescuers who will probably find your vehicle or your camp before they find you (hint: if you had remained in camp, you'd be rescued by now). On the note leave the name, address, and phone number of everyone in your party; a description of clothing, equipment, and supplies being carried; the date and time you set off; the intended direction of travel and your intended destination; and a description of everyone's condition of health and special medical needs. The latter may insure special supplies (insulin, for example) are immediately on hand when the rescue is finally made.

A NOTE left on the dashboard will give searchers a huge head start in finding you. Be sure to identify yourself, provide contact information, and indicate your intended route.

Understanding how to manage a survival emergency helps make the process of living through a crisis a more organized, effective, and comfortable endeavor. Doing the right things in the right order can easily shorten your ordeal considerably, and it may even save lives.

SETTING PRIORITIES

When it comes to survival, is it more important to have food, water, shelter, or fire? There is a common belief that shelter is always the highest priority, followed by fire, followed by water, and then food. Logical arguments can be made that shelter, fire, water, and then food is the correct order, but survival situations are not always that simple. Let me illustrate.

If the problem is that you fall overboard in 40-degree Lake Manitscold, the most important survival consideration is to stay afloat until you are rescued.

If the problem is that you accidentally shot your buddy through the leg with your killer broadhead, first aid becomes the first priority.

If the problem is that you're lost in the woods with night coming on, everything depends upon whether it's August or February and the woods in question are on Oahu or the north end of Vancouver Island.

You get the picture. There are many factors involved in making the determination about what is the most important survival technique to work on. But because you can only do one thing at a time, you have to know how to decide where to start and why. This is really a question of knowing how to set priorities.

Establishing priorities is extremely important to the successful outcome of a survival situation because if you don't know what's most important, you're likely to work on the wrong thing.

In order to establish a reasonable priority list, you must evaluate the following elements of your situation realistically:

- ▶ Immediate threats to life
- ▶ Long-term threats
- ▶ State of physical health—illness or injuries
- ▶ Mental and emotional condition
- ▶ Terrain—swamp, mountains, desert, etc.
- ▶ Location—do you know exactly where you are?
- ▶ Weather—immediate and long-term outlook
- ▶ Number of people in the survival party
- ▶ Available resources—equipment, food, water, medical supplies
- ▶ Natural resources—shelter, fire, water, food
- ▶ Likelihood of rescue

Once you clearly understand the situation you're facing, you can begin to formulate a survival plan. But you can only do this if you honestly understand the first and second points on our list—immediate and long-term threats to life.

In chronological order, the human body is threatened in the following ways:

- ▶ You can die almost instantly from any number of things, such as drowning, animal attack, a fall from a cliff, being overrun by a wildfire, etc.
- ▶ You can die from exposure to heat or cold in a matter of hours or even minutes.
- ▶ You can die from lack of water intake in a few days.

▶ You can die from illnesses or injuries on a varying schedule that ranges from almost immediately to months, depending upon the seriousness of the malady.

▶ You can die from starvation in a month. You probably won't live long enough to die from starvation if you fail to take care of more urgent needs. However, if you can't get enough nourishment, your ability to think and function will be severely hampered, and that will play a detrimental role in your ability to survive.

From this, we might be tempted to jump to an unfortunate conclusion and make a general assumption that food is not as important as shelter. But survival situations can be so varied that items on the priority list can easily swap positions. There may actually be a situation in which food is the priority because every other item on the list is either not critical at the moment or is satisfied already. Example: You're marooned in good health on Survivor Island, where the temperature is always pleasant and a freshwater spring is right at your camp—all you need right now is food to bolster your energy and comfort you psychologically. Work on a lightweight shelter after lunch, then try to figure out some signal devices.

Obviously, we can't carve priority lists in granite. There is no one-size-fits-all list, because each situation must be evaluated on its own merits. Only then can priorities be established. But being able to accurately identify your most urgent needs is where the whole survival process begins.

SURVIVAL IS IN THE DETAILS

It was just one of those things than can happen so easily around camp, when George accidentally cut his arm. Ordinarily, it would be a small matter requiring a bit of first-aid treatment. But these were not ordinary circumstances. The time was 150 years ago, and George Donner was the leader of a pioneer company headed west toward the Sacramento

Valley. The party, which included women and children, was caught by an early snowfall in the Sierra Mountains, and they began to starve and suffer from exposure. As the snow piled higher, the immigrants ran out of food and resorted to eating their oxen. When the meat was gone, they ate the ox hide. The longer they were trapped by the snow, the weaker they became, and soon members of the party started to die. It was a poor time for the slip of a hand to carry a sharp blade into one's arm.

Small problems, such as the slip of a hand, have enormous consequences in a survival situation. In George Donner's case, with poor nutrition, inadequate sanitation, and limited medical attention, his wound lingered and became infected. Over time, he grew so weak that when the rescue party finally arrived they couldn't save him.

Ah yes, there was a rescue. It began with the heroic efforts of ten men and five women—only two of the men and all five of the women survived the journey—who fashioned crude snowshoes and trekked the rest of the way over the mountain and down into the Sacramento Valley, where they rallied a rescue effort that went back over the mountain to bring the survivors to safety.

But the consequences of the slip of George Donner's hand didn't stop just because rescuers arrived. He was weakened by the infection, and when it became clear that he was not strong enough to be carried to safety by the rescue team, his devoted wife, Tamsen, chose to stay by his side rather than leave him. It was a lonely and tragic moment as the two of them watched the survivors disappear over the mountain, leaving them behind to face the wilderness alone. On that day, the grim reaper bought two for the price of one. In the end, of the eighty-seven pioneers in the Donner Party, thirty-nine perished on the mountain and forty-eight survived.

The story of the Donner Party is sad, yet instructive. During the trip west, a number of small individual mistakes were made by members of the wagon train that, taken alone, were seemingly inconsequential. But in the end, those small slipups along the trail resulted in delays that put the group behind schedule. Errors in judgment took a toll. Equipment breakdowns slowed the pace. Each day of getting out of camp late put the travelers behind schedule, and the accumulation of these minor mistakes ultimately trapped the pioneer company in the early snow of the Sierra Nevada Mountains. And then there was George's wound.

What is really at issue here is not the injury itself. That is only an example of how little things have a huge impact in a survival situation. Small details make the difference between a pleasant outdoor experience and a full-blown, life-and-death survival incident. So the first step is to pay attention to the details and constantly be aware of what's going on. You can have no plan for survival until after you have a clear understanding of your situation. Without the assessment, you can't even begin to take care of the important details. So the first step is to sit down and engage in some frank discussion with everyone in your party—or with yourself if you're alone—to figure out how to handle the situation.

Let's quickly scan a few of the critical issues that will determine your ability to survive. Later chapters in this book will go into greater depth about these topics, but here are some brief highlights to illustrate the importance of paying attention to the seemingly minor details.

Fire

Perhaps you remember the scene in the movie *Jeremiah Johnson* when Robert Redford's campfire was suddenly snuffed out by a pile of snow that fell from the branches of a tree. Proper choice of campfire location is just one of many details to be dealt with. Here are some others. (Again, see Chapter 3 for a complete discussion of fire-building techniques.)

▶ Fuel must be dry and abundant.
▶ The fire base must be on dry mineral soil (hard dirt or rocks) to prevent the fire from igniting underground roots or other organic materials and getting away from you. If the ground is moist, build up a dry platform to serve as a fire base, because the convection current of rising air created by the fire will suck up the moisture and can weaken the blaze. Contain the fire within a ring of rocks or mounded soil to prevent it from accidentally spreading.

BEFORE starting a fire, prepare a fire ring in a safe location and collect as much wood as possible. The rule of thumb is to gather three times as much wood as you think you'll need to get you through the night.

▶ Look overhead to make sure there is nothing that might catch fire or fall into the flames.

▶ Consider the prevailing night wind direction so you aren't sleeping in the smoke.

▶ Consider the purpose for the fire. Is it for signaling (bright flames by night and smoke by day), cooking or boiling water (small fire with good bed of coals), or warmth (large and built with a reflector surface behind it)?

▶ Protect the fire so it doesn't get drowned by falling rain or by rising water.

Shelter

Many of the following details concern natural hazards or nuisances that may be in the area where you're thinking of building your shelter. (The topic of shelter in wet, cold, and hot weather is covered thoroughly in Chapter 2.)

▶ Look down. You're looking for ants, ground-dwelling wasps, or other insect colonies that may already inhabit the construction site.

▶ Look up. You're looking for wasps or beehives, as well as for widow makers (branches that can fall out of an overhead tree or rocks that may slide off an overhanging cliff). You're also looking for evidence of water that might stream over the edge of a cliff during a night storm.

WIDOW makers are dead limbs in the trees above your camp that might fall and cause damage or injury. Before setting up camp, always look up to make sure nothing can fall on you.

▶ Look around. Check the area for snake habitat, scorpions, and spiders. Make sure your shelter site isn't in a drainage that could fill from a distant storm and wash you away in a flash flood.

▶ Try to locate your shelter where it may be seen by search-and-rescue teams. If possible, place the shelter within easy access to firewood, water, and food supplies.

▶ Take advantage of existing shade in hot weather, open exposure to the sun in cold weather, natural windbreaks, etc.

Organization

Keep all items of equipment clean, organized, and in good working order. In a survival situation, the loss of a knife can be disastrous, but it is equally serious to allow the knife to become inoperable by misuse or neglect. This applies to every item of equipment, every piece of clothing (your primary shelter against the elements), every bit of food, and every drop of water.

▶ Take inventory of what you have.

▶ Think of every secondary and tertiary use for each item. This is a creative process in which you discover many uses for your bootlaces other than merely holding your boots on. Can your belt buckle be used as a signal mirror? Do you have any paper in your pocket that might help with fire starting? You get the idea.

▶ Make a place for every item, and be continually aware that everything is still in its place.

▶ Immediately repair anything that becomes dull, broken, torn, or in any way damaged. This is what you do in survival camp when you have no TV to watch.

Sanitation

This is more than simply washing your hands before eating. Field sanitation must become a way of life, whether you're camping or fighting for your life in a survival situation.

▶ **Avoid living in the dirt.** Build up a platform of natural materials to live on, whether it is a log floor, matted grasses, bark slabs, or pine duff raked together into a "nest."

▶ **Live clean.** Take advantage of every opportunity to wash body and clothes. It makes you feel better, and your clothing lasts longer if it is clean. It's enough trouble to do this that you'll start thinking of ways to avoid getting filthy in the first place, which is a benefit in itself.

▶ **Food and water.** Don't be paranoid. You can eat lots of things you never thought possible. But at the same time, be careful with your food and drinking water because carelessness here can contribute to failure to survive. Don't experiment with the menu. Some wild plants are deadly, and unless you know what it is, don't put it in your mouth. Starvation is probably not going to kill you, but the wrong plant may. Boil drinking water,

KEEPING yourself and your clothes at least somewhat clean will help keep your spirits up and even help keep you healthy. Clean socks, for example, will help prevent foot problems.

because illness brought about by ingesting *Giardia* or *Cryptosporidium* can lead to dehydration. (See Chapter 4 for water-finding and purification techniques and Chapter 5 for information on the safety and availability of food in the wild.)

Constant Awareness

It is vital to be continually aware of the details in what you're doing and what's going on around you. Remember what happened because of the slip of George Donner's hand. Ask yourself, "Where will the blade end up if the knife slips? Where will that boulder go if it falls off the cliff above my shelter? What will happen if my fire suddenly flares up and scatters sparks?" Ask yourself that type of question about every detail of what's going on around you, and then come up with a plan to minimize the risks. In the end, survival is measured in small increments. The devil is in the details.

Safety Tips

Think back to pioneer times and how folks survived all the hazards that faced them as they crossed the vast wilderness, camping under the stars every night, then settling empty lands to begin farming or ranching or just raising their families. Those were days of danger, to be sure, but the unfortunate truth is that life is perhaps even more menacing for us today.

Contrary to Hollywood's version of pioneer life, relatively few travelers or settlers were killed by wild animals. As dangerous as wild predators could be, they were far less of a risk to life and limb than accidents, disease, or bouts of extremely foul weather. Today, we have better equipment to help prevent some of the risks of yesteryear. Medical science banished most of the diseases that took down people by the thousands only a century ago. We have high-tech clothing and shelter to help protect against the weather. But there is an unfortunate rise in predatory activity. A different kind of predator may be circling camps, lurking in parking lots, stalking neighborhoods, waiting for an opportunity. It's the human predator. Even our country's semi-wilderness areas are impacted by an increase in population, and some of those who wander the backcountry exhibit less than exemplary moral character, making it necessary to take extra precautions while we travel and camp.

The very nature of exploring the wilderness poses certain challenges to personal safety and the security of our property. Along with preparing for the rare appearance of a grizzly at the weenie roast, there are other precautions we should take to protect against accidents and injuries or assaults on ourselves and our property.

WHEN camping in bear country, always stow your food high above the ground some distance from camp. Rig up a bear wire by stretching a rope between trees and then tossing the line that holds the food bag over the first rope and hoisting the bag at least 10 feet off the ground.

▶ Ideally, don't camp or hike alone. I know there are some who prefer to go solo, but doing so increases personal risk. Alone in the backcountry, something as simple as a stumble can result in a debilitating injury that can leave you stranded. An encounter with a predator, animal or human, that is bent on mischief is much less likely to result in a bad outcome if you travel in company with other people.

▶ If neighboring campers start to get rowdy, which can happen in even a remote and pristine campground, be ready to break camp quietly and leave. Confrontation with a group of testosterone addicts who feed their egos by showing off to friends is worthless and dangerous.

▶ Always secure your toys while in camp. Remove ignition keys from motorcycles and four-wheelers, and lock them up inside your primary vehicle's love box. Use chains and heavy padlocks to secure these things to trees or logs or to your primary vehicle.

▶ Keep your vehicle locked and valuable stuff inside hidden beneath blankets.

▶ If you're camping in bear country, always secure food in a container hung in a tree some distance from your camp. Garbage that cannot be burned in your campfire should be hung in the same manner as you hang the food until you are ready to leave camp and can hike the refuse out. (For rules regarding encounters with animals in the wild, see Chapter 10.)

Take responsibility for your personal safety and the security of your property while traveling and camping. It takes only a little extra preparation and awareness to eliminate some of the hazards.

Basic survival strategies

A child wanders away from the family camp. A hunter races off in hot pursuit of a big buck and loses his way. The weather unexpectedly turns violent and leaves a camping family stranded in the wilderness. A vehicle breaks down on a lonely trail miles from civilization. Outdoor survival situations arise in many different ways, but regardless of the cause, the results are often tragic.

What is easily forgotten as we pack the car with tents and sleeping bags is that we are leaving the comfort and safety of home and heading into a more unpredictable environment where things can get out of control if we are not careful. Sometimes what begins as an unfortunate incident evolves into a full-blown survival situation.

There are steps we can take to either prevent or at least minimize the seriousness of problems that may arise. Packing along some items of safety equipment, as well as spending a little time on special training for everyone in the group, goes a long way toward making outdoor experiences safe and happy ones.

Little accidents are common around camp—bumps and bruises, a sliver or scrape, a burn from a campfire ember. Those who venture into the outdoors need to be prepared with knowledge and the right equipment to take care of these minor medical emergencies. For those who really want to be prepared, taking a Red Cross first-aid course is a good place to start. At the very least, a well-equipped first-aid kit is an essential item that should always be close at hand. This can be purchased as a kit or assembled at home to meet any special medical needs

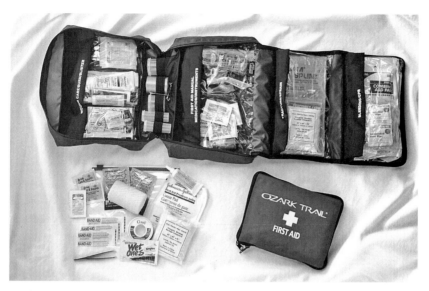

THE first-aid kit at the top is large and comprehensive and is suitable as the main camp emergency medical kit. Lower left is a sample of first-aid supplies that can be carried in a cargo pocket. The small kit at the lower right fits on a belt.

of family members. Depending upon the size of your group, you might choose to have a large expedition kit, but at the very least you should have a personal-sized kit that you can put together yourself and stow in a plastic baggie in your pocket.

One of the most serious situations that arises is when a member of the family wanders away from camp and becomes lost. This is particularly terrifying when the person lost is a child. Each child should be taught that wandering away from camp is not allowed. It is helpful to take a family hike through the entire campground, taking the time to point out landmarks and how they relate to the location of the family's camp. If the children are permitted to hike around and explore, teach them to turn around and look back at the tent every now and then just to make sure they haven't wandered out of sight of the main camp.

Each member of the group should be outfitted with both audible and visual signal devices. A lightweight and inexpensive but powerful whistle such as the Storm Safety Whistle sold by outdoor equipment

SHOW children around the campsite, pointing out landmarks they can use to identify where they are in relation to the tent, and specify boundaries that the kids should not go beyond.

retailers is claimed to be many times louder than U.S. military whistles. If someone becomes separated from camp and can't find the way back, the whistle is used to call for help. The nice thing about audible signaling devices is that they can be used day or night. For visual signaling during daylight hours, it's hard to beat a small, unbreakable signal mirror, available at sporting goods outlets for less than $10. The flash from a properly directed mirror in bright sunlight signals the location of a lost individual across many miles—much farther than an audible signal carries.

These small, inexpensive, and lightweight devices are a tremendous help in locating a lost individual. But it is necessary that those who have these items of equipment know how to use them. A fun family outing could be built around a simulated survival incident in which each person must actually use the audible and visual signal devices to get "rescued." This is on the same order as running fire drills at home so each person knows how to react in an emergency.

Whenever you head into the backcountry, stop and think, "What if we have to stay longer than planned? What do we need to survive?" This is a key concept, because you never know when you will unexpectedly end up in an emergency situation that turns into a survival incident. Hope it never happens, but prepare for the worst.

If a trip suddenly becomes a survival situation, here are some basic things to consider:

EQUIP each child with a signal whistle, and explain when it's appropriate to use it. Teach the kids that this is an important piece of survival gear that should only be used in an emergency.

▶ Exposure to the elements poses a threat to human existence. In a survival situation, maintaining proper body temperature is critical. Shelter from the elements—rain, wind, sun, insects, etc.—is vital. Clothing is the first line of defense when it comes to shelter. Clothing with long sleeves and long pant legs is important in both hot and cold weather because it helps control body temperature and dehydration. Long clothing also helps prevent sunburn, scrapes, bites, and other minor injuries. Every person should have windproof and waterproof clothing (an inexpensive pocket poncho works), as well as insulating layers to preserve body warmth.

▶ Food is important. Even though a healthy individual can survive for long periods of time without eating, the problem with going too long without food is that the person literally runs out of fuel and can't function efficiently. It might take several weeks to actually die of starvation, but in the meantime the victim will be operating at a very low level men-

ANOTHER potentially lifesaving piece of signal equipment that children can use is a small, plastic mirror. Children should be taught how to use the mirror to attract attention if they become lost or injured.

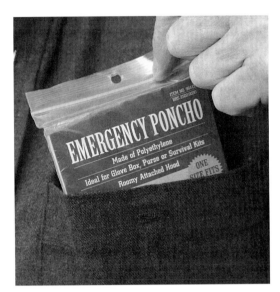

ALWAYS be equipped with some emergency shelter. A pocket poncho is lightweight and compact, yet will protect the wearer from precipitation and wind, two of the factors that lead to hypothermia.

tally and physically. No matter how long your trip is planned for, take along enough compact, high-calorie emergency food to last a few extra days. It's good insurance.

▶ Water, on the other hand, is essential to survival. Each person should have a couple of quarts of drinkable water every day—and more if there is much exertion or the ambient temperature is high. Take three times as much water as you think you need for the outing, because you just never know when you'll need it. For greatest safety, a portable water purification system should be included in the equipment inventory. These are available in backpacking stores or from outdoor equipment mail-order catalogs. The system should do more than just improve water flavor with a carbon filter. The one you want actually removes dangerous waterborne microorganisms, such as *Giardia*, by means of a high-quality filter or kills them by means of chemical action.

▶ Take redundant methods of starting a fire, so you can have one in the pocket of a jacket, pants, fanny pack, etc. You don't ever want to be without a means of starting a fire just because you happened to leave your jacket or pack in camp, then wandered away and got lost. Fire can be used as a signal, for cooking food and purifying water, for warming up and drying out, and for cheering up a gloomy night. Teach children of appropriate age and maturity the proper and safe use of fire, and how to put one out.

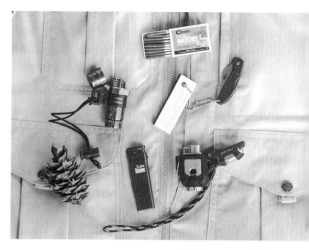

ALWAYS carry multiple methods of starting a fire and spread them around among your pack, your pants, your jacket, and your shirt pockets so you will never be without at least one.

▶ File a flight plan with people back home. Tell them where you're going, when you'll be back, and any side trips you have in mind. Include information about who you're traveling with, what vehicles are being used, and what type and color of equipment you're carrying. That way, if you don't show up back home in a reasonable time, a search can be initiated. Don't alter the plan unless you call and notify the people back home that you are doing so. This might seem like a lot of trouble, but it is nothing compared to being stranded on your own.

▶ Once you're in camp, don't just wander away without letting someone know where you're going and when you expect to return. Discuss your plans with a responsible adult who can organize a search if you don't return at the appointed time.

▶ Talk with everyone in the group about the rules of conduct in camp. If there are children along, make sure they understand that everyone needs to know where each person is all the time.

Related to this, there should be some agreement about when to call in the search-and-rescue people. My friend Steve and I enjoy going on long hikes, ski treks, and mountain bike rides. These often last until the wee hours of the next morning. Our instructions to our wives are "Don't call search and rescue until at least 10:00 A.M. tomorrow." It's our nature to explore. We know there is a better-than-even chance we will be late getting back. Everyone expects it.

On the other hand, if the kids are playing down at the fishing hole and one of them turns up missing, conduct an immediate search, looking for footprints and calling out to the child. If your efforts don't result in finding

the missing child, don't waste any more time before calling for reinforce-
ments. While you're waiting for the search-and-rescue team to arrive,
continue to search actively.

▶ Prepare each person with knowledge and basic equipment for survival
alone in the wilderness. Each person should have an age-appropriate kit
that could include some of the following items: a pocket full of emergency
rations, a bottle of water, a small first-aid kit, a whistle, a means of starting
a fire, an emergency shelter, a knife, a small flashlight, and a signal mirror.
Youngsters of responsible age can be taught how to prepare an emergency
campfire, add moist fuel to the blaze to make smoke as a signal, use a
pocket poncho for shelter, and make their position obvious to searchers
through audible and visual signals and other means.

STAY OR GO?

Worst-case scenario: You drive so far back in the mountains that civilization is only a vague memory. Without warning, your vehicle breathes
its last, leaving you stranded. This is the stuff of which headlines in
tomorrow's newspaper are made.

In fact, the newspaper headlines carried just such a story in the winter of 2006, when the James Kim family became stranded in the mountains of Oregon after their car became stuck in the snow on a lonely
forest road. After waiting for rescue for nine days, James left his wife,
Kati, and their daughters, seven-month-old Sabine and four-year-old
Penelope, to seek help. Clearly, James Kim was trying to do the right
thing and, in a heroic effort, even though he was weakened from more
than a week without food, he made what was probably the most difficult decision of his life—to leave his wife and children behind while
he went for help. The story had a tragic ending, with James dying of
exposure. But the good news is that Kati and the children were rescued
in remarkably good condition. The best that can come of this story is
for it to serve as a learning experience for the rest of us. I will discuss

more of this incident later, so we can see what went wrong and what went right.

Regardless of the kind of vehicle we use for mobility in the back-country, it can be both a blessing and a curse. On the benefit side, our wheels make it possible to cover a lot more ground in less time, be rested when we arrive at our destination, haul camping, hunting, and fishing supplies, and take passengers along for the ride.

But at the same time, the ability to cover a lot of ground means that we can get ourselves deep into trouble pretty fast. Also, most of us become almost totally dependent on the vehicle, complacently expecting it to always work perfectly. When the vehicle breaks down or gets stuck, the situation becomes ugly if the driver and passengers aren't prepared to face the possibility of either a long-term stay in the wilderness awaiting rescue or a long hike to get help. Preparation is the key to survival in the wilderness, but when it relates to a vehicle breakdown, there are a lot of things that need to be considered before any final decisions are made about hiking out for help.

A critical part of preparing for any trip is to make sure somebody knows exactly where you are going, where you intend to spend each night, and when you are expected to be back home. If you fail to notify friends and relatives about these important details of your itinerary, nobody will know where to look for you or when to activate a rescue effort. When you prepare a "flight plan" of your trip, be sure to adhere to it. Violating the plan creates chaos if you don't get home on time and you end up someplace nobody is expecting. That throws search-and-rescue efforts into commotion, as time and energy are spent searching for you in the wrong place. If you must change your plans, notify all those people with whom you left your original itinerary so they will be aware of the new plans.

But stuff happens. Something unexpected comes up and attracts us in another direction. Murphy's Law demands that breakdowns occur in the most unlikely, inaccessible spot, miles from where we're supposed to be. The Kim family, for example, did the right thing by notifying their friends of their travel plans—their intended routes and overnight destinations. The trouble began when they missed an exit on Interstate 5 in central Oregon. Rather than turning around and taking the intended exit that would lead them safely through the mountains to the coast, they continued on the interstate and took the next off-ramp. This put them on a route that was different than their plan specified. Later, when the car became stuck in the snow, the friends who had the flight plan in their hands had no way of knowing that a search of the intended route would not place the search teams anywhere close to where the Kim family was stranded.

When the worst happens, you have decisions to make and things to do. In this scenario, you are stranded and you can't get the vehicle back in running condition.

Step One: Take a deep breath, relax, and evaluate the situation. It probably isn't as bad as you think. Is anyone in your party dead? Is there an immediate threat to anyone's life? (I'm talking immediate, as in, the jaws of a famished grizzly are snapped firmly on the tail pockets of your companion who is scrambling up the nearest tree.) In all likelihood, none of these conditions exist. Count this as a major blessing.

Step Two: Realize a couple of facts. The fact that you drove there means that other people can also drive there, and you may end up being accidentally rescued by another passerby. Also, recognize the fact that your vehicle is much more visible than you are. Be aware of how important that is. It will help you make one of the most critical decisions you will face—whether to stay put or try your hand at self-rescue (which, in terms of success, ranks right up there with do-it-yourself dental surgery).

Here's the brutal truth: if your decide to leave your vehicle and try to hoof it out, rescue teams in the air and on the ground will have far more difficulty finding you. We're talking the needle-in-haystack level of difficulty. They will probably find the vehicle but miss seeing you. This is especially true if you hike cross-country rather than following the road.

When James Kim decided, after nine days, to leave his family with the vehicle and try to find help, he started out doing the right thing by following the road back the way they had come. Unfortunately, the effects of hypothermia, caused by exhaustion from more than a week without food as well as the cold, wet conditions, led to a breakdown in his ability to make good decisions. Within a couple of miles of the car, he left the road, for reasons nobody can understand, and decided to hike cross-country. That was his death sentence. Within hours after James left his family, rescuers located the car, Kati, and the girls. Two days later, after intensive searching, they located James. It was too late.

It's decision time. Do you stay or go? In favor of staying with the vehicle and awaiting rescue are the following:

▶ The vehicle is a ready-made shelter.
▶ All your supplies are at the vehicle site.
▶ By staying put you conserve energy, meaning you need less food and water.
▶ The vehicle is more visible to rescuers than a hiker is.
▶ The vehicle serves as a psychological attachment to civilization, helping ward off feelings of panic.
▶ By staying right where you are, the entire party can work together to improve the camp, maintain signal fires, gather firewood, water, and food as well as bolster each other's spirits.
▶ Sticking to camp is less risky from an injury standpoint than hiking cross-country.
▶ If you remain with the vehicle, you run less risk of getting lost.
▶ Staying with the vehicle allows you to exploit all the resources of the locale, whereas a hiker can never take full advantage of the natural resources for survival because he is constantly moving.

If you decide to stay and make camp at the vehicle site, exert every effort to make the place visible to aircraft and to search parties on the ground. If scraping all the paint off the roof of the truck, down to shiny bare metal, will make it more visible, do it. Have signal fires ready to ignite (smoke by day, flames by night). Clear brush away from the vehicle. Arrange brightly colored items on the ground to attract attention. Remove mirrors and use them for signaling.

The decision to leave the vehicle and attempt to hike out for help should be made only if every item in the following list can honestly be met:

▶ You are absolutely certain that nobody is going to come looking for you at this location. (I firmly believe that James Kim reached this point. And I can understand why he did, after nine days with no evidence of a rescue attempt, so I do not criticize him for his decision.)

▶ Your health and fitness levels, and those of your party, permit the rigorous journey.

▶ You are positive of the direction and distance to reach help and know you can overcome every terrain obstacle along the route.

▶ After taking inventory of your supplies, you determine that you have everything necessary to successfully make the hike.

If you decide to leave the vehicle, it is important to leave a note in a highly visible place notifying rescuers of the following:

▶ Your name, address, phone number, and next of kin—and the same for every member of the party.

▶ Your age, state of health, and condition of fitness—same for everyone else.

▶ A detailed description of your clothing and equipment.

▶ A detailed hike plan, including the time and date you left the vehicle, your intended destination, direction of travel, and intended campsites along the way.

The decision to leave a disabled vehicle and hike out is a difficult one. The wrong decision sometimes means the difference between simply an unexpected stay in the wilderness and a true survival situation.

Unless there are compelling reasons to abandon the camp, the safest policy is to stay with the vehicle and continue your signaling efforts until help arrives. In the end, the cursed vehicle that broke down in the first place may well be the very thing that attracts the attention of search teams. All things considered, even a disabled vehicle can be a blessing in the backcountry.

Surviving the Elements

2

In virtually every survival situation that does not involve a medical emergency, obtaining protection from the elements rises to the top of the priority list. The human body quickly and easily suffers from overexposure to the sun, wind, cold, humidity, or lack thereof. While there are tales of heroically surviving extremely brutal conditions, suggesting that the human body can endure a great deal of torment and deprivation (which is true), it is far better to prevent the suffering than to endure it. Proper shelter, established early in the game, is one of the best ways to avoid unnecessary physical and psychological distress.

Survival requires an organized approach to life in the wilderness. Step by step, you must always stay ahead of the game. Here are a few of the basics that will be covered in greater detail as we go along in this chapter.

▶ Be prepared with proper clothing and equipment.
▶ Stay dry.
▶ Stay warm or cool as the season demands.
▶ Use what's available for emergency shelter.
▶ Sleep off the ground when possible.

The shelter you wear

Unlike some other members of the animal kingdom, we are without feathers and, for all practical purposes, hairless. We cannot sink into the mud and dehydrate into a state of suspended animation until the next rain, then magically reemerge. We cannot eat one final feast, crawl into a cave, and hibernate until spring. Of all animal life, human beings are among the most delicate. Our skin is unsuitable to deflect stings and bites or the effects of a harsh sun, a thorny plant, or a chill wind. A few degrees up or down in body core temperature spells death.

Because we are so unfit to endure harsh conditions dressed as we came at birth, our survival depends on the ability to manipulate our environment by using shelter and clothing. When we leave the protection of a structure or a vehicle, clothing becomes our primary shelter.

Naturally, season is a concern, but proper clothing protects against more than just heat or cold. It is a barrier against anything that causes damage, such as sun, wind, abrasions, bug bites, and stings. Life outdoors calls for "real" clothing. Don't be fooled by popular TV programs depicting beachwear in survival situations. In reality, long sleeves, long pants, and sturdy footwear offer the best protection against nature's

DURING warm weather, zip-off cargo pants offer excellent flexibility, providing leg protection with the option of shorts when full coverage is not needed.

A WIDE-brimmed hat is preferred to limit exposure to the sun, but if a wide brim isn't available, use a piece of cloth tucked in the back of your hat (or just draped over your head) to shade neck and ears.

weapons. In mild to hot conditions, my personal preference is a pair of lightweight cotton/nylon-blend, zip-off cargo pants because they provide good protection and give me the choice of long or short when it's hot or cold. A lightweight long-sleeved shirt (with sleeves that can be rolled up and secured by a button) worn over a T-shirt provides the warmth of layering, protection against bugs and brambles, and the option of removing or adding what I need as the situation changes.

Hot-weather clothing shields against exposure to the sun and allows your body to cool itself through evaporation. Look for lightweight, light-colored fabrics that will reflect rather than absorb the sun's rays. Ventilation is important to minimize overheating and perspiration. A loose fit is more comfortable and allows air to circulate over your skin to promote cooling. Boots or sturdy shoes not only protect against impact injury but also prevent sun- or heat-blistered feet. To defend the neck and ears, wear a broad-brimmed hat or drape a handkerchief around the sides and back of a baseball cap, French Foreign Legion–style. UV-protective sunglasses complete your daytime wardrobe. But be prepared for cold temperatures at night by having an insulating layer you can add when needed.

In cold weather, proper selection of clothing material is especially important. There is an old saying among veteran outdoorsmen about winter clothing: "Cotton kills." Sounds grim, but the truth is that cotton absorbs and retains moisture. One of the leading causes of hypothermia is moisture that is held next to the body, so cotton is a fabric that, under the wrong conditions, can get you into trouble. But the fact is that a lot of today's clothing is made of cotton or a cotton/polyester blend. This is even true of clothing on the racks of good outdoor equipment stores. If you have a choice, select other materials, but if you are wearing cotton in the outdoors, take extra precautions to keep the clothes dry. For clothing that will be worn in cold and/or wet weather, the best materials move moisture away from the body through wicking action. There are both natural and man-made fabrics that offer superior wicking action; wool is the best natural fiber for this purpose, but polyester blends and polypropylene lead the game when it comes to synthetics. For those who think they have to settle for synthetic fibers to avoid the itch of wool, the good news is that lightweight merino wool garments are excellent for use as the layer closest to the body or for mid-layers, and they are soft as brushed cotton against the skin. Some of today's wool clothing can be machine washed for added convenience. If you want wool clothing but can't find it at your local outdoor retailer, search the Internet for places such as Cabela's (www.cabelas .com), L.L. Bean (www.llbean.com), or REI (www.rei.com).

It is best to wear cold-weather clothing in layers that are loose enough to trap air in order to retain body heat. By dressing in layers, you can add or subtract clothing as required by the conditions. The three primary layers are the base layer, an insulation layer, and an outer shell. If each layer is capable of being opened (with a zipper, buttons, etc.) rather than being a pullover, you have the flexibility of venting body heat and moisture to help prevent the buildup of moisture next to your body.

The primary purpose of the undergarment layer is to hold body-temperature air next to the skin while wicking moisture away from the skin. One of the most important characteristics of each insulation layer (you might wear more than one, depending upon conditions) is loft that traps warmed air. Some natural insulation materials, such as down, are superior when dry but soak up water and lose loft when wet and become poor insulators. In damp conditions, synthetics are best. Ideally, the shell layer should be windproof, waterproof, and breathable, preventing moisture from entering from outside while allowing body moisture to move through the fabric to the outside atmosphere.

Rapid heat loss takes place from the head, neck, and wrists, so important features of cold-weather clothing include:

IN cold weather, multiple layers of clothing trap air and provide valuable insulation. A base layer that wicks away body moisture is covered by an intermediate insulation layer, and that is covered by a breathable but windproof shell layer.

- ▶ A hood that can be positioned and adjusted over the head and around the face to control air movement at the head and neck.
- ▶ Sleeves with adjustable wrist closures.
- ▶ A drawstring at the waist and another one at the bottom of the shell to prevent air movement around the body.
- ▶ The shell layer should be long enough to cover your hips.
- ▶ There should be adjustable vents to permit the escape of perspiration moisture.

As an example of my cold-weather clothing, I wear Thermax undergarments, then either a wool shirt or a combination of fleece insulation items, such as a vest and a lightweight long-sleeved jacket. When I

WHEN your hands or feet get cold, cover your head. This old woodsman's adage describes how important it is to keep body heat from escaping from your head and neck, areas of your body that lose warmth rapidly. A hood adds valuable protection.

need an outer shell, I wear a hooded and oversized shell parka that is windproof, waterproof, and breathable. It is long enough to cover my hips, has a snow skirt in lieu of a drawstring waist, a bottom drawstring, wrist closures, and pit zips to ventilate the armpit area. Beneath the shell's adjustable hood, I wear a fleece hat with side covers that can be folded up over the top or lowered and secured beneath my chin to protect my neck and ears. To protect my lower body, I wear Thermax undergarments, then a pair of wool pants. Depending upon the conditions, I might forgo the wool pants and wear trousers made of synthetics, then add a windproof shell layer. The best windproof pants are made of waterproof, breathable material that allows your body's moisture to escape while keeping rain or snow from penetrating from the outside.

When it's extremely cold, I prefer mittens rather than gloves. Inside a mitten, fingers share warmth with each other, whereas inside gloves, fingers are isolated and can become cold. My choice of hand protection in moderate conditions is a pair of Windstopper gloves. In cold and windy weather, I put on a neoprene face shield that wraps around my head and secures in the back for protection against frostbite.

The feet need lots of protection because they (and your hands) are the first parts of your body to suffer in cold weather. Depending upon conditions, your choice of footwear can range from waterproof hiking boots to Sorels with felt liners to arctic mukluks over wool socks. Be careful to avoid forcing your feet into boots that are too tight, because this inhibits circulation and leads to frostbite.

GLOVES are great, but mittens are even better in extreme cold.

Dress carefully. Your clothes are your first line of defense against the elements—they're really a wearable shelter.

THE SHELTER YOU CARRY

Anyone venturing into the backcountry and intending to spend even a single night will normally carry a shelter system consisting of a tent and a sleep system. This shelter you carry is among the most basic of "survival gear" and so must be chosen with due consideration of the anticipated weather, with "anticipated" going beyond what's really expected to include what might be anticipated in a worst-case scenario. True, adequate emergency shelters can often be constructed from available materials in the wild, but these may not be as effective as gear designed for the purpose, and the effort that must be expended in materials gathering and construction can sap valuable energy.

Tent

When it comes to shelter, the next step up from clothing is a tent. I confess that there was a time when I leaned toward a primitive outdoor lifestyle, and I've spent time sleeping under the truck or in a cave to get out of an unexpected midnight drizzle. That works, but nowadays I think it's better to have a tent.

Actually, no single tent is perfect for all occasions, so I have a couple to choose from, depending upon circumstances and the number of people in the party. There are times when I hit the trail knowing full well that when the truck is parked, I'm going to slip a backpack over my shoulders and head deeper into the wildlands. Other times, the whole family is going to camp right next to the vehicle. Those are the situations that tell me whether to take my super-lightweight backpack tent or the big cabin tent.

Size and shape are not the only fundamental differences between tents, so let's take a look at the most important factors to consider when trying to choose a tent. Some of the questions you need to ask yourself are:

▶ What will be the most frequent use of the tent—backpacking or camping close to the vehicle?

▶ How many people will be using the tent at one time?

▶ Is cost a big factor?

▶ Is multi-season use a consideration, or will the tent be used mainly during summer months and mild weather?

For those who never intend to backpack, there are tents that fall into the category for "car camping." Tents in this category are relatively large and heavy because weight and bulk are not extremely important when the vehicle is doing all the hauling. Some of these tents have vertical walls on all sides and a ceiling height that can reach seven feet—plenty of room to stand up and move around, and the vertical walls allow space for cots. Almost all the comforts of home. Such a tent can measure 10 by 20 feet, feature room separations inside, sleep twelve people, weigh in the neighborhood of 50 pounds, and cost several hundred dollars. Of course, you can also find a nice cabin tent that measures 9 by 12 feet, sleeps five, weighs less than 25 pounds, and costs much less. There's a lot of variety.

Maybe you prefer a dome tent, which is very suitable for family use. Domes are interesting for a couple of reasons. They are freestanding, meaning they don't need to be staked to the ground or have guy lines to hold them up. In fact, a dome tent can be erected in one place, then easily picked up and moved to another spot. And they stand up well to severe winds. A typical 8-by-8-foot dome is compact when broken down, weighs about 10 pounds, and sleeps four people.

One of my shelters is the Kamp-Rite Tent Cot that I bought from Paha Qué Wilderness, Inc. (www.pahaque.com). This is a two-minute shelter that I can set up in sixty-one seconds (yes, I timed it) from the time I take it out of the vehicle until the moment I crawl inside it and out of the weather. Add another minute to install the rain fly. It goes on something like a fitted sheet, with a couple of tie-downs on each side. As the name implies, the Tent Cot is a cot with a tent built over the top. It has zip-open doors on both sides and both ends, with zippered no-see-um screens for protection against the bloodsuckers. This arrangement gives total control over ventilation, privacy, and protection against wind and rain. The cot is up off the ground about a foot, so nothing creepy or crawly can bother, and it eliminates direct contact

A FAMILY tent with bug screens provides lots of protected space for everyone to spread out and relax.

WHEN the group consists of only two to four individuals, a compact dome tent offers adequate sleeping space.

with wet, cold, or lumpy ground. The Tent Cot is rugged enough for the military. In fact, Paha Qué received a letter from a soldier serving in Iraq, who wrote that he had been using a Tent Cot for sixteen months in that combat theater. He praised the company for making such a tough and capable product. The downside is that the Tent Cot is bulky and cumbersome to carry. It works well if you're carrying it with a vehicle, but it's not a feasible backpacking shelter.

At the other end of the scale are the ultralight backpack tents, which are excellent for use when minimal weight and compact size are important. What you sacrifice with this type of tent is spaciousness and stand-up room. These tents are basic shelter with low profile and are intended primarily for sleeping or taking refuge from a storm. Obviously, tents are not sold by the pound, because a superlight, tiny, high-quality backpack tent can cost more than a big cabin tent.

A TENT cot provides shelter and raises you off the ground. They're handy for camping with motor vehicles but too cumbersome for backpackers.

After you've decided general size and shape, choose the correct type of material. An error here can result in misery. The problem is that people are humid creatures, and when sealed up in a waterproof tent we quickly fill the air with enough moisture that

BACKPACK tents offer high mobility because they are lightweight and very compact. There's only enough room inside for sleeping, but there is often a protected vestibule for storing boots and packs.

it will begin to condense on the inside of the material and create our own little indoor rainstorm. Realizing this, tent manufacturers develop methods of getting the humidity out without letting bad weather in by clever use of appropriate materials and by designing ventilation openings in the structure.

Early tents were made of canvas, and some still are. The material is porous enough to allow interior humidity to pass through to the outside. When soaked by water, the fibers swell and seal the pores enough to make the shelter fairly water resistant, although a hard rain can cause some moisture to penetrate. Touching the canvas when the outside is wet causes capillary action to draw water through the fabric to the inside, creating a leak. Canvas is heavy and bulky, especially when it has absorbed a lot of water. And it will mildew and rot if packed away without first being thoroughly dried out.

Nylon is a common tent material because it is so lightweight and durable. It dries quickly after a storm and resists mildew and rot. There are a couple of different types of nylon used in tent manufacture. Taffeta is heavier and more durable, so it is generally waterproof-coated with urethane and used for floors and rain flies. Ripstop nylon has distinctive reinforcing threads that crisscross about every quarter inch. Being lighter and less durable than taffeta, ripstop is generally used for tent walls and roofs. Uncoated ripstop nylon is not waterproof, so a waterproof rain fly is used to cover the roof when there is a threat of rain.

There are high-tech materials such as Gore-Tex that are waterproof and breathable. A roof and walls made of these materials shed water but still allow interior moisture to pass through to the outside, making it possible to do away with the rain fly. These tents are more expensive and require careful handling to prevent damage but are generally lighter and more compact (because there is no fly) and allow for an easier setup.

When shopping for a tent, be aware that there are a couple of different ways that tent material is stitched, and one is better than the other. Double-stitched felled seams are preferred for strength and can be recognized by examining the seams: they have two rows of stitching, and the edges of material are overlapped and folded together to interlock the fabric prior to stitching. Examine the workmanship of the seams to see that there are between 6 and 12 stitches per inch (fewer than 6 stitches doesn't give enough strength to the seam, and more than 12 tends to weaken the fabric). Stitching should be straight and pucker-free. Cotton/polyester thread is best because it swells slightly when wet to help seal the stitch holes. Nylon thread is too hard and can cut the fabric when tension is applied.

Some of the important features to look for in a tent include:

▶ A waterproof floor that extends about 6 inches up the walls on all sides.
▶ Screened door and vent windows to provide cross-ventilation while keeping bugs out. Dark-colored netting is easier to see through than light-colored netting.
▶ An awning over the entry to keep rain away from the door.
▶ Interior pockets to hold small items such as eyeglasses or other miscellaneous stuff.

Hollow support poles that are connected to each other with elastic cord are easier to erect and keep track of than poles that are separate. Unless you are an expedition camper, you probably won't need special features like snow tunnels or cook holes in the floor.

Life in a tent requires a bit of care to keep from destroying the fabric. Clear away anything on the ground that might damage the floor before erecting the tent. Consider spreading a tough, plastic tarp over the ground for added protection and then set up the tent on the tarp. It is good policy to remove shoes or boots before entering, to keep from wearing holes in the floor. A small whisk broom is handy for sweeping out dirt, bugs, and leaves that manage to sneak inside. Operate the zippers slowly and carefully to prevent damage to the bug screens. And when the trip is over, set the tent up in the yard or garage to clean it, air it out, and dry the fabric before storing.

Properly chosen and cared for, a good tent will last nearly a lifetime, and it beats the heck out of sleeping under the truck. Now the next thing you need is a good sleeping bag.

Sleeping Bag

Some memories (especially the most miserable ones) refuse to die. Take my first Boy Scout outing, for example. Armed with a brand-new sleeping bag that was stuffed with a material called kapok, I marched into camp and buttoned my shelter half to one belonging to another boy. As I unfurled my sleeping bag, the other kid asked a technical question: "What's in your bag?" That's when I suffered a momentary lapse. All I remembered was that the material started with the letter k, so I blurted out the first thing that came to mind. Unfortunately, the word I came up with had nothing to do with sleeping bags—being more commonly employed as a feminine hygiene product. On that camping trip, I nearly died twice. Once from embarrassment and again because I almost froze to death in that dang sleeping bag.

The good news is that today's sleeping bags are light-years ahead of the old technology. The bad news is that, unlike my old kapok-filled bag, a high-quality sleeping bag drains your wallet of several hundred

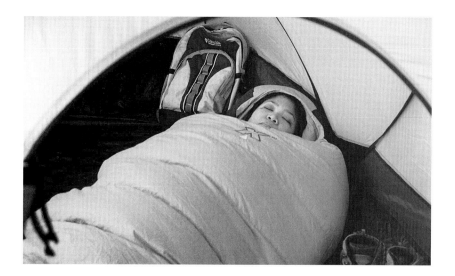

A GOOD sleeping bag is among the most valuable gear you can own, because it can preserve valuable body heat in cold weather. Goose down provides the best insulation value for weight, but some synthetic materials come close and are even preferred in certain situations.

dollars. But then you have to ask yourself, what is the value of comfort? Personally, the older I get, the more valuable comfort is.

One of the most important items of outdoor equipment is a good sleeping bag. It can save your life, serving as shelter that not only protects you from the elements but also helps you retain critical body temperature. The question is, what are the qualities and characteristics of a good sleeping bag? Here are some things to be aware of as you're shopping for your next sleeping bag.

- ▶ **Insulation value.** Match the insulation value of your bag to the seasons and locations you will use it. A minus-20-degree expedition bag is not what you need for summer camping in the Deep South.
- ▶ **Weight.** Lighter is better if you are backpacking, but not if you carry your gear in a vehicle.
- ▶ **Loft.** *Loft* is the term used to describe a measurement of the fluffy thickness of a sleeping bag's insulation. Good insulation with lots of loft traps air between the fibers, and it's the dead air that keeps you warm.
- ▶ **Fit.** This is a totally personal matter, but for optimum warmth, a cozy fit that still allows you to move around comfortably inside the bag is best. The foot box should provide ample room for feet and toes. Make sure you have

adequate room for your shoulder and chest and sufficient length for your height. Some manufacturers offer bags designed specifically for women, cut slightly narrower in the shoulder area but with more generous space for hips.

▶ **Details of construction.** A cold-weather bag should have an insulated draft tube running the length of the zipper inside the bag to prevent cold air from coming through the zipper. The zipper needs to have large pull tabs, so you can grab them even with gloves on. A layer of stiff material in the lining adjacent to the zipper helps prevent catching the bag lining material in the zipper. There should be a fully insulated hood that is adjustable by using a drawstring. Comfort is increased if there is extra insulation in the foot box and torso. Look for construction technique that ensures that there are no sewn-through seams that create regions of poor insulation.

▶ **Accessories.** Get a waterproof stuff sack to keep the sleeping bag dry and protected from damage.

▶ **Maintenance.** Most bags stuffed with man-made insulation material can be machine washed, but down bags cannot. When it comes time to have the bag cleaned, follow the manufacturer's recommendations. Day-to-day treatment includes opening the bag and allowing it to air out—all bags are happier if they are stored open, permitting the insulation material to expand.

▶ **Insulation material.** Mother Nature wins this contest. Pound for pound, the best sleeping bag insulation is prime goose down. The other thing goose down does best is compress, making it easy to stuff the bag into a small sack. If these were the only factors involved in selecting the best sleeping bag insulation, we would look no further. But life isn't that simple.

Even with all its good qualities, there are a few downsides to down. One, when it is wet, down stops insulating. Two, when it is dry, if the bag gets ripped, the down will escape and leave voids in the insulation layer. Three, under some conditions, down clumps into lumpy globs, leaving areas without insulation. And four, even the fluffiest goose down compresses under the weight of your body, leaving you without much insulation or comfortable padding under you.

Make no mistake, I'm not condemning down bags outright. In fact, I own one. But to make sure the bag does its job, I make sure it never gets wet (I don't take it on canoe trips, for instance), and I use an insulating pad under the bag to provide extra insulation and comfort when my weight compresses the floor of the bag. I also keep it away from the campfire, where sparks can burn through the cover and release the feathers.

There are some high-tech, man-made materials like Polarguard 3D that are nearly as good as down when it comes to insulation. Among the good characteristics of this material are that it doesn't clump and it won't escape if the bag gets ripped or burned. Being synthetic, the material does not absorb moisture. If it gets soaked, it can be wrung out and continues to insulate even when damp.

Bags made with synthetic insulation are quite a bit less expensive than their down counterparts. As a comparison, a 15-degree Lamina bag made by Mountain Hardwear that weighs in at 4 pounds, 14 ounces costs about $140. Match that against a 15-degree Phantom down bag from the same company that tips the scale at only 1 pound, 15 ounces but drains the wallet to the tune of $350. It costs a lot to buy a 3-pound weight savings. The question to ask is, what could you do with the $200 savings—perhaps buy a nice waterproof bivvy or some upgraded clothing?

Admittedly, the dark side of synthetics is that they are bulkier, and it takes a heavier bag to equal the insulation of down. On the other hand, with a layer of less compressible synthetic insulation beneath your shoulders and hips, you might be able to get away without having to add the weight and bulk of an insulating pad that is (in my book) absolutely required with a down bag.

WHEN shopping for a sleeping bag, look for the temperature rating tag and the information about the type of insulation material.

If money is no object, choose the best bag to suit your location, activity, and mode of transportation. If you're kayak camping during the rainy season and you know getting soaked is a possibility, go with synthetics. On the other hand, if you're backpacking into a dry camp where you'll be sleeping on a mattress in a tent where you're assured of staying dry, down is the choice.

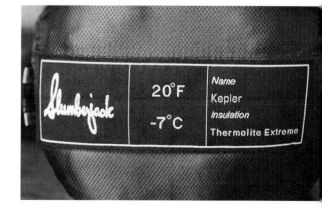

Pads

How much more comfortable will you be if you add a closed-cell foam pad or a self-inflating mattress under your sleeping bag? From the standpoint of heat loss, any insulation under your bag is better than lying on the bare ground. Conduction is the method of heat transfer that you suffer when you are in direct contact with a cold object (like the ground). Any dry insulation layer that keeps you from direct contact with the cold object offers resistance to thermal loss through conduction. This resistance is called the material's R value. The higher the R value, the better.

Here are the characteristics that make for a good sleeping pad or mattress.

▶ **Weight vs. comfort.** The most comfortable pads are the heaviest. If you're backpacking, you have to make some compromises.
▶ **Durability.** Air mattresses and self-inflating air/foam mattresses are comfortable but require care to prevent punctures. Closed-cell foam pads are puncture-proof but provide less comfort.
▶ **Size.** For best performance from the pad, you want protection under the full length and width of your body, so use a pad or mattress that is large enough to give full coverage.
▶ **Winter camping.** Some experienced cold-weather outdoorsmen combine a closed-cell pad and a self-inflating mattress. By placing the pad beneath the mattress, extra comfort and thermal protection are provided.

A SLEEPING pad adds comfort and insulation beneath a sleeping bag. Closed-cell foam pads (right) are less expensive and more durable than inflatable foam pads (left), but bulkier. Inflatable pads offer better insulation and comfort.

This system also protects the self-inflating mattress from damage. If you're using this technique, slightly overinflate the mattress, because additional air increases the insulation value.

THE SHELTER YOU MAKE

When a tent is not available, you must either find or construct an emergency shelter. Erecting a suitable shelter actually plays several critical roles. First, it protects against the elements. Second, it can be constructed to serve as a visual signaling device that aids in a search-and-rescue operation. And third, it provides a powerful psychological benefit by allowing the individual to enjoy the relative comfort of a secure camp. "Now we're just camping" is the mental cushion on which the individuals involved comfort themselves. That alone makes a huge difference in the way everyone feels about the situation.

The best shelters are those that are tight against the wind and offer protection against precipitation. Those elements are enemies of the human body, so staying dry and protected against the blistering heat of the sun or the chilling wind is extremely important. A secondary concern is that the shelter is secure from (or at least is located so it doesn't promote) invasion of insects and animals. Another desirable element is that the shelter be highly visible so it can attract the attention of potential search-and-rescue teams. Sounds like a colorful expedition-quality tent, doesn't it? But a high-zoot piece of camping gear may not always be available, so the survivor must know how to improvise.

Protection against the elements may be offered by something as primitive as a rocky outcropping, a pile of driftwood, an overhanging ledge, or the protective

WHEN a tent isn't available, use whatever nature provides as a means of erecting a shelter. The base of this overturned tree could provide a solid support for a lean-to.

BE creative in the use of every natural resource. Depending upon the season, you might need shelter from the hot sun, a cold wind, or precipitation.

wall created by the upturned root system of a downed tree. These natural shelters can be further improved by using available brush, rocks, limbs, slabs of bark, or whatever can be found to enclose a protective space. By paying attention to the direction of the prevailing wind and utilizing what nature provides, a cozy enclosure can be constructed.

Of course, natural shelters are usually pretty well camouflaged. If you're hoping for rescue, you need something to make it stand out against the backdrop of the natural landscape so searchers will see it. Place colorful equipment (a backpack, sleeping bag, jacket, etc.) on or around the exterior of the shelter to attract attention.

If you're lucky enough to have a few things with you to employ in making an emergency shelter, life will be much easier. Something as inexpensive and lightweight as a pocket poncho or an emergency blanket will perform extremely well at shielding you from wind and rain and is the fastest and easiest way to make a lean-to shelter. And if it is brightly colored or shiny, so much the better from the standpoint of attracting the attention of search teams. In forested areas, use tree branches to make

BARK slabs can often be pulled from fallen trees for use as covering for an emergency shelter.

WHERE there are cliffs or rock formations, look for an over-hang or cave where you can take shelter. Always check for unfriendly animals or insect pests and make sure that the roof is secure.

sloping rafters for the lean-to, then tie the emergency blanket or poncho to the poles. If there are no tree limbs to use as supports, secure the upper and lower corners of the poncho or emergency blanket by weighting them down with rocks, then stretch the roof as tight as possible.

If you're near a vehicle, the best shelter might be inside if the weather is mild. However, if you're dealing with extremely high or low temperatures, taking refuge inside is exactly the wrong thing to do. A vehicle interior can become hot as an oven or cold as a refrigerator, so it is often better to move outside where you can position yourself in the shady path of a breeze or where you can keep a warm fire burning. The vehicle is still useful, though, because you can remove the hood and prop it up to form a makeshift lean-to shade shelter. Or, you can strip out the carpeting, headliner, or door panels and put them to use as part of the shelter. When it comes to survival, don't worry about a little cosmetic damage to the vehicle—you're trying to save your life.

It's important to be careful about where you set up the shelter. Make sure it is on ground that is not infested with ants, subterranean hornets, or other insects, and where the natural drainage of rainwater won't flood the camp. Try to establish a shelter whose opening takes

A LEAN-TO shelter can be erected quickly of poles made from small downed trees. If you can find a natural ridgepole, use that. Or lash a pole between two trees to make the ridge. Then angle a pair of braces up to the ridge to support the roofing materials.

USING bootlaces or pieces of cordage, an emergency blanket can be tied across the ridgepole and down the side poles to form the roof. This type of shelter can be erected in a matter of minutes after the supporting structure is built.

THE tarp lean-to will provide shelter from sun, snow, or rain. For more protection, use other forest materials to form sidewalls, and position the shelter to block the wind. Then build a fire in front of the opening so the warmth will reflect down on you from the roof.

advantage of the prevailing climate. North-facing is best in hot weather to avoid the direct glare of the sun. During cold weather, the shelter should face southeast to catch the earliest warmth of morning sunshine. This is all presuming that you are in the Northern Hemisphere. Opposite directions apply to the Southern Hemisphere.

Once the elements are no longer a threat, turn your attention to making the shelter as visible as possible to aid in the search-and-rescue effort. Do anything that will attract the eye of a searcher. Clear foliage from around the area. Make tracks that lead to the shelter. Set up "unnatural" objects such as piles of rocks, or arrows on the ground made of rocks that point toward the shelter, or a message drawn in the hard soil. If you have a Space Blanket or other bright fabric, use it as an attention-getting cover for the shelter or simply spread it on the ground and weight it down with rocks or logs so it won't blow away. Something as simple as that can be seen from a distance and may be just the thing that attracts a rescue party.

Sleep off the Ground

As you work to improve your situation, one consideration should be getting yourself up off the ground. Trying to sleep on damp, sloping, lumpy ground can be miserable. Not only that, but sleeping on the ground might put you in harm's way if you're in snake country or where there are scorpions, spiders, ants, or other critters that will come looking for a meal or a warm place to cuddle at night.

AFTER the shelter is made, lay out trail markings to direct searchers to your location. A simple arrow made of loose stones or branches will do the job.

There are a couple of options for getting yourself up off the ground. Perhaps the easiest is a hammock. If you don't have one, see if you can improvise one by using whatever you can find. A length of rope tied to each end of the seat cover fabric scavenged from your dead vehicle will work.

If a hammock is out of the question, consider building a sleep shelf by lashing the ends of two parallel poles to a couple of supporting logs and then adding crossbars to form the shelf. (Lashing techniques discussed in Chapter 9 will be useful in building this type of shelter.) Lay on some dry grasses or pine duff to soften the bed, and then build your shelter over this shelf.

It's worth every minute you spend building an emergency shelter and then working to constantly improve its protective capability and comfort level, because this is what will shield you from the elements and turn a survival situation into a much more tolerable experience.

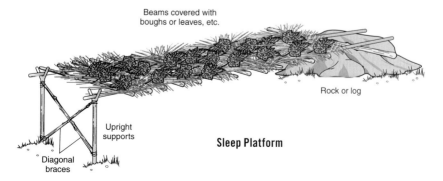

Beams covered with boughs or leaves, etc.

Rock or log

Upright supports

Diagonal braces

Sleep Platform

LASH poles together to make a sleep shelf. This keeps you off the lumpy, cold ground and away from ground-crawling insects.

Who knows, one day your ability to erect a shelter from the natural materials you can find around you may even save your life.

WET-WEATHER SURVIVAL

Human beings must stay dry to remain healthy. This is especially important in a survival situation, when it is often difficult to control our environment. Getting wet leads to misery and sometimes even to death from hypothermia.

The fact is that even a warm, tropical rain that does not feel uncomfortable can lead to hypothermia. Moisture on your skin is nature's air conditioner and serves an important purpose during hot weather. As the moisture evaporates, it cools the body and helps keep the core temperature in the right range. But during cool weather, moisture on the skin is a threat to our survival. That's when it becomes a top priority to get dry and stay warm.

It takes the application of solid survival technique to survive in wet weather, and if you have the added benefit of good equipment, it makes the whole ordeal easier. Let's talk about equipment first. Clothing is your first line of defense against the elements. The best clothing will keep outside water from coming through your clothes while allowing perspiration moisture to escape into the outside atmosphere. This characteristic is called breathability and is available in quality outdoor gear ranging from boots to hats and everything in between.

Since your feet are the most likely parts of your body to be in contact with water, start with waterproof boots. Wet feet are not only uncomfortable but are more prone to injury than dry feet. It literally can mean the difference between being able to hike or becoming lame and unable to help yourself with all the other survival duties. The most important consideration when choosing boots is that they fit well and serve the purpose. This is a form-over-function thing, so color and style are not important.

Inside your boots should be the best socks you can buy. Cotton socks absorb and hold moisture, keeping your feet cold and clammy. Wool or polyester socks are a better choice. Wool insulates even when damp and tends to wick moisture away from the skin. Polyester refuses to absorb moisture and dries quickly. Consider wearing a lightweight sock inside heavier socks as a blister prevention method.

Moving up, dry pants are next on our list. Hiking through a damp forest or beating your way through tall, wet grasses or bushes soaks pants. Wearing waterproof, breathable pants is ideal but expensive. An alternative to high-priced Gore-Tex is to wear nylon wind pants over wool pants. The nylon sheds water and dries quickly, and wool resists absorbing moisture that manages to get through the nylon. One bonus provided by wool is that it continues to insulate even when damp.

A waterproof coat is worth its weight in whatever precious metal you can name. Mine is a hooded shell that is both waterproof and breathable. It is sized large enough to fit comfortably over an assortment of insulation layers. Sometimes I wear it by itself as a rain jacket, but at other times I add insulation layers to keep me warm and dry. Under the arms are "pit zips" that can be opened for ventilation, because exertion can cause perspiration. Hypothermia doesn't care whether you get wet from rain or from sweat, so dress with openable or easily removable layers to make it easy to vent heat and moisture and to regulate your body temperature.

Becky and I have lightweight rain suits that are both waterproof and breathable for those times when rain but not cold is the prime concern. A rain suit should be large enough that it easily fits over other clothing. Also in my wardrobe of stay-dry clothing is a poncho that can be folded and stuffed in a cargo pants pocket. This gear doesn't have to be expensive; we bought ours at Wal-Mart for a reasonable price.

In addition to clothing that keeps you dry, you need a shelter that will do the same. A waterproof tent is an obvious choice, but in an emergency you might have to improvise. A tube tent, a compact poncho, or a Space Blanket can be pressed into service as an emergency shelter from the rain.

STAYING dry is the first step to staying warm. A lightweight rain suit protects against falling rain and also protects your pants from getting soaked while walking through wet brush or tall grass.

Choosing a suitable campsite makes all the difference in wet weather. A poorly selected site leaves the shelter wet and miserable. Select a spot that naturally drains water away from the shelter. Elevated ground offers a good chance for a dry camp, but stay off of ridges or hilltops where the wind will be a nuisance and lightning strike a danger.

If you are caught completely unprepared and have no equipment at all, you must understand techniques for making the best use of what nature provides. Study the topography, looking for ledges or caves that provide cover. Observe the direction of the wind and rain, and seek the lee (downwind) side of anything that offers itself as a windbreak. I've hunkered down in the lee of a large boulder that shielded me from cold, wind-driven rain. Study the vegetation, looking for dense thickets that shed water. In a pinch, I have taken shelter beneath a tight clump of bushes and found dry ground. Look for a cluster of downed trees or a large tree with bark that can be peeled off in slabs and laid against the horizontal trunk to form a lean-to.

In a downpour or even a steady drizzle, it is best to seek some kind of existing shelter rather than working on the construction of a shelter in the rain and becoming soaked to the skin. I'd rather hunker down in an uncomfortable but dry spot and wait for the rain to subside and then improve the situation later when there is less risk of becoming soaked. If there is nothing available that offers immediate protection, use whatever materials are at hand to make a shelter as quickly as possible. Look for some dead branches that can be propped up against a log to serve as roof rafters. Then interlace lighter limbs through the rafters so they will stay put, and finish by roofing the structure with bunches of long grass, piles of leaves, bark slabs, or anything else that will deflect the rain and wind.

The point is to be creative and use whatever is available to get out of the wet. An example of this is the day Becky and I took Ryan and Shane, our youngest boys, for a canoe ride on a lake in Wisconsin. The day was warm and sunny, but there were billowing clouds to the west that I kept my eyes on. Suddenly, a gust of wind hit us, and I looked over my shoulder to see that we were being overtaken by a fast-moving storm with black skies threatening heavy rain. Our first priority was to get off the lake as fast as possible to avoid the danger of capsizing. We reached the nearest shore just ahead of the storm, and before we had a chance to seek protection from the rain, the clouds opened with a vengeance. Quickly, we dragged the canoe to higher ground and rolled it over. Then we all crawled under the protection offered by the overturned canoe. The storm left as quickly as it had come, and we resumed our canoe trip, dry and safe.

In addition to wearing the proper clothing to protect yourself from wet weather, there are a few simple but effective techniques that will help you remain dry:

▶ Remain inside the shelter as much as possible while the rain is falling.
▶ Keep a small fire burning so you can stay warm and use the heat to dry articles of clothing that have become wet.
▶ To keep your supply of firewood dry, move it inside the shelter.

▶ As you walk through wet grass or underbrush, use a walking stick to knock the water off the grass and leaves and to part the way before you.

▶ Walk carefully, choosing the path that will keep your feet and legs as dry as possible.

▶ Do not sit on or lean against wet objects.

▶ Before sitting, spread a poncho, tube tent, or emergency blanket to keep the back of your pants dry.

▶ Make good use of breaks in the weather to gather firewood, improve the shelter, or move to a new campsite.

SURVIVING COLD WEATHER

We become so accustomed to flipping a switch and turning up the automatic temperature controls in our vehicles that it's easy to become complacent. I've known people who fail to take so much as a jacket along while traveling in winter conditions, rationalizing that they are only going a short distance and they'll be back home soon enough. It's a foolish assumption to make. It's much better to be overprepared than to leave ourselves vulnerable. Give yourself a fighting chance at survival by putting together a winter emergency travel kit and always dressing appropriately for the weather conditions. Contact local authorities to find out about dangerous road conditions. Consult weather information on the radio, TV, Internet, or other sources to learn about incoming weather systems that might hamper your travel plans, and be willing to change your plans or alter your routes of travel if conditions are not safe. (For tips on weather forecasting and weather safety, see Chapter 11.)

Gear to Carry in Your Vehicle

Those who live in parts of the country known for long winters and deep snow routinely carry emergency supplies in their vehicles. Here is a basic list of equipment that should be kept in your vehicle while traveling in snow country in the winter. Add to the list as you see fit.

SELF-RESCUE GEAR

▶ four-wheel drive with a winch

▶ tire chains

▶ shovel

▶ high-lift jack

▶ tow straps

▶ snowshoes or cross-country skis

SHELTER

▶ tent

▶ sleeping bags

▶ blankets

▶ warm clothing

▶ deep-winter boots

▶ gloves or mittens

▶ warm hat with ear and neck protection

▶ neoprene face mask

EMERGENCY FOOD

▶ high-energy stuff like GORP or power bars (see Chapter 5 for more information)

▶ a metal cup for melting snow for drinking water

FIRE-STARTING EQUIPMENT

▶ lighter

▶ waterproof matches

▶ emergency candle

▶ road flares

▶ backpack stove and fuel

COMMUNICATION

▶ notification of family or friends before starting out

▶ cell phone

▶ CB, FRS (two-way Family Radio Service radios), or ham radio and extra batteries

▶ signal mirror

▶ flashlight and extra batteries

▶ colorful cloth panels

▶ PLB (personal locator beacon; see Chapter 6 for more information)

Stay Warm, Stay Alive: The Hot Rock Bed

Cold-weather survival doesn't always involve snow, high mountains, or Arctic tundra. Even deserts can be bitterly cold and deadly.

It was supposed to be nothing more than a day hike on a crisp winter afternoon. Our destination was a cave where a thousand years ago the ancient people of the Four Corners slickrock country might have taken shelter. The very thought of it was intriguing. The sky was clear, and no foul weather was forecast. So we left our gear in the vehicle and headed down the canyon without a care in the world, figuring to be back by nightfall. That was a mistake.

Near the end of the down-canyon hike, Becky's foot blistered from a combination of ill-fitting socks and boots that were too new and stiff. At first, it was just a hot spot on her heel, and she decided to ignore it for a while. By the time she told me about her foot, we were almost to the cave and she was starting to limp. We removed the boot and sock to have a look at the injury, and I knew immediately that we weren't going to be hiking back up the canyon until her foot had a chance to recover somewhat.

So there we were, five miles from our vehicle. Night was only a few hours away, and we had nothing except the clothes we were wearing to keep us warm. Our clothing was simple—blue jeans, long-sleeved shirts, and jackets. Not the best, but after all, we hadn't planned on spending the night. And that's exactly how many survival situations begin—people trek off into the backcountry, sometimes less prepared than they should be, because they're not expecting problems to arise.

From the looks of the weather, the night was going to be clear. And that meant cold air at our elevation of nearly 6,000 feet, even though we were far enough south to see the Utah-Arizona border. I had seen this kind of thing before, and shuddered at the thought. On this night, the water in the creek would freeze hard, and I knew it would seem like an eternity before the sun rose to warm the earth again. The situation possessed all the potential of a real disaster.

Our choices were either to sleep on the frigid soil in our lightweight clothing or to come up with some other plan. The priority list read something like this—stay dry, get out of the wind, get a fire going so we can keep warm. Fortunately, all the natural resources were at hand to accomplish everything that needed to be done. But some special survival techniques also came into play.

Because the weather was fair, all we had to do to remain dry was stay out of the creek. During the hike, we took precautions to keep our feet dry, even though we crossed the stream several times. We looked for shallows where we stepped from rock to rock, and we used narrow spots to jump across. In a few places, we had no choice but to hike up and around terrain where there was no natural ford. This made the way more difficult, but it was far preferable to the consequences of getting wet.

A breeze will follow a canyon and funnel through it like a wind tunnel, so one of our concerns was to get out of the wind to conserve body heat. If you wait until you feel the cold, it's already late in the game. Not necessarily too late, if you have the means of restoring lost body heat, but it's far better to conserve than to restore.

As we covered the final distance to the cave, we made use of natural windbreaks as much as possible, moving in the wind shadow of boulders and brush. Suddenly, the cave was an even more important destination than it had been before, because now it was to be our shelter, not just an attraction for the sake of curiosity.

Cold air sinks to the bottom of a canyon, while warmer air rises. Staying in the canyon bottom exposed us to the bitterest cold the night offered, so we were fortunate that the cave was located midway up the side of the canyon wall. If the cave had been near creek level, we would have sought the protection of a rocky overhang or some other form of shelter at a higher elevation, where the ambient air temperature was more survival friendly. But with a topographic map in hand, I knew almost exactly what we would find when we turned the final corner and saw the cave a hundred feet upslope, where the air was warmer.

The final need was to add heat to our environment by making a fire—not just a little campfire that warmed our faces and hands while our backs froze all night long, but something that allowed us to sleep in comfort without the need to keep feeding the blaze. We didn't want to sit there and shiver through the endless gloom of one of the longest nights of the year waiting for a reluctant sun that seemed like it was never going to rise again.

We had to come up with a plan—assess the situation, look around and discover what was available, and do the best we could to improve our conditions. At the back of the cave where the sandy soil was loose and soft, we scooped out a shallow trench that was about eight feet long, four feet wide, and a foot deep. A shallow grave. Next, we lined the bottom of the trench with stones—not creek stones that might have moisture trapped inside that would turn to steam and shatter the stones when heated, but dry rocks from the area around the mouth of the cave. Then I went in search of firewood. Because of the technique we were using, we needed only enough firewood to keep the blaze going for a couple of hours.

We spread the wood throughout the trench and ignited it. We kept the fire going strong for about an hour to heat the stones thoroughly and to warm up the soil beneath them. Yes, it was smoky in the cave, but the convection current carried the smoke up against the cave ceiling and out the entrance, so all we had to do was stay low. In the gathering darkness and chill of night, the light and warmth of that fire felt very comforting.

After an hour or so, we moved the remaining bit of fire to a location we had prepared for a small campfire that provided light until we fell asleep. With the fire out of the trench, we raked the previously excavated sand over the hot rocks, covering the stones to a depth of eight or nine inches. Then we sat around our new campfire and waited for the heat from the rocks to penetrate the covering layer of sand, driving out any moisture remaining in the soil. Because the soil came from way back in a desert cave, there was very little moisture in it, but we gave it half an hour anyway. After thirty minutes, we stretched out on the warm sand that covered our hot rock bed.

Hot Rock Bed

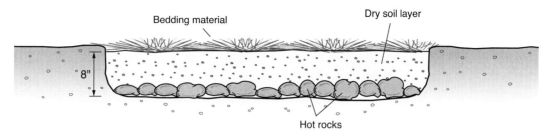

Bedding material

Dry soil layer

8"

Hot rocks

It felt so good to lie on the warm ground and feel our muscles relax. At first, we each had to lie beside our hot rock bed, because it was too toasty for us to lie directly on top. As the night progressed and the ground slowly lost its warmth, we gradually migrated toward the middle. By morning, we still felt a little bit of heat from the ground beneath us. We slept comfortably through a frozen night on soft, warm sand and were ready for a slow hike out of the canyon, going easy on Becky's injured foot.

It doesn't really matter whether there's a cave available, or you use a downed tree's root system as a wall to build a shelter against, or you find a rocky ledge. The techniques for surviving a cold night (or longer) in the wilds are the same. And they are not difficult, if you have a clear understanding of the priorities. Stay dry, protect yourself from the wind and other elements, and get a fire going. If you are without camping gear, use your ingenuity and the natural resources at hand to make the best shelter and fire you can.

Unexpected things happen in the outdoors, and it is important to be prepared with the equipment (a knife and fire-starting equipment) and techniques (such as building a hot rock bed) to get you through difficult situations.

The rule is: stay dry, stay warm, stay alive.

A HOT rock bed is an excellent emergency measure for surviving a cold night when no tent or sleeping bag is available.

Shelter in the Snow

In winter conditions, you have several shelter options. A tent is the fastest and easiest type of shelter to erect, and it will protect you against the snow and wind. But tent material is thin and doesn't provide very much protection against the cold. That doesn't keep expeditions to extremely cold places like Mt. Everest from using them, though.

A vehicle provides protection that is similar to that of a tent, but the inside temperature resembles a refrigerator at night because there is almost no insulation value to the sheet metal and glass. Snow can be used to improve the insulation value of a tent or a vehicle if the snow is piled over the top. A vehicle is able to support the load of snow without a problem, but the tent would have to be very sturdy to hold up under the weight of the snow. If you are able to reinforce the tent to withstand the load, a snow layer up the sides and over the top will help hold the warmth inside. In essence, the tent becomes similar to a snow cave, except that the roof won't melt and drip on you. But you want to be very careful about mounding snow over a tent, because if the structure collapses it might trap you inside. The best way to avoid the problem is to layer snow on thinly at first and then see how the tent holds up under the load. You don't need several feet of snow on the tent to improve the insulation; even just a few inches of snow will do wonders to help contain the warmth inside the tent.

Snow Cave. When the subject of snow shelters comes up, most people immediately think of snow caves. These are excellent shelters if conditions are right for their construction. The best place to build a snow cave is into the side of a deep snowdrift. To look for the deepest snow, check the lee side of a hill, and the snow on the north-facing slope will generally be deeper because it is more protected from direct sun that melts the snow on the south-facing side. It's also possible to find a suitable drift on the lee side of a boulder, where the wind-blown snow has accumulated.

To construct the snow cave, tunnel straight into the lowest part of the drift. The tunnel should be just large enough for you to crawl in and out easily. The reason you are tunneling low on the drift is to make it easy for the cold air to escape and the warmer air to be captured inside the cave. Keep the floor of the tunnel level as you burrow deep into the drift. After you have dug the tunnel straight for several feet, start to dig upward to create an interior dome that follows the contour of the slope. Strive to keep the roof consistently a couple of feet thick so you don't break through to the outside as you create the cave. As the cave interior is enlarged, sculpt a sleeping platform at a higher level against the back wall, making it long enough and wide enough for you to sleep comfortably. The raised platform will allow you to stretch out in the warmer air that collects in the upper part of the cave.

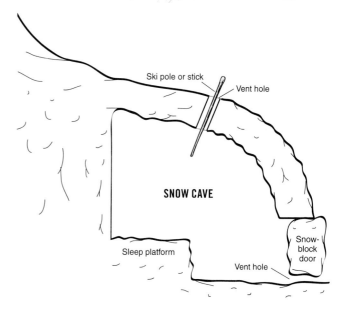

BY digging into the side of a deep snowdrift or a snow-covered hillside, you can carve out a cave that will protect against the bitter cold, wind, and snowfall. Make a vent hole in the roof and at the entrance to allow the free flow of fresh air to prevent suffocation.

The only other feature for the snow cave is the ventilation hole in the roof. You can make the hole by using a ski pole or a long stick. Poke the stick through the roof, and create a vent hole that is three or four inches in diameter. Then leave the stick protruding through the roof so you can use it to keep the hole open and free of snow, and to serve as a warning to anyone outside to prevent them from walking on and destroying the shelter. And finally there is the door. If you have a backpack, you can use it to block the doorway to help hold the warmth inside. If not, use snow blocks. Don't totally blockade the doorway, but leave another ventilation opening that will allow the heavier cold air to drain out.

The snow cave should not be warmed too vigorously or the roof will begin to melt and could collapse. A single candle is sufficient to bring the interior temperature as high as the snow cave can safely endure. Even though it's not really warm inside, the value of the snow cave is the protection it gives against the wind and weather outside.

The hardest thing about building a snow cave is trying to stay dry during construction. While crawling in the tunnel as you're carving the snow and shoving it outside, it is virtually impossible to stay dry. The only chance you have is to move very slowly and deliberately, paying close attention to avoiding contact with the snow. Pace yourself to prevent perspiration from soaking your clothes. If you get wet, your chances of survival diminish.

Quinzhee Mound. Another type of snow shelter that is similar to a snow cave is called a quinzhee mound. This is basically the same type of shelter but is built on level ground where no slopes or drifts exist. The quinzhee is constructed by mounding the snow into a huge heap and allowing it to settle naturally for a couple of hours. One of the drawbacks to this type of shelter is that you must suffer outside in the cold while that waiting period passes. To try to burrow into the snow mound too soon only invites a collapse of the structure. After the mound has had time to settle and firm up, you simply dig out the inside of the mound as you would for building a snow cave.

A QUINZHEE mound is similar to a snow cave, except that it is constructed by piling up snow on relatively level ground and then hollowing out a cave-like interior chamber. Create a sleep shelf so you can rest in the warmer air near the top of the shelter. Don't forget the airholes.

If the quinzhee will be built where there is a deep bed of snow, but it is all on level ground, the mound doesn't have to be extremely large. You will take advantage of both the mounded snow and the depth of snow below the mound. For example, if there is very little snow, and it will all have to be scraped together to make the mound, the diameter of the mound should be ten feet to accommodate a single occupant. If the snow is two feet deep, the mound need only be six feet across.

After mounding the snow and allowing it to settle, go to the downwind side of the mound and dig down as deep as possible into the snow several feet outside the perimeter of the mound, creating steps that lead down to the lowest level right below the outer edge of the mound. After digging down, dig horizontally toward the center of the mound for several feet into the mound.

Quinzhee Mound

Ski pole or stick

Vent hole

Sleep platform

Then start digging upward in an arc to carve the dome inside the shelter. To keep from breaking through the roof, pincushion the dome from the outside with sticks that are as long as you want the roof to be thick (about a foot long is good). As with a snow cave, shape the inside of the dome to follow the contour of the mound, and when you encounter the pincushion sticks you know you've scooped away enough snow and will be leaving about a foot of snow thickness to make the roof strong. As you remove snow from the floor area, create a raised sleeping platform that will allow you to rest up in the warmest air. Because the entrance doesn't allow the cold air to drain out the way it would in a snow cave, the lower level of the floor will trap the cold and hold it, making the raised sleeping platform all the more important.

Anytime you're scooping snow off the ceiling, as you do in a snow cave or quinzhee mound shelter, you are going to get wet from the falling snow. It is extremely important to minimize the amount of dampness in your clothing. Wear a poncho if you have one, and work slowly to prevent perspiration from dampening the clothes from the inside.

Covered Snow Trench. Faster and easier to build than either the snow cave or the quinzhee, the covered snow trench offers protection from wind and snowfall, but not as much insulation as the other two shelters. The covered snow trench can be built on level or sloping ground in any condition where the snow is deep enough to be scraped together to form a low wall structure.

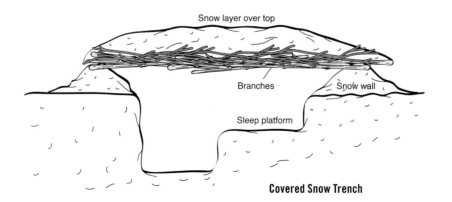

Snow layer over top

Branches

Snow wall

Sleep platform

Covered Snow Trench

A COVERED trench is the easiest snow shelter to build; it even works when the snow isn't very deep. Dig down and use the excavated snow to form walls around the trench. Place branches across the walls, then cover them with a layer of snow.

Begin by forming a trench in the snow that is about a foot longer than your body and three feet wide. Use the snow that is excavated from the trench to create a three-sided wall structure around the trench, with the opening facing downwind. Ideally, the trench should be about three feet from the floor to the top of the walls. An alternative method is to mound up what little snow there is to form walls on three sides of a trench-like space.

During construction, form a sleeping platform that is slightly higher than the floor so you can have a place to rest that is up out of the coldest air. Cover the platform with soft branches from evergreen trees, if they are available, to provide some insulation from the snow.

When the trench is complete, cut branches from trees and lay them over the walls and across the open trench to form rafters. Make this part of the structure strong, because it will bear the weight of snow that you will pile on top. If you have some kind of tarp material (a spare emergency blanket or poncho), spread this over the rafters to form a roof, and then carefully layer snow on top to provide insulation. If you have no man-made roofing material, keep laying on tree branches to strengthen and close the gaps between the rafters. Finish with lush evergreen boughs, and then carefully add a layer of snow until it is about a foot deep.

Use a backpack or a snow block to seal the entrance. Be sure to make a ventilation hole in the roof and the doorway, as you would for a snow cave or quinzhee mound.

Trapped by Snow

The weather is fickle and tricky and sometimes mysterious. Storms come and go, often behaving in strange ways that leave even the meteorologists scratching their heads. It wouldn't be so bad if head scratching was the worst that happened. But sometimes the unexpected storm traps people, leaving them with no way out. Taking every reasonable precaution is no guarantee that a storm system won't move in without warning and catch you unprepared. In Chapter 1, we visited the situation that engulfed the James Kim family, trapping them in their car miles from help. And they are not the only ones. It happens to many people each year all across the country. Sometimes they live. Sometimes they don't.

Severe winter storms can drop huge amounts of snow very quickly. At high elevations, it is not uncommon for a single storm to dump several feet of snow in a few hours. You might go to sleep in your truck camper with the ground only lightly covered with a thin scrim of snow but awake in the morning to find that the truck, camper, and everything else is covered by three or four feet of snow. Under those conditions, you're not going anywhere. If the campground, road, or rest area where you stopped is not critical to daily travel, it might be a long time before a snowplow clears the way to safety. Even if the road is normally used by traffic, a widespread storm might tie up the snowplows for several days before they can get to you. It's up to you to be able to survive until help comes.

The question is, what are you supposed to do if you are trapped by snow in your vehicle? In every survival incident, the first thing to do is assess the situation. Until you know the true nature of the situation, you are in no position to make decisions about what to do next. If you can listen to the radio, perhaps you can find a weather report that tells you if the storm is over or if more is coming. Try to determine where you are, how many miles it is to civilization, whether or not you expect someone to come along this route with a plow, or whether you're on your own. Take inventory of the supplies you have in the vehicle; look for blankets or sleeping bags, water, food, and a means of communication.

Ah yes, communication. That's a good place to start. After all, if you can "reach out and touch someone," the rescue effort can begin immediately. Maybe you'll be home before dinner. Do you have a cell phone or a CB radio? While it's certainly worth the effort to try one of these methods, you have to realize that CB radios and cell phones are very limited as to range of operation. On the other hand, amateur radio operators (hams) can transmit and receive messages across the country or around the world and use a relay system to get a message back to local authorities. In 2007, it became easier to become an amateur radio operator because, from that point on, Morse code was no longer required for testing. With my two-meter handheld ham radio that operates on a VHF (very high frequency) band and is, therefore, limited to line-of-sight transmission range, I have been able to talk with people more than 100 miles away. A small HF (high frequency) band radio that can be installed in a vehicle as easily as a CB has no range limitation and can contact people around the world. I encourage everyone to become a ham operator and carry a portable transceiver in the vehicle. It provides one more method of calling for help when you need it. The licensing process is simple—all you do is study the manual and take a written test. The best way to become licensed is to find an amateur radio club in your area, and they will help you get ready to pass the test. To find out more about this, go to www.arrl.org (the official website for the American Radio Relay League, the national association for amateur radio).

Do you have a PLB (personal locator beacon), as we discussed earlier? If so, and you are convinced that your life is in danger, now's the time to activate it. Take a look at Chapter 6 to read more about signaling. All of those techniques apply to this situation, and you should put as much effort as possible into sending a distress signal. Any way you can do it, signaling for help is a top priority, because the sooner you make contact with the outside world, the sooner you will be safe.

Also occupying the top of the priority list is taking steps to prevent cold-weather injuries like hypothermia and frostbite. Stay dry, stay out of the wind, do everything you can to prevent heat loss from your body. Dress warmly. Keep your head, neck, wrists, hands, and feet covered. Don't touch anything cold with your bare skin. Stay inside the vehicle or shelter, because it will protect you from wind, cold, and wet. If you have one, crawl into a sleeping bag. Keep yourself hydrated by drinking plenty of water. Eat high-energy foods to keep the caloric fires burning. (For information on field treatment of hypothermia, frostbite, and cold-water immersion, see Chapter 7.)

And now for the conundrum. Staying inside a vehicle can be good or bad, depending upon the situation. On the good side, it is a fact that the vehicle represents a dry and somewhat comfortable space that serves as a shelter against moisture and wind. It will serve as a ready-made snow cave, if there's enough snow to cover it to a depth of a couple of feet so the snow provides insulation. However, if there's just enough snow to keep you from traveling safely but not enough to cover and insulate the vehicle, then the sheet metal and glass enclosure starts to resemble an icebox.

It is tempting to run the engine so you can operate the heater, but there are both pros and cons to this tactic. On the pro side, the heater provides warmth to help ward off hypothermia and frostbite. On the con side, eventually the vehicle will run out of fuel and within a very short time the vehicle will be cold again due to lack of insulation. Rather than run the tank dry, you might want to save enough fuel to allow you to drive to safety after the snow melts or you find a way to extract the vehicle. Not only that, but operating the engine when the vehicle is trapped by snow might channel carbon monoxide from the exhaust system into the interior. Carbon monoxide poisoning puts you to sleep before you're aware of the danger and then does its deadly work. It's not a sure thing (nothing is, in a survival situation), but it's enough of a danger that it should be weighed in the balance as you're making decisions. (See Chapter 7 for a complete discussion of the dangers and prevention of carbon monoxide poisoning.)

If you're stranded very long (remember, the James Kim family were stranded for nine days before being rescued), you must figure out other ways to stay warm. At some point, you might need to establish a camp outside the vehicle so you can keep a fire going while at the same time use the vehicle for whatever shelter it can offer from wind and precipitation and for a comfortable place to sleep or rest. Staying near the vehicle offers two benefits: it is a powerful psychological connection with civilization and is the most highly visible object searchers will be looking for.

One of the most important tasks is to create signal devices—and here comes that conundrum again. Snow piled on the vehicle to help insulate the interior acts as camouflage, making it harder for searchers to spot from an aircraft. If you clear the snow off the vehicle, its colorful paint or shiny surfaces can be seen more easily, but there goes your nice snow cave.

Another way to make yourself more visible without having to uncover the vehicle and lose valuable insulation is by tying a piece of colorful cloth to the radio antenna as a signal to the first snowplow that comes by. If you have tools, consider removing the vehicle's hood and piling it on top of the insulating snow layer that is covering your vehicle, where it can serve as a colorful visual signal without removing the snow layer that's helping to keep you warm.

Forget about trying to hike out to civilization. Fighting your way through snow that's deep enough to trap your vehicle will only result in your becoming wet and exhausted and hypothermic and dead. Difficult as it is, be patient. Do the best you can to establish visible signals by keeping a fire going, making smoke, and using color and motion. (See Chapter 6 for effective signaling techniques.) Then stay near the vehicle, sit calmly, and conserve your energy.

Avalanche

Every winter people are killed by avalanche. One might think this is because those folks are out looking for adventure and sometimes they find more than they were looking for. But that's not the only scenario. Consider what happened in Colorado in early 2007, when record snowfalls piled on the mountains until the mountains could hold no more. When the snow let loose and roared across U.S. Highway 40 like a white freight train, cars were swept off the road and buried.

If you're caught in an avalanche, the situation is far different from merely being stranded by heavy snowfall. Being hit by an avalanche is like being run over by a cement truck. There's nothing soft about the snow when it hits you like spilled concrete at a hundred miles per hour or more. There may be injuries or deaths to deal with. Your vehicle might be swept over the edge of the canyon. If you're not in a vehicle, you or your entire camp might be slammed by the snow slide and tumbled hundreds of feet before coming to a stop buried under tons of snow, so you might not be visible to others. It's a grim thought, but it happens.

Surviving an avalanche is largely a matter of luck, because there's nothing much you can do to save yourself while the snow is sliding. If you're in a vehicle, it will be rolled and tumbled and crushed; you may or may not be able to extricate yourself without the aid of a rescue team.

If you're on foot or in camp when the avalanche hits, the situation is even worse. We've all heard the advice about trying to "swim" to the surface of the snow before it stops sliding and sets up like cement, but avalanche survivors say that is nearly impossible. You're at the mercy of one of the most awesome forces in nature, and trying to swim out of it is like trying to swim across a raging white-water river. You might get lucky, though, so there's nothing to lose by trying.

If the avalanche is small enough or moving slowly enough, you might be able to crawl toward one side of the slide by using a swimming motion. Along the edges of the slide, the snow is moving more slowly, making it easier to extricate yourself. But if you're caught in the middle of a big one, you have no choice but to ride it out and hope for the best. Just before the snow stops sliding, it will still be fluid enough to allow you to move your arms and legs a bit. Use that sliver of time to attempt to clear a space around yourself; at least around your face and head so you can breathe. The pressure of the snow, once it stops moving and solidifies, will be crushing, and you may not be able to move so much as a finger. But you must try to dig out in the direction of the brightest light, which will be the thinnest covering of snow. The trouble with all this is that it is easy to exhaust yourself and work up a sweat that will only hasten the onset of hypothermia. This is the most difficult situation in which to remain calm, but that is what you must do. Control your breathing and pace your work. Of course, this is the time when you really need to have an avalanche beacon on your body, so others who also have that type of equipment can locate you beneath the snow. Just as a PLB can save your life when you're lost or in trouble, an avalanche beacon is your one best shot at survival in this dire situation.

Let's jump forward and assume that you have survived the initial avalanche. Your immediate concern now is to assess the situation. Who is alive? Who is dead? Who is injured? If possible, treat the injuries—at least get the bleeding stopped. If you're in a vehicle that has been swept over the edge of the mountain, work on extricating yourselves. You may have to dig your way out, so if you are traveling through snow country, it is a good idea to have a small shovel in the vehicle. Once you are outside and the injured are stabilized, your job is to move to a safe location and then do everything you can to make contact with the outside world.

Where one avalanche happens, another can follow. A second slide could come down the same slope at any time, so you must move to a safer location. To move across deep snow, snowshoes or cross-country skis are extremely helpful. Struggling through chest-deep snow without these aids to travel will quickly leave you wet, cold, and exhausted. Hypothermia and frostbite are almost inevitable, death possible. If you don't have skis or snowshoes, you might be able to improvise a set of expedient snowshoes by lashing broken tree limbs together and tying them to the bottom of your feet. Almost anything you can do to enlarge your footprint will help, so be creative. When the Donner Party became stranded in the deep snows of the Sierra Nevada Mountains, the thing that finally helped save the survivors was improvised snowshoes. Even in their weakened condition, after a long period of starvation, a small group of men and women fashioned makeshift snowshoes and trekked over the mountains to California, where they roused a rescue team to go back and save the remaining survivors. So it can be done.

When you get to a safe place, if there is no one around to rescue you, set up camp. Use the tent, sleeping bags, and blankets carried in your vehicle (you do carry them, don't you?). If you can get back up to the highway and out of the avalanche zone, this is the best place for camp, because it is the route traffic follows, and it is the path rescuers will take. Call for help by using the cell phone or radio equipment, set up visible signal devices, or activate the PLB.

Hunker down, get a fire going, and stay dry and warm. Keep yourself hydrated and fed so you don't lose energy. Stay put and keep the signal efforts going until rescuers arrive.

SURVIVING HOT WEATHER

Memorial Day weekend, several years ago, we were camping along the shores of Lake Powell in the slickrock desert country of extreme southern Utah. The land here is solid stone, and the sky was filled with a blistering sun that heated the rock like a skillet. Even though this is a recreational paradise where sun-worshipping weekenders skim the lake on personal watercraft and camp in houseboats, it is also a place where trouble can come easily to the careless.

The sun had an unfair advantage, rising before we were ready, getting a head start on heating the air to a fever. But this offered us an opportunity to practice the fine art of survival in the searing heat of a desert summer. Although the cool waters of Lake Powell transform this country from a no-man's-land into a popular playground, people still manage to get themselves into heat-related problems here. Lost in their recreational fantasies, some seem to forget that staying alive under such torrid conditions is an outdoor survival skill.

Before technology transformed this part of the desert into a recreation area, the native people lived here quite successfully (as is the case all over the world), taking advantage of what nature offered while avoiding mistakes that spell disaster. To the experienced desert dweller, staying cool in hot weather becomes instinctive. It's just life, it isn't a survival adventure. He doesn't stop long enough to think about every step he takes, where he places his bare hand, how he paces his labor. He simply does what is right and works with what he has at hand and what nature offers.

For those of us who are only occasional visitors to the desert, advanced preparation for camping in hot weather is the key to comfort. When civilized materials are unavailable, knowing how to make do with what nature provides is the key to survival.

Staying cool in hot weather is more than just an issue of comfort. It's also an issue of safety and avoidance of serious conditions such as dehydration, sunburn, heat exhaustion, and heat stroke. The tactics employed to prevent these problems include the concepts of reflection, insulation, hydration, and evaporation, as well as pace and timing of energy expenditure. Those are all big words that sound pretty technical, but as you'll see, none of this is rocket science.

Reflection

For our purposes, reflection is nothing more than preventing a certain amount of the sun's rays from reaching your body or your living space. A tent, a bush, a rock overhang, and your clothing all provide reflective protection against the sun's energy to one degree or another—sending that energy in another direction by reflecting it away from you. Complete protection from the sun is difficult to achieve unless you're in a cave, but every little bit helps.

Depending upon the reflective quality of the material at hand, it may or may not take a massive barrier to turn away the solar energy. Highly reflective material, such as a thin layer of foil, is very effective. Light colors reflect more efficiently than do dark colors, which absorb heat. This concept goes right down to your choice of clothing, the color of your tent roof, etc. For summer use, choose light colors with tightly woven fabric that will not permit light penetration. At the same time, the material should allow ventilation that assists in cooling through evaporation, which we'll discuss in a moment.

Reflection is important in the battle against sunburn as well as overall thermal gain, so the more complete the covering, the better. Wear a wide-brimmed hat that shades the entire face and head, a handkerchief draped from the hatband so it covers the back of your neck, long sleeves and long pant legs, and full-coverage shoes or boots instead of sandals or bare feet. Include even covering for the hands if possible. Your clothing is nothing more than a wearable shelter that you can carry with you everywhere you go. Choose your shelter wisely.

Insulation

If highly efficient reflection isn't available, then putting a lot of insulative material between you and the heat is a priority. A heavy stone overhang offers shade and protection from the sun by absorbing its energy.

Stacking brush on a hastily built wikiup framework may result in fairly low reflectance, but the insulation value is protective.

In this regard, clothing, even if it isn't highly reflective, offers protection. Note that the Bedouins of the Arabian Desert often dress in dark clothing, but it is heavy, full-coverage clothing that insulates them from the harsh heat and sunshine.

In an emergency, people have been known to bury a large part of their body in the soil to escape the blistering sun, covering their exposed face with shade protection so they can still breathe. The deeper you go in the soil, the cooler it is because of the combined reflective and insulation values of the ground.

Hydration and Evaporation

Keeping your body well hydrated is vital for sustaining the delicate balance of fluids and avoiding dehydration. Nothing serves as well for this purpose as pure water. One of the uses to which the body puts its internal supply of water is directly related to hot-weather survival, and that is evaporation. By allowing some moisture to come to the surface of the skin where it is in contact with the atmosphere, evaporation cools the body. It's nature's little air conditioner. But the body's water supply is also used for many other critical functions, so we need to keep a steady flow of water into the system in order to take advantage of evaporative cooling without placing other body functions at risk.

Lake Powell, or any other body of water, helps the cooling efforts by allowing you to apply an external dose of water for evaporation. Go jump in the lake to cool off, and when you come out of the water stand around and let the air evaporate the moisture. It's the quickest way to get cool, but you still need water on the inside to carry on bodily functions.

Ventilation is good, up to a point. You want enough ventilation in your clothing and in your shelter to help maximize the cooling effect of evaporation. But you don't want to be subjected to a blast furnace of hot wind that dries you out, heats you up, and makes you miserable. Shelter yourself against excessive wind.

Pace and Timing

Directly related to hydration and evaporation are the concepts of pace and timing of energy expenditure. Because it is so important to guard your internal water supply, it is critical to pace yourself to avoid excessive perspiration. Rest during the heat of the day and labor or travel only during the cool periods of early morning and late evening. I am not an advocate of traveling through the night unless you have a reliable light source to help prevent injury from stumbling, wandering into sharp plant life, or trespassing on dangerous wildlife. Work and travel during the cool part of the day, but only while you can still see what you're doing. (For information on prevention of and field treatment of heat cramps, heat exhaustion, and heat stroke, refer to Chapter 7.)

General Rules for Hot Weather

We may find ourselves camping in deserts, mountains, or tropical environments during the heat of summer. The success of our journey depends upon how well we follow these general rules for hot-weather survival:

- ▶ Slow the pace.
- ▶ Schedule laborious activities during the cool of the day.
- ▶ Drink plenty of water.
- ▶ Inhale and exhale through the nose to minimize dehydration of the mouth and throat.
- ▶ Wear full-coverage, lightly colored clothing.
- ▶ Take every opportunity to be in the shade.
- ▶ Take full advantage of evaporation and mild ventilation.
- ▶ Protect yourself from hot wind.
- ▶ Avoid touching hot objects.

Blending these survival concepts into each day's activities helps prevent problems that might otherwise transform the excursion from a fun camping trip into a grim survival situation. Practice these techniques and, before long, staying cool in hot weather will become instinctive.

Fire

The ability to make a fire and keep it going in all kinds of weather conditions is one of the hallmarks of a person skilled in the ways of the outdoors. Under certain conditions, all that stands between life and death is the ability to make a fire. Although cold weather may certainly increase the need for a fire that keeps us dry and warm, it doesn't have to be midwinter for a fire to be critically important.

Death from exposure (hypothermia) can occur at 50°F if other conditions exist, such as being damp, fatigued, improperly clothed, not having sufficient caloric intake, and being exposed to a breeze. Under these conditions, a fire is very important in the effort to save your life. Not that simply placing a hypothermic patient in front of the flames will save his life, but heating food and drink, drying the clothing, warming the air surrounding the victim—all of these things are beneficial when they are combined with the other steps that are taken in the prevention and field treatment of hypothermia.

Of course, most campfires are used for purposes other than emergencies, making it useful to know how to build a fire that accomplishes the task at hand. A properly managed fire can be used as a signaling device to assist in a rescue operation. A good campfire provides illumination for the camp, purifies (boils) drinking water, cooks food, dries clothing or equipment that is damp, heats water for purposes of hygiene or sanitation, and provides a psychological aid for the camper. It's amazing how frightening a dark and lonely night in the forest can be and how a cheery campfire calms the heart when things look bleak.

A properly built and managed fire doesn't necessarily require a lot of wood, but the trick is knowing what kind of fire is best for each purpose and then how to go about building and managing it. There's more to building a fire than some folks might think—things like deciding on the appropriate type of fire for the occasion, collecting enough of the right kinds of fuel, properly laying the fire bed, making tinder and kindling, getting the fire going, and maintaining it for an indefinite period of time.

Before launching into a discussion about fire-building technique, we need to face the fact that there are valid environmental and safety reasons for not starting a fire, especially when many of the functions of a campfire can be handled instead by a camp stove or lantern. So, why have a fire?

To answer that question, let's ask a couple more: What happens when you are without a camp stove, lantern, or other equipment, and a situation arises that demands a fire? What if you wander away from camp into the backcountry and find yourself in a situation in which you need to purify water, cook food, signal for help, stay warm, dry your clothes, or just make it through a dark and lonely night? At times like that, nothing takes the place of a campfire. By applying proper fire-building techniques, almost all of the negative aspects of having a fire in the backcountry are eliminated.

TYPES OF FIRES

A proper fire almost never needs to be very large. In fact, an old woodsman's saying goes, "You can tell the size of the fool by the size of his fire." A small, well-built fire is almost always adequate, especially if it's built properly for its specific purpose. A cooking fire is not the same as a warming fire, and a warming fire is different than a signal fire. To the neophyte, the distinctions are subtle, but each type of fire has its own important characteristics.

Cooking Fire

For cooking, it is preferable to have a relatively small fire. Trying to cook on a large fire usually burns the food on the outside while leaving it raw on the inside. A big blaze is also a menace to the chef, who suffers each time he gets close enough to tend to the meal.

Slow cooking is best, and that is accomplished by keeping the fire small and concentrated. The heat of a fire can be concentrated in a small area by enclosing it between two wet or green logs or by circling it tightly with a ring of stones. The logs or stones are also useful to support containers of food or water.

In some circumstances, you may want to use a long fire, with coals at one end and active flames at the other. This allows you to cook several items at once instead of having to wait for one thing to finish cooking so another can take its place over the heat.

A keyhole fire allows you to have a main campfire and a cooking fire (consisting of active coals) all in one. With a keyhole design, the main fire occupies the larger round end of the keyhole shape, and the cooking area is in the elongated part. As coals are formed, move them from the main fire into the cooking area.

Active fire

Embers

Keyhole Fire

A KEYHOLE fire allows you to maintain a lively blaze in the circular portion along with a protected bed of coals for cooking in the elongated section.

Warming Fire

When a warming fire is needed, use some type of reflective surface to concentrate and direct the heat. A large boulder is an excellent reflector if the fire is built at the base of the rock. Even better, position the fire between a pair of large boulders so the heat is reflected from one to the other, then stand in the middle and be warmed from both sides. A stone surface absorbs heat and slowly releases warmth throughout the night, even if the fire dies down.

In the absence of boulders, employ the face of a cliff. However, when making camp at the base of a cliff, look up to see what hazards may fall from above.

With effort, a reflector wall can be erected of damp or green logs stacked atop each other and supported by upright posts. Be creative. Build an L-shaped reflector wall that also serves as a fine windbreak.

Positioned between two reflectors, you can enjoy warmth both front and back. Lacking a reflector, you can still enjoy warmth on both sides of your body if you position yourself between two or more small fires. Another technique is to build a long, low fire and stretch out in front of it to warm the entire length of your body at once. If the ground is cold, let the fire burn for a couple of hours to heat the ground beneath it, then move the fire three or four feet away and position yourself on the heated ground.

Other hints:

▶ Once a good bed of coals is built up, add medium-sized fuel that burns slowly and steadily through the night. Use long logs and push the burning end farther into the blaze as necessary.

▶ Keep a supply of wood close at hand so you don't have to leave the fire to get more fuel. Position the supply of wood close enough to the fire to dry it out, but far enough for safety.

Signal Fire

When you're trying to attract attention, the rule is "smoky fire by day and bright blaze by night." Add bits of green or damp foliage into the flames to create smoke. If you suspect that there is a search being conducted from the air, three fires arranged in a triangle or a straight line is a recognized distress signal. A bonus is that you can position yourself between these fires for warmth, and the smoke keeps the mosquitoes and flies away.

When maintaining a signal fire, it may be difficult to gather enough fuel to keep a full blaze going all the time. But it's important to be prepared to bring the fire to life on a moment's notice if

Reflector Fire

THE best way to add warmth to a shelter is to build a reflector fire that faces toward the shelter entrance. Position the fire near enough to be effective yet far enough away to allow easy entry and exit and so that it doesn't threaten to ignite the shelter.

Triangle Signal Fire

THREE fires laid out in a triangular formation is a recognizable distress signal, but to maintain all these fires requires more firewood. The solution is to keep one fire burning and the other two ready to ignite when you believe searchers are close enough to see the signal.

you hear the drone of a search plane or distant noise of rescue teams. If the situation is serious enough to justify a signal fire, don't be caught with dead ashes. Keep a small fire burning and have plenty of fuel and smoke-producing green foliage on hand to enable you to have a full-blown signal fire going within a few seconds. (For a complete discussion of signaling techniques, see Chapter 6.)

Night Fire

Once you get a fire going, avoid having to start it over and over again. One effective method of keeping a fire alive overnight is by banking it. This is done by building up a substantial bed of coals and raking them together in a heap. Lay a couple of medium-sized logs over the coals to provide fuel for the night, then cover the logs with ashes and more coals. To keep air from getting to the coals, cover the whole thing with a mound of dry soil.

In the morning, uncover the coals. They will still be glowing, and the logs will have begun to be consumed by the heat. All you have to do is add fine kindling and blow the coals into flame. Bank a fire anytime you want to more easily restart the fire in the morning without having to start from scratch.

BUILDING A FIRE

In spite of differences between the structural aspects of various fires, there are certain things that are common to all fires. Let's begin with the foundation, or fire base. A fire base gives firm support to the fire and keeps the burning fuel off damp ground. It also helps contain the coals and prevents the fire from spreading out of control beyond intended limits. A fire base can be built up of flat stones or green logs laid together tightly, or it can consist of nothing more than hard ground that is scraped level and cleaned of burnable debris. In some cases, if precipitation is not expected, a fire base may be built in a shallow hole that will focus heat for cooking. In other instances, it may be preferable to build the fire base above ground level to keep burning fuel and embers from contact with the flammable forest floor or damp ground. With a proper base, it is possible to build a fire on hard-packed snow or swampy ground. Most of the time, soil that is scraped clean and

Fire-Base Platform on Snow

TO BUILD a fire on snow or on moist ground, you must construct a solid fire base. Even though a log fire base will eventually be consumed by the fire, most of the heat from the fire rises upward, allowing the wood fire base to last a long time.

A STONE floor is an excellent platform to protect the fire from moisture from below. The stones will absorb heat that will last many hours. Wrapping one of the hot stones in clothing and taking it to bed will help keep you warm through the night.

surrounded by a ring of stones is a sufficient fire base, but conditions don't always allow this simple approach, so it's good to keep other options in mind.

The ground around any fire base should be cleared of combustible debris to a distance of at least three feet from the edge of the fire. If the fire base is directly on the ground, make sure there is nothing combustible in the soil beneath the fire.

Place the fire where it will provide the most convenience and efficiency and the least hazard. Don't build a fire near an insect nest, because that will stir the bugs up and give them an attitude. Observe which direction the prevailing night wind blows, then position the fire so the smoke drifts away from your shelter. Look skyward for overhanging branches that might catch a spark and become a torch. In winter, overhanging branches loaded with snow can unexpectedly unload on a fire below, becoming an instant extinguisher.

Finding Dry Fuel

There are times when it is difficult to find dry fuel, especially after a storm. Finding dry wood is easier if you look for standing dead trees. A fallen dead tree that is supported off the ground by other fallen trees or rocks provides better firewood than a tree that has been lying on the ground soaking up moisture. Moisture is drawn by capillary action up a

SEARCH for dry firewood by pulling dead twigs and limbs out of standing dead trees or look for downed trees with branches that are not touching the ground where they can absorb moisture.

dead branch that is touching the ground, leaving part of the branch damp.

Even after a serious storm, a live tree contributes dead twigs and branches because the upper part of the tree tends to shield the trunk and lower limbs. Because trees grow from the top up, the best place to find old dead wood on a living tree is near the bottom. Select only those twigs and branches that snap off easily when bent.

Find something to use as a club to knock dead twigs and branches from a standing tree. Before trying to break large branches, test them to see if they are likely to give up easily. Don't wear yourself out pounding on a strong branch when your time and energy can be more profitably used attacking smaller stuff. Avoid the temptation to jump up and down on a dead branch to break it off, because that's an invitation to injury.

Some wood is short grained, and an old dead limb that is even bigger around than a baseball bat can be easily broken off in chunks by hitting it against another log or a rock. Other types of wood have a long, flexible grain that causes the wood to splinter. Fortunately, both splintered wood and blocked wood are useful for a campfire. Thin splinters are excellent for kindling, and blocks are added soon after the kindling catches fire. Regardless of the type of wood used, the concepts are the same, so let's discuss the three main types of fuel needed for a successful campfire: tinder, kindling, and fuel wood.

Tinder

When you are gathering fire-building materials, the first component needed is an ample supply of good tinder. With the right kind of tinder, you can start a fire with just a spark. Without it, you may not be able to get a fire going, even with a box full of matches.

Proper tinder is highly combustible stuff, fluffy, very fine in size, almost hairlike, and perfectly dry. Unless you capture a delicate bird's nest made of very fine materials, a perfect tinder bundle does not often occur naturally, so it needs to be created. Fortunately, the raw materials for making excellent tinder can be found almost everywhere. The dry stalks of many weeds contain fibers that can be broken down and bundled together for tinder. In the fall of the year, thistles produce copious amounts of "down" that can be collected and added to a tinder bundle. Thistle down by itself ignites instantly when touched by a hot spark or even a small flame, but it fails to hold the flame for very long, so it is best added to a fine-grass tinder bundle where it can flare up quickly and help ignite the rest of the bundle.

Shredded bark from trees such as the cedar, palm, or juniper or from bushes like sagebrush make excellent tinder. Dry grasses, twisted and wrapped together, can be formed into a tinder bundle. Some dry grasses make excellent tinder, but not all are equal in this regard. If the stalks are thin and thready, they'll work, but if they're gross and straw-like, they are less desirable unless they can be broken down into a finer form. To use rough grasses for tinder, break the fibers down into very fine strands but take care not to pulverize the materials into dust. In rain forest areas where you might expect dry tinder to be rare, the moss that grows heavily on tree limbs

TINDER is very fine, hairlike, and exceedingly dry. Dry grasses or other feathery plant material can be twisted to form a "bird's nest" for a tinder bundle. Kindling ranges in size from the diameter of a pencil to that of a finger. Split wood is best for kindling.

makes excellent tinder if it is dry. Even in a rainstorm, the tree might offer enough protection to keep the moss on the trunk or on lower limbs dry enough to serve as tinder.

As you're moving through the environment, whether it's desert, forest, seashore, or mountains, always be on the lookout for possible sources of tinder material. Collect them and stow them away in a dry pocket or pack for use later. You'll never be sorry you collected and preserved too much tinder.

For a tinder bundle to work best, tightly form it into a simulated bird's nest, then place it at the bottom of the fire's framework, where the blaze will be started. By placing the tinder at the bottom, the heat and flames will ignite the overlying superstructure of kindling, which will then ignite the larger fuel wood.

Kindling

For best results, you need varying grades of kindling, ranging in size from thin slivers the diameter of a toothpick to ragged splinters the diameter of a finger and about a foot long. Dry twigs found along the protected side of the trunk in the lower levels of a tree make good mid-sized kindling. To create small kindling, shave thin slivers from a piece of dry wood or shatter a brittle branch by smashing it with a large stone. You want long, thin splinters, not short chunks. Splintered wood is better than whole, round pieces. The more shattered fragments that are sticking out to catch the small flames coming from the tinder bundle, the better. Wood with a heavy sap content is excellent, and you can smear your kindling across the sap that is dripping from a tree wound to make it catch fire quickly and hold the flame for a long time.

A fuzz stick makes it easier to get a fire started. Create a fuzz stick by shaving a thumb-sized stick all around its circumference and from end to end in such a manner that the shavings remain attached but flare out like small feathers. A few fuzz sticks included with the small kindling, propped up over the tinder bundle, will increase your chance of success when starting the fire.

Fuzz Stick

MAKE a fuzz stick by slicing leaf-shaped shavings from a dry stick, leaving the bases attached to the stick. These shavings will catch fire easily and help with the transition from quick-burning tinder to the more enduring kindling.

Fuel Wood

In like manner to kindling, prepare fuel wood in varying sizes. Begin with pieces that are not much bigger than the largest kindling. Think of this as a transition size between kindling and larger fuel wood. Then increase to heavier pieces of wood as the primary fuel. It takes a mature bed of white-hot coals to sustain a fire that is capable of burning large blocks of wood, so be patient and don't start piling on the big wood too early or you'll kill the fire.

Because you can't plan in advance where you're going to be when a survival situation arises, you must be prepared to burn whatever is available. Sometimes what's available isn't the best, but you have to deal with reality and use whatever you have. In every event, however, there are a few characteristics about firewood that you can count on.

- ► Split wood burns better than whole logs.
- ► Wood that has been previously charred ignites more easily than "inexperienced" wood.
- ► Wood that is saturated with old sap (called pitch wood by old-timers) burns even when wet and ignites faster than normal wood. Look for splintered remains of dead trees and search among the broken pieces for heavy wood, stained orange and black with pitch.
- ► Avoid punk (semi-rotted) wood.

Gather sufficient fuel to keep the fire going long enough to perform its function. There's a big difference in the amount of wood needed to sustain a momentary lunch fire that you'll soon abandon and the amount needed for a warming fire that's supposed to last through the night. In any case, gather double what you think you'll need, and stack it near enough to the fire to be convenient (close enough to be warmed and dried by the flames) yet far enough away that it is out of danger. Every once in a while, turn the wood over so the other side can dry.

Lay long pieces of fuel wood that can't be broken or cut into smaller pieces across the fire so they will burn in two. Or place the end of the log into the fire and let it burn, then push the log farther into the fire.

Long Logs on a Fire

IF a fire log is too big to break into smaller pieces, drag it onto the fire and allow the blaze to burn it in two, leaving you with more manageable pieces.

Structure

Heat and flames rise, so the best shape of a fire structure is somewhat vertical. This allows the flames to climb upward and ignite the fuel that is placed on top. Tinder belongs at the bottom, with small kindling next. Arrange the kindling in a loose crossing pattern that allows the fire rising from the tinder to lick each finely slivered piece of wood with tongues of flame. Next, lay on the transition pieces of larger kindling and small fuel wood. Keep all this burning furiously until a healthy bed of coals has accumulated, then add larger pieces of fuel wood.

Be sure there is ample airflow through the fuel. A fire that can't breathe from the bottom will starve for air and die. Use either a tipi-shaped structure or one that resembles a log cabin, leaving air spaces between the sticks to promote good breathing. Revive a dying fire by opening up holes in the stack of burning fuel to increase airflow or by rearranging burning sticks that have fallen over so the structure takes on a somewhat vertical aspect again.

If you are building a fire on snowy ground or in a swampy area, it will be necessary to construct a solid platform for the fire base. The platform can be made of small- to medium-sized green logs, planks of wood, or large, flat stones that are placed close enough together to keep the fire from eating its way down into the soggy or snowy ground. The fire will gradually burn down into any combustible materials used to make the platform, so if you're using logs, be prepared to replace platform materials when necessary. The other reason to have a platform under the fire in such conditions is that the heat of the blaze will create an updraft that will literally suck the moisture up out of the ground, and that can be enough to kill a fire.

In windy conditions, kneel on the windward side of the fire base that you have prepared. If you're wearing a coat, pull it out as wide as possible to form a windbreak as you huddle over the tinder and kindling. Before striking the match, feel what's happening for a moment to make sure you have formed a protective windproof environment. When you're certain everything is ready, strike the match and hold it for a moment, pointing downward with the flame at the bottom and the stick up at a diagonal. This will allow the flame to stabilize and begin to gain strength as it burns the matchstick. Carefully move the flame into the tinder bundle and adjust the smallest splinters of kindling to take advantage of the growing blaze.

Feed kindling into the fire until a strong blaze has been established, then begin to feed the smallest fuel wood first, working gradually up to the larger stuff. Be sure to have a sufficient supply of fuel wood to keep the fire going for awhile, and when the fire is well established, be diligent about searching for additional firewood to add to your supply and stacking it near enough to the blaze to dry it if it's wet but not so close that it ignites. Collecting firewood is an ongoing process that requires your constant effort.

A good fire is one of the greatest benefits in a survival situation, so take time to build it right. By starting with good tinder, kindling, and fuel wood, and making sure the fire structure is properly erected, you will enjoy a warm, cheery fire in no time.

Fire without matches

There are a few reasons why someone should know how to start a fire without the use of matches or conventional lighters. One is that eventually you run out of matches or your lighter runs out of juice. Another is that you might find yourself without either matches or lighter, in spite of all my preaching about always carrying redundant numbers of these most important items. When that happens, knowing how to strike a fire by another method could save your life. A third reason to practice matchless fire-starting techniques is that it's more fun than simply striking a match or spinning the wheel on a lighter.

Fun aside, it is unquestionably more difficult to get a fire going by using primitive techniques. When your life depends on getting fire going quickly, that is not the time to be scrounging through the woods looking for materials to make a bow drill, hand drill, fire plough, or any other primitive fire-starting equipment. It's also not the time to have to rely on having a bright sun that can produce fire through a magnifying glass, nor to count on having a vehicle battery and a set of jumper cables available. When you need a fire to save your life, there is hardly anything else that will do, and you don't want to delay the process.

But when instant methods are unavailable, it is not only possible but essential to start fires by other means. I encourage you to practice these techniques, but please don't let this chapter lull you into a sense of complacency about carrying redundant modern fire-making tools.

The Bow Drill Method

It was deep in a remote canyon of the southern Idaho desert where I experienced the magic of making my first fire by "rubbing two sticks together." But I must warn you, that magic is not easy to come by. The technique is commonly referred to as the bow drill method. We should actually call this a bow, drill, fireboard, and hand socket method, because those are the parts that make up the equipment set. Each piece in the set must be perfect or a fire will not be achieved. If the drill or fireboard are made of the wrong materials, the fire will fail. If the notch in the fireboard is not properly made, there will be no fire. If the bow string is too loose or too slippery, if the hand socket is not formed to allow friction-free spinning of the drill, or your technique is jerky or you give up too soon, you'll face a dark, cold night without the benefit of fire.

This is not an easy technique. Even though I've made many fires by this method over the years, I am almost tempted to call the whole process impractical for most readers. It's not that the method doesn't work, but that few folks ever learn it, practice it, and master it. And if you don't master it ahead of time, you can't expect to suddenly find success when the snow is falling, the rain has made everything wet, the wind is blowing, and the night is black and cold.

For those who want to learn the method, here are the step-by-step details to getting a fire going with a bow drill set.

The Tools. One of the things that makes this method so difficult is that you can't always find the right materials. The native people who use primitive fire-starting equipment don't wait until they need it. They build their bow drill set when the right materials are available and carry this equipment with them. It's their version of a disposable lighter, except they never dispose of it—they just replace parts that wear out. When you find yourself in a predicament and want to make a bow drill set, you might be in an area where the right materials are not available. To solve that problem, when you come across some good materials for making the set, grab them and take them with you. Don't expect to be able to find what you need at the moment you need it.

Let's start with the drill and fireboard. These can be made of the same or different materials, but they both must be made of the right kind of wood. If the wood contains a lot of resin (pine, for example), a glaze coating will form where the drill and fireboard meet, and that will interfere with the creation of the powdery dust that forms the coal used to start the fire. If the drill and fireboard are made of the same type of wood, the rate of wear of both pieces will be about equal, and the equipment will last longer. If one or the other is made of a softer wood, that piece will wear faster and require earlier replacement. That's not necessarily a bad situation, though, because the softer wood will create more friction to form the coal. Some of the woods I've used for my drills and fireboards include yucca, willow, cedar, sage, and cottonwood. While practicing the technique, experiment with a variety of woods that are common in your area.

The bow can be made of a stout stick a couple of feet long and maybe as thick as your little finger. The bow should be stiff enough to resist bending excessively when you put pressure on the string, yet supple enough to bend a little without breaking. It's called a bow for a reason—it should act like one. If your bow stick has a small fork on one end and a knob where there used to be a branch on the other end, those features will make it easier to tie on the string and keep it from slipping.

The hand socket (sometimes called a hand hold) is used to apply pressure to the top of the drill as it is spinning on the fireboard. I call this piece a socket because it must have a cavity to receive the pointed end of the drill and allow it to spin with minimal resistance. A hand socket can be made of stone or wood. Smooth stone offers the advantages of low friction to impede the spinning action of the drill, as well as durability. The disadvantages are weight and the difficulty of creating a suitable cavity. A wood hand socket is lighter to carry and faster to fabricate, but the wood-to-wood contact between the socket and drill will create some friction that will slow the drill. Using a very hard wood for the hand socket will help reduce the friction problem.

Additional materials include something to catch and hold the hot dust as it pours from the fireboard so it can form a coal that can be easily transferred to the tinder bundle. And, of course, there's the tinder bundle. You must have excellent tinder that is super dry and made of very fine materials. Form the tinder bundle into a shape resembling a bird's nest, with a depression on top into which you will transfer the coal.

If you have good materials to work with, fabricating the pieces is not too difficult, but it is extremely important that they be made correctly. Let's start with the fireboard, because that's where most of the challenge lies.

The fireboard should be flat on top and bottom so it will rest firmly on the ground without twisting or rolling when you're spinning the drill. Split the fireboard out of a stalk (yucca or willow) or limb (cottonwood or other nonresinous softwood) so that you end up with a plank-shaped piece that is about half an inch thick, a couple of inches wide, and maybe a foot or so long. If it's too long, it will be difficult to stow and carry. On the upper surface of the fireboard, you must make a crater-shaped depression in which the drill will work. Use a knife or sharp stone to start the formation of this depression, and later on you will use the drill itself to enlarge and deepen it. This depression should be far enough from the edge of the fireboard that the wall of the crater doesn't breach the edge as it becomes larger with use, but near enough that you can cut a notch from the edge of the fireboard that penetrates all the way to the center of the depression. I like to use a notch that is about $\frac{1}{16}$- to $\frac{1}{8}$-inch wide and is cut straight in from the edge of the fireboard to the center of the crater. On the bottom of the fireboard, the notch is widened into a cone-shaped funnel that allows the hot dust to collect and be concentrated in a tight pile. The accompany-

THE notch in the fireboard must be shaped to allow hot dust to flow freely down to form the coal. The notch is wider at the bottom and is cut in toward the center of the depression where the spindle works.

THE spindle (or drill) is rounded at the bottom to create lots of friction at the fireboard and pointed at the top to reduce friction with the hand socket. Periodically trim the spindle to maintain these characteristics.

ing photo shows the bottom surface of the fireboard, but the notch is not finished: it will be cut deeper toward the centerline, narrowing to about $\frac{1}{16}$ inch at the end.

The drill must be pointed on top and blunt on the bottom. The tip rides inside the cup of the hand socket, while the blunt end works in the depression on the top of the fireboard. The upper tip shouldn't be so sharp that it's fragile; it's OK to have a bit of a blunted point, but you want it to glide effortlessly in the hand socket cup. The bottom of the drill should be slightly rounded to flat so that it makes maximum contact with the depression in the fireboard. Actually, a slightly flatish blunt end seems to create more heat and wears away the fireboard more slowly. Use this end of the drill to put the finishing touches on the fireboard by spinning the drill in the depression.

I made my hand socket out of a smooth stone. By using another rock, I pecked away at the stone until a cup was formed. This took quite a while, but when I made this set I was in a desert area where there was little timber to use for a wooden socket. No matter which material you use, it doesn't hurt to lubricate the inside of the socket with a light coating of animal fat to help reduce friction.

Aboriginal peoples who relied on bow drills used a thin leather thong cut from some animal hide as the bow string. Common practice among the rest of us is to use a bootlace. Keep in mind, however, that

THIS hand socket is made of stone that I shaped by peck-ing it with another rock. Wood hand sockets are faster to make, but the wood-on-wood contact has the potential to create undesired friction.

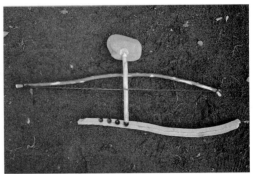

THE bow drill set consists of a hand socket at the top, the spindle (or drill) that is spun by the bow in the center, and the fireboard at the bottom. This fireboard has been used many times, with each of the older friction craters having started many fires before it was necessary to make a new friction point.

this puts your bootlace at risk, because there's a lot of friction and wear created by sawing back and forth with the bow, and the lace will wear through over time.

Using the Fire Drill. Now to put it all together. Pick a level spot where you can comfortably kneel on one knee while the other foot is placed on top of the fireboard to secure it. Let's pretend you're right-handed for this explanation. If you happen to be left-handed, just reverse sides in this description.

▶ Kneel with your right knee on the ground.
▶ Place a leaf or some other materials to catch the coal, such as a piece of fabric, paper, or cardboard, on the ground beneath the notch in the fire-board. Don't worry, the coal is not hot enough to ignite these materials.
▶ Position your left foot on top of the fireboard, close to the depression where the drill will work, but far enough back to allow movement of the bow with-out interference.
▶ Take the drill in your left hand and the bow in your right.
▶ Thrust the top of the drill into the bow between the string and the stick, then take a single wrap of the string around the drill.

TO use a bow drill, plant one foot on the fireboard, hug your knee with the arm that holds the socket, and smoothly move the bow back and forth to spin the drill while increasing tension on the bow string with your thumb.

▶ Place the bottom of the drill in the depression on the fireboard, and hold it there with your right hand while you pick up the hand socket with your left.

▶ Rest the hand socket on top of the drill, with the cup over the drill's point.

▶ Hug your left knee in the crook of your left arm, and place your left wrist close to your shin so you can hold the drill vertical on the fireboard and keep it from wobbling as you move the bow.

▶ Now take up the bow in your right hand and, while applying downward pressure on the drill with the hand socket, slowly saw the bow back and forth to spin the drill. If the bow string slips around the body of the drill, apply pressure on the string with your right thumb until the drill spins easily. A coating of pine sap on the string will help prevent slipping around the drill.

▶ Gradually increase the speed of the bow and the pressure on the hand socket, and keep sawing with the bow until smoke appears from the drill and fireboard. Notice that black dust is starting to be created by the friction. If the notch in the fireboard is properly formed, this dust will exit the bottom and be collected in a tight pile on the leaf. If the dust is scattering or collecting on top of the fireboard, the notch needs to be opened up more to allow the dust a proper exit.

A LEAF is placed beneath the fireboard to catch the hot black dust and enable you to transfer the coal that forms to the tinder bundle.

AFTER the coal has been transferred to the tinder bundle, gently blow on the tinder until smoke turns to flame. Be sure to have the kindling ready to accept the flaming tinder, because this burns very quickly.

▶ Don't get excited, just keep the bow moving smoothly and maintain pressure on the drill. When the smoke is strong and steady, keep going for another minute, then gradually slow to a stop and remove the drill from the fireboard.

▶ Gently remove the fireboard from the leaf and observe the pile of black dust. If there is still a wisp of smoke, there's a good chance that you have a coal that can be moved to the tinder and blown into flame. If there is no hint of smoke, start over and sustain the process longer than last time.

▶ When moving the coal to the tinder, be careful not to drop or scatter the dust coal. This is a very delicate commodity, so treat it like nitroglycerin. Place the coal into the heart of the tinder bundle, gently wrap some fine tinder over it, and blow into the bundle. With luck and proper technique, the tinder will begin to smoke and then suddenly burst into flame.

▶ Be ready with more tinder and a stack of very dry kindling already set up in your fire location. Now, go celebrate. You've created the miracle of fire.

Flint and Steel

Moving into a less primitive technique, but one that still does not use matches or lighters, there is the modern flint and steel set. Actually, there's no flint involved, but the technique is similar to what you could do if you had a real piece of flint rock and a steel striker. Under totally destitute conditions in which you have no other way to strike a spark, it is possible to do it by hitting just the right bit of angular rock with something like the spine of a knife (the back edge of the blade). But the odds of your finding just the right rock are so low that you should carry something more reliable with you.

Someone might ask, why carry a modern flint and steel set when I could just as easily carry another butane lighter instead? My answer is by all means to carry the lighter, but realize that the butane will eventually run out, whereas the flint and steel set will keep working. But don't just carry the flint and steel set as an unused backup to your primary fire starter—practice with it every chance you get, because there is definitely a proper technique.

MODERN flint and steel sets come in all shapes and sizes. In this photo are (left to right) the ToolLogic SL3 Fire, Light My Fire, the Doan magnesium block, and the BlastMatch.

There are several different products on the market that utilize the spark-producing flint and steel concept. The simplest type has a bare sparking rod with a plastic grip at one end. To create the sparks, you can use the sharp edge of a knife spine or the small steel blade that comes with the sparking rod. The most renowned sparking rods are made of a material called Swedish FireSteel (developed for the Swedish Department of Defense), and with proper use they are capable of creating a shower of sparks with a temperature of 5,000°F. This emergency fire starter is very compact, lightweight, and has a hole in the handle so it can be attached to a keychain or a lanyard to hang around your neck. The one I use is the Scout model

THE Light My Fire flint and steel set is a simple stick of Swedish FireSteel and a serrated striker. The large plastic knob makes it easy to hold the firesteel, and a lanyard keeps the striker from getting separated and lost.

DOAN Manufacturing Company makes this magnesium block with an embedded spark-producing rod along one side. Shave the magnesium into the tinder to serve as a fire-assist element prior to striking the spark.

BLASTMATCH is a spring-loaded sparking rod with a striking steel positioned alongside. Forcing the rod down sharply into the tinder bundle that is resting on a solid surface and pressing down on the striking steel with the thumb creates the sparks.

made by Light My Fire that has a lanyard to keep the serrated steel component from getting lost.

Another type that is made by Doan Manufacturing Co., Inc., is bulkier and heavier. It incorporates a block of magnesium that can be shaved into the tinder before striking the spark to assist with the ignition process. The magnesium shavings catch the spark easily and burn incredibly hot. The sparking rod is embedded in one edge of the magnesium block, and a hole in the block allows a lanyard or keychain to be attached. Attached to mine is a small folding knife with a serrated portion of the blade that serves as an excellent striking steel and can also be used as a backup knife.

The BlastMatch, made by Ultimate Survival Technologies (www .ultimatesurvival.com), has a large rod of sparking material inside a plastic grip, and the steel striker is built into a sliding handle that is part of the grip and is pushed down to create a powerful shower of sparks. To use the BlastMatch, flip open the protective handle, use your thumb to press down on the part of the handle that contains the striking steel, position the end of the sparking rod in the tinder bundle that is supported on a rock, and thrust the spring-loaded handle downward.

I also have a ToolLogic (www.toollogic
.com) SL3 Fire folding knife with a wet/dry
magnesium alloy sparking rod that fits in
the handle. To operate, pull the fire starter
out of the handle, open the knife blade, and
use the special scraper notch at the base of
the blade to produce a lively cluster of hot
sparks. The thing I like about this knife is
that besides being a knife with a plain and
serrated blade and having the flint and steel
feature, it also has a built-in signal whistle
in the handle.

Differences between the products aside,
the technique for using a flint and steel set
to start a fire shares some common ground:

TOOLLOGIC SL3 Fire is a folding knife with a sparking rod
in the handle. Strike a spark by swiftly shaving the special
notch in the blade against the rod. The knife handle also
features a built-in signal whistle.

▶ Prepare excellent tinder ahead of time. Because the sparks are tiny and fly
all over the place when they are produced, the tinder bundle must be tight
and dense. To help catch the sparks, a small piece of tissue paper tucked
into the tinder bundle is very useful.
▶ Hold the end of the sparking rod near the tinder.
▶ When passing the steel over the sparking rod,
the movement must be steady and firm or the
sparks will be weak and few in number. Use
the sharpest edge of the steel and forcefully
scrape the length of the sparking rod.
▶ Except in the case of the BlastMatch (with
its plunger-style mechanism), there are two
different motions you can make to produce
sparks. Choose the one you like best for the
conditions and the tinder you are working
with. One method is to stroke the steel down
the length of the rod toward the tinder. The
other is to hold the steel still while you swiftly
pull the striking rod upward. Using the first

IT might take several attempts to get a spark from a flint and
steel set to catch in the tinder. It helps if the tinder bundle is
tightly packed, or if you have a small piece of tissue paper to
catch the sparks.

method, you run the risk of scattering your tinder if you are too vigorous and overrun the end of your rod with the steel. In the second method, the risk is that you are not able to maintain strong enough contact between the steel and the rod, and the sparks are weak.

There is another type of flint and steel that most folks don't think about. If you happen to have (or find) a lighter that has run out of butane but operates with a serrated steel thumbwheel that strikes a spark against a "flint," don't discard it. The sparking device might be able to produce a strong enough spark to ignite tinder, especially if you can spruce up the tinder with a little bit of gasoline salvaged from a vehicle fuel system. Because the lighter was designed to ignite a wick that is soaked with fuel, the sparking mechanism did not need to be particularly powerful. But if you can place the wheel and flint in close proximity to either some extremely fluffy and dry natural tinder or a bit of cloth with some gasoline on it, the chance of producing a fire is good.

Caution: If you're working with gasoline, use only a few drops to help the tinder catch a flame. Position yourself well away from the source of the fuel so you don't accidentally ignite escaped fumes. Also, be ready to move quickly away from the tinder, so as not to burn yourself if the fire flares up.

THE flint and steel in an old butane lighter that is out of fuel may still be able to strike enough of a spark to start a fire, especially if you have a few drops of fuel such as gasoline available. Hold the business end of the lighter down in the tinder and give the thumbwheel a spin to create the spark.

Magnifying Glass
It is possible to ignite a fire by magnifying and concentrating the sun's rays. Some methods of magnifying the sun's rays include the use of a small magnifying glass, a camera lens, eyeglasses, or anything else that will focus the light. To be successful with this method, the sun must be very bright. Any overcast will kill your chances.

▶ Prepare your tinder. To catch the hot, focused light produced by a magnifying glass, the tinder needs to have a somewhat consistent surface. A bundle of dry grass is more difficult to ignite than a small piece of tissue, for example. But have a regular tinder bundle ready to receive the burning paper.

▶ Hold the glass at a right angle to the sun, and experiment with the distance you need to hold it above the tinder. What you want is the smallest, brightest pinpoint of light possible. If the glass is concave (such as with eyeglasses), adding a small amount of clear water will help create a more efficient lens to focus the light.

▶ If your hands are shaky and move the focused point of light around, there won't be enough heat in any one spot to ignite the tinder. It might be possible to prop up the glass on some arrangement of piled rocks or pieces of wood to suspend the glass and then tuck the tinder in the beam of light at just the right spot. That way, you won't have to sit there and hold the glass.

IF the sun is high and hot, a fire can be started with a magnifying glass. Because it's difficult to focus the beam against loosely woven tinder, a small piece of tissue paper is beneficial.

Vehicle Battery Method

A vehicle battery can be used to produce a hot spark that can ignite tinder. But a huge dose of caution must be used when employing this method, because batteries are explosive under the right conditions. Under certain conditions, wet-cell batteries can produce and release a small amount of hydrogen gas in the battery compartment. If a spark occurs in that atmosphere, a dangerous explosion can happen. That's why the recommended method for attaching jumper cables to start a car with a dead battery is *not* to attach both jumper cables to the battery terminals, but to attach the positive lead to the positive terminal and the negative lead to an electrical ground point some distance from the battery where the hydrogen gas will be weaker or nonexistent.

The same holds true for using a battery to create a spark for starting a fire. For safety, the spark must be produced as far from the battery as possible. Here are the steps for hooking up the jumper cables.

▶ Roll out the jumper cables, and attach the red and black clamps at the end farthest from the vehicle to a stick of wood, keeping the clamps about a

A SPARK can be produced with battery jumper cables, but this is potentially dangerous. First clamp the far ends of the cables to a piece of wood a foot away from each other, then attach the near ends to the battery.

foot apart. This prevents them from accidentally making contact with each other and creating a spark while you're attaching the other ends of the cable set to the battery.

▶ Attach the other end of the jumper cable clamps to the positive and negative terminals on the battery. For this operation, it doesn't matter which cable is attached to which terminal, because all you're trying to do is create a spark, not match polarity as you would need to do when jump-starting another vehicle.

▶ Prepare your tinder bundle, kindling, and firewood.

▶ An effective (but not necessary) aid to starting this type of fire is a bit of cloth with a very small amount of gasoline on it. You might be able to obtain gasoline from the vehicle's carburetor by disconnecting a fuel line or directly from the gas tank by using a rag attached to a long piece of stiff wire.

▶ When everything is ready, unclip the far ends of the jumper cables from the piece of wood, and touch the ends together in a striking motion. Do not hold the ends of the jumper cables together, because that creates a dangerous short circuit that can result in a battery meltdown and vehicle fire. You're just trying to start a little fire, not one the size of a truck. In close proximity to the tinder, strike the cable ends across each other to create the spark.

FIRE STARTERS

Warmth, light, the ability to dry your socks, cook your food, purify your water, signal for help. All these are benefits of having a nice campfire. But getting that fire started is often a daunting task. And that's why there are fire starters.

When we talk about fire starters, we aren't discussing waterproof matches or butane lighters—those are ignition systems. The kind of fire starters we're talking about are special materials (both man-made and natural) that can be used to almost guarantee that you'll end up with flames, sometimes even when the fuel is damp. Think of these materials as accelerants, because they catch fire quickly and easily, then speed the progress of the blaze.

Accelerants exist in nature, so you might be able to find some good fire starters right near camp. Pitch, for example, is a great aid to starting a fire. It is a resinous material that occurs naturally in some evergreen trees, especially those that have suffered a wound in the distant past. The wound filled with sap as the tree attempted to heal itself. Over time, the sap was absorbed into the wood fibers, passing through a natural distillation process whereby it became thick and heavy and

GETTING a fire going in the wilderness is often a difficult task if natural, dry tinder and kindling are unavailable. As a backup, carry store-bought accelerant-type fire starters in a plastic bag.

hard. The result is what backwoodsmen call "pitch wood," and it is highly prized as a natural fire starter because it catches a flame and holds it, even in adverse weather conditions.

The old wound often leaves the tree weak and vulnerable to breakage. If you find a tree that has been shattered by wind or snow load, take a closer look and see if you can find slivers of heavy, darkly stained pitch wood that can be pulled loose and carried in your pack or pocket until you need to use some as a fire starter.

Even if the tree hasn't had time to develop pitch wood, fresh evergreen sap is volatile and can be used to make a good fire starter. So, if you find a tree that is oozing sap, collect some on several twigs to use at the base of your fire. The more you use, the better. Sap on the surface of a twig won't necessarily make the twig itself more flammable, but it will serve to hold the flame longer and give you a better chance to ignite the tinder and kindling that you prepared. Like any volatile liquid, the sap eventually burns away, but by the time it does, hopefully you have the fire well ablaze.

If you want to prepare your own homemade fire starter, you can do it by using lint from your clothes drier filter and candle wax or paraffin. Here's the way I do it. Tear off enough lint to form a marble-sized ball. Light a candle, and drip ten to fifteen drops of molten wax into the lint. Be sure to use enough wax to saturate the lint ball. Then, while the wax is still warm enough to be pliable, wad the lint into a pellet. Make lots of them, and store these pellets in a small zip plastic baggie until you need them. On its own, the lint is a good tinder material that catches fire easily, but it burns with a fleeting flame and never burns completely. When the wax is added, the pellet catches a flame easily, burns more vigorously, and lasts longer.

I also like another method using lint from a clothes dryer, a birthday candle, and an empty toilet paper tube. Loosely wrap the candle with lint, allowing the wick to protrude so you can set it on fire with a match or lighter. Stuff the lint-wrapped candle into the tube, place this package under the firewood, and ignite the wick. The candlewick lights easily, and soon the candle melts into the lint, eventually catches the tube on fire, and the tube helps keep the whole thing together.

PITCH wood, wood saturated with pitch from an old wound in a tree, is a natural accelerant. When you find some in the wilderness, collect some slivers and carry them with you for future use.

This system is easier to put together than the individual pellets, but the drawback is that it takes up more space in a backpack.

If you're not a do-it-yourselfer, there are fire-starter products available at your local hardware store or sporting goods retailer. First to the hardware store. People who have wood stoves at home often use compact fire starters to ignite the kindling. These products are equally useful in the campground setting or in the backyard barbecue. One starter is called A-OK Fire Log Lighter. It comes in a box of 48 sticks that each break into four cubes, giving you 192 pieces.

Now to the sporting goods store. For camping trips and as an emergency fire starter in my survival kit, I use WetFire Tinder, manufactured by Ultimate Survival Technologies. This product is a solid cube that weighs a little over an ounce. Each cube is individually wrapped in foil, can't leak, is nontoxic, and leaves no residue. The cubes burn without smoke and ignite even in high wind and wet weather. As the name implies, WetFire burns while floating in water and by some miracle burns even longer when wet.

Impressive is the fact that it isn't always necessary to use a whole cube to get a fire going. WetFire burns at over 1,300°F, yet cools almost instantly when snuffed out. A small pile of shavings is enough to start a campfire or pre-warm a backpack stove at high altitude. Just sprinkle a small amount of shavings around the backpacker stove burner, and it lights instantly.

If you can't find WetFire at your local sporting goods store, order it directly from the manufacturer by going online to their website www.ultimatesurvival.com.

There are a lot of different commercially available fire starters on the market. Using any of these products, your life in camp will be easier. When the weather is foul, these products give confidence that you'll actually be able to get a fire going. In every condition, lighting a fire becomes a quicker and easier chore. And that means dinner gets hot faster, you have the comforting warmth and light of the fire when the sun goes down, you can dry your wet clothing, and you'll be regarded as a hero in camp. (For further discussion of essential fire-starting gear, refer to Chapter 9.)

FRESH sap on a twig will catch and hold a flame like a torch. These little twigs added to the tinder bundle or kindling pile will help ensure that the fire has enough strength and endurance to burn successfully.

CAMPFIRE LESSONS

We were hunkered for the night beneath a stone overhang, and the sun was going down fast. More than a dozen miles from civilization, our car had run out of fuel. Later investigation showed that there was a hole in the gas tank, probably put there by a sharp rock we ran over earlier that kicked up and smacked the tank. Worrying about that could wait. All we cared about now was making it comfortably and safely through the night, secure from the weather beneath this natural shelter. (Why not just stay in the car? Because being outside, with a fire, was better.)

The fire was there for several reasons. One was to provide some light, as the sun was heading over the horizon. The illumination of the fire served a couple of important purposes—to allow us to see what we were doing and to help calm any growing anxiety about being stranded in a strange and wild place. To make the most of the flickering light, we placed the small blaze near the stone wall of the overhang. The illumination reflected off the wall and the overhanging ceiling, spreading soft light over a much wider area than a fire sitting alone in the middle of the space could have done.

If the situation were truly an emergency, the light from the fire could have been arranged to serve the most important function of all—to signal for help. After all, if you attract the attention of someone who can rescue you, you don't need to spend a lot of time in a survival situation. Signal fires are useful both day and night. By day, you want the fire to produce lots of smoke (add bits of green or damp foliage to produce white smoke, burn oil or rubber to make black smoke). A column of smoke is visible for many miles and usually attracts the attention of everyone in the vicinity. If you keep the smoke rising hour after hour, someone is surely going to come and check it out.

By night, the smoke is less visible, so what you need is a bright blaze that puts a lot of light into the sky. Naturally, a large signal fire should be built in a clearing where there is no danger of setting the whole forest on fire. But rather than one big fire, a trio of smaller, more manageable fires is even better. Three fires arranged in a triangle make an internationally recognized distress signal. Besides that, you can position yourself between the fires to stay warm all the way around—which brings us to the next topic.

Within a few minutes after the sun went down, the air was noticeably colder. We hadn't planned on the car breaking down in this remote spot, so we didn't have camping gear with us—no sleeping bags, tent, or warm coats. The cold became a concern. The way things were going, this was shaping up to be a long and miserable night. So, in addition to providing light, the fire suddenly became very important as a source of warmth. But that little campfire wasn't going to be much of a heat source—unless we modified it.

Without sleeping bags or even blankets, and knowing that a campfire is famous for toasting one side of you while allowing the "dark side of the moon" to freeze, we needed to come up with a solution. One solution to the problem is to position the fire a moderate distance away from a reflective surface (like the rock wall at the back of our overhanging ledge, for example), allowing a space for us to get between the blaze and the wall. With the fire in that location, the wall effectively reflected some of the heat onto the side of us that was not facing the fire. Enhancing the effect of the reflector fire even more, we erected a stone wall on the far side of the fire to turn even more heat back toward us. There we sat, surrounded by the glow and the warmth of the fire, until morning brought the light of a new day and eventual rescue from our dilemma.

The reflector system is among the easiest methods for increasing the effectiveness of a campfire. There are other techniques, such as the hot rock bed mentioned in Chapter 2, but for us on that night, the reflector fire did the job. It was quick and easy to set up and proved why it has been a fundamental survival strategy used by outdoors people for centuries. If there is no rock wall available, use other techniques and whatever is available to construct a reflector. For example, a reflector can be made of the upturned root base of a downed tree. If the fire is kept at a safe distance, even combustible materials, such as a stack of logs, can be pressed into service as a reflector. If you can do nothing more than erect some sort of framework from which to hang a Space Blanket, that will also work as an effective reflector.

Staying warm on a chilly night is one of the primary functions of a fire, but cooking is another important reason to have a fire. Not only cooking food, but also boiling water to purify it. For this, a small fire with low flames and a good bed of coals is preferred. To concentrate the heat of the coals, build a ring of stones around the fire base. A few small stones placed in a triangular formation within the coals serve as a trivet to support a cooking pot or a pan.

If you have the luxury of choosing your firewood, keep in mind that pitchy woods are useful for getting a fire going, but cleaner-burning hardwoods are better for cooking. Gather wood before darkness falls and stack a sufficient amount to see you through the night. If the wood is damp, stack it near enough to the fire to dry, but far enough away so that it won't burst into flame.

Don't Set the World on Fire

Remember the headlines about the camper who became lost in the San Bernardino National Forest and started a fire to signal for help, but ended up igniting a raging forest fire that took several days to extinguish? During the battle, nearly four hundred firefighters, four helicopters, and four air tankers were called in to fight the blaze. When something like this happens, hundreds of thousands of dollars are spent, and men's lives are placed at risk to undo a mistake that never should have happened.

In a separate yet related incident, a lost camper used a flare to signal for help but ended up igniting a raging forest fire. That fire became the largest and most deadly fire of the season, as locally gusty winds that exceeded 60 mph fanned the flames and sent the inferno 30 miles to the west and south into a heavily populated area near San Diego. When the toll was counted, there were thirteen fatalities, and more than two thousand homes were destroyed.

Be very careful when working with fire, because it takes only an instant for it to get away from your control. Sparks rising from the blaze when you toss wood into the coals can be caught by the wind and sent a great distance, settle into dry grass or leaves, and start a wildfire. Combustible material beneath the fire base might hold a smoldering coal only to burst into flame long after you've left camp. Always be certain the fire base is totally dead, all the way down to mineral soil, before leaving the area.

Water

In order of importance to keeping the human body alive, clean water ranks right behind air and shelter. Without air, you die in a few minutes. In certain situations, if you lack shelter, you expire in a matter of hours. And in some conditions, if you have no drinking water, you perish in just a few days. You must be able to find a reliable water source if you are going to survive for very long.

It's possible to locate water in nearly every wilderness, but you need to understand where to look. Water almost always ends up in the lowest part of the landscape—in canyons, rock crevices, valleys, and other low areas such as lakes or swamps. I say "almost" only because water pockets that are discussed later in this chapter are often found on the tops of mesas, where a person might not think to look. But in most cases you want to look for topographic drainages where water will naturally collect as streams or rivers that are fed by lakes, mountain snowmelt, or glacial melt higher up. Natural drainages also channel runoff from local or distant storms and are the eventual path for water to take.

Because water naturally seeks the low ground, that's the place to look first. Even if there is no water on the surface, the ground in the lowest spots of the drainages will be the place where water was last to be found. As you examine the drainage, try to imagine what the water would do if it were there—where it would flow, where it would form pools. Go to those places and dig down to see if you find any indication of moisture in the soil. If you do, continue digging until the hole is a couple of feet deep, and then take a breather and wait for water to seep into the hole. It may, or it may not. Not every hole in every likely spot will produce water, but it is worth a try.

Of course, if you come across some damp ground, you know there is water in the soil. All you need to do is dig a hole, allow the water to seep in, and give it enough time for the particulates (mud and silt) to settle and leave clear water. But be cautious about every water source. If there is moisture in the soil, but nothing is growing around it, and there are no animal tracks leading to and from the watering hole, the water might be toxic. Do not use water from that source. Be aware that some methods of purification are not enough to remove all the toxic elements. Boiling, for example, will kill all the microorganisms but will not remove toxic minerals or chemical contaminants.

One indicator of the presence of water in the soil is the growth of especially green vegetation. If you see a place where the plants are growing more thick and lush than in surrounding areas, that will be a good place to search for water in the ground. Large plants such as willows or cottonwood trees are good indicators that are easy to spot from a distance.

Watch the patterns of animals, birds, and insects as they move about your area, because they all need to go to water periodically. Birds often circle water sources, and insects tend to stay fairly close to a reliable water source. Animal tracks may lead to water, but the source might be miles away, especially if the tracks are of large animals that range widely. If you come across a cluster of tracks that seem to aim in one direction, that is a clue worth following.

Sound is another indicator. I once found a hidden water source by listening to the frogs at night. I noted the direction of the croaking songs from my camp, and the next morning I hiked in that direction and found the concealed pond. In the mountains, sound is often the first clue to the presence of water, as you may be able to hear a small waterfall or a rushing stream that is invisible through the dense foliage.

If you have a sensitive nose, it might also lead you to water, as the odor of mud is detectable. To be successful, you must use your senses of sight, hearing, and smell to detect the clues that are around you. By employing logic and a keen awareness of what's around you, the water can be found. But that's only half the battle, because unless the water is falling right out of the sky into your mouth, you must consider it to be contaminated and in need of purification.

WATER PURIFICATION

For health reasons, drinking water must be pure. Ingesting contaminated water leads to problems that increase dehydration or even worse. Some waterborne organisms cause dysentery, which leads to prolonged diarrhea, fever, and weakness. Or you might end up with cholera or typhoid fever. Then there are flukes that will bore into your bloodstream, where they live as parasites and cause disease. It's even possible to swallow a leech, which hooks onto the throat or crawls up into the nasal passages, where it sucks blood and creates a wound that may become infected.

Basically, there are three categories of waterborne pathogens that cause disease. According to U.S. waterborne disease statistics for the years 1999–2001, there were 431,846 reported cases of illness in the United States as a direct result of these three categories we're about to discuss. Waterborne disease is a big problem that can get out of control and race through the population like a wildfire in dry prairie grass. Of course, all those victims of disease weren't camping or hiking when they got sick. No, most of them were using municipal water supplies. And if municipal water systems can become contaminated, just think what can happen in the streams, rivers, and lakes where the water is untreated.

▶ Bacteria, which are microscopic in size, are often single-celled organisms that typically cause illnesses such as typhoid fever, cholera, and dysentery. One of the most well-known bacteria is *E. coli*. In just one incident in Walkerton, Ontario, 2,300 people became ill and 7 people died from waterborne *E. coli* when it got loose in a municipal water supply. Fortunately, bacteria are easily killed by the use of chlorine as a chemical water purifier.

▶ Viruses are infectious organisms that reproduce when they invade living host cells. Viral infections lead to diseases such as hepatitis, polio, and meningitis, as well as gastrointestinal and respiratory illness and even paralysis. These little beasts are so tiny that they easily pass through water filters but can be killed by use of chemicals or by boiling.

▶ Finally, there is the category that includes protozoan parasites, single-celled organisms that feed on bacteria that are common in humans and animals. Among the common causes of waterborne disease are *Giardia* cysts and *Cryptosporidium* oocysts. These parasites are resistant to treatment with chlorine but are large enough that they can be trapped in a high-quality water filter or killed by boiling.

In case you think a little bout of dysentery is a fair price to pay for a great outdoor adventure, listen to the story of our friend Trudy who went on a two-month camping trek across a portion of the high plains and mountains of Wyoming. During the trek, she experienced occasional diarrhea but thought that was only normal, given the camp diet. After she returned home at the end of October, mild diarrhea continued on and off until January. She didn't feel sick, but not well either. Then in January, things got really bad and then got worse. By March, she couldn't get out of bed. There was blood in her stools. Her husband took her to the hospital emergency room, where she was diagnosed with ulcerative colitis (bleeding ulcers in the colon). In three months, she lost thirty-five pounds and was put on prescribed doses of prednisone and other drugs. After being bedridden for three months, she gradually began to feel a little better but was still extremely weak. The doctors told her that there was no cure and she would be on medication for life. A visit to another doctor resulted in discovery of the *Cryptosporidium* parasite in her colon. Almost no nutrient was being absorbed by her digestive system, and she would have slowly descended through malnutrition, dehydration, and death. After six years, she is fortunate to return to near-normal health. However, she isn't finished with this yet. She must have annual colonoscopies, and she has a permanently compromised immune system, occasional recurring bouts of dysentery, and the diagnosis that she now has a 50 percent greater chance of colon cancer. This is nothing to play with.

After a review of the different disease-causing organisms, it is obvious that more than one approach to water purification is necessary. So, let's talk about how to sanitize your drinking water so you can get rid of the bad stuff that can make you sick. The first consideration is the water source. If you're able to catch rainwater, you don't need to worry about purifying it. But if the water has touched anything other than the air and your clean container, treat it as if it were contaminated.

Filtration

The intent of filtration is to screen out harmful substances. If the bad stuff is stopped before it gets to your mouth, you're safe. Thanks to modern technology, today's submicron level of filtration can effectively screen out protozoa, bacteria, some chemicals, and pesticides. There are highly effective filter systems that are lightweight and easily portable for backpacking and camping. High-quality filters are expensive, but they are capable of purifying several hundred gallons of water, so

A COMPACT water filter that can be carried in a pack can remove many harmful biological, chemical, and mineral toxins, making most water sources safe and potable. Viruses, however, are too small for most filters to trap.

they last a long time for an average outdoorsman. And, they work. But you have to be careful before buying a water filter. Some units are nothing more than "taste improvers" that will remove a foul odor or flavor but not much more. Words like *bacteriostatic* sound impressive, and uninformed consumers may think this is a guarantee that the filter removes bacteria from the water. Actually, the big *B* word just means that the filtering element impedes bacteria growth within the unit itself, not that it removes waterborne bacteria. When it comes to filtering raw backcountry water, the words you want to look for are *Giardia* and *Cryptosporidium*. Because these pathogens are so small, it takes a very tight filtering medium to physically remove them, and such filters don't come cheap.

There are two types of filters worth considering: membrane and depth. Membrane-type filters employ porous sheets that allow water to pass through but block anything larger than the pore size. The good thing about membrane-type filters is that they are easy to clean. But the downside is that they clog up pretty quickly.

Depth-type filters employ a dense yet porous filtering element (such as a ceramic block) to screen out particulates as the water is forced through the material. These filter elements are cleaned by scrubbing or backwashing. If the system includes a carbon filter component, it is also able to eliminate certain chemicals and heavy metals. The only caution is that the filter elements need to be treated carefully to prevent them from cracking.

I've tested a variety of water filters and have found that they all keep me healthy when I'm forced to rely on unreliable water supplies. My rule is, don't leave home without one. There are some filter systems that are integrated into a water bottle, eliminating the need to operate a pump. Simply fill the bottle and drink filtered water through an integrated straw.

Chemical

The whole idea behind chemical treatment of drinking water is to poison all the little critters that are swimming in your drink. Iodine and chlorine are the old standbys in the water purification game. Make no mistake about it, chemical water treatments are toxic, at least to the organisms being treated. The key to safe use of these products for human consumption is to carefully follow manufacturer recommendations. Exercise additional caution, because some people have chemical sensitivities or are allergic to some of these substances (particularly iodine).

The effectiveness of a chemical purifier depends on product freshness, water temperature, water clarity, exposure time, and dosage. Check the expiration date on the product package to make sure the chemicals are fresh. For more effective purification, raise the water temperature to 60°F or above. Pre-filter or let the water stand overnight to allow sediments to settle, and then treat only the clear water. Allow the recommended treatment time and use the full dose of chemical.

Chlorine is used by municipalities all across the United States to treat city water before it is delivered to residential taps. For camping situations, products such as Halazone have been popular through the years. Regardless of what product you use, always follow directions.

Iodine comes in both tablet and liquid form. Use tablets as directed. The recommended dosage for liquid iodine is five drops of 2 percent

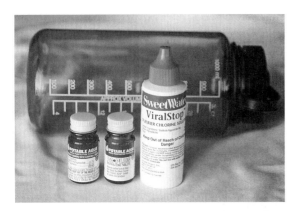

CHEMICAL water treatments are compact and lightweight enough to carry in a pocket. Chlorine and iodine are the chemicals used, but some people have an allergic reaction to iodine. Neither chemical is 100 percent effective against all pathogens, and they leave an aftertaste.

tincture of iodine in a quart of clear water. If the water is cloudy or especially cold, increase the dosage to ten drops. Shake the container to disperse the iodine, and then let it stand for half an hour before drinking.

Chemical (iodine or chlorine) treatment has always been popular as a means of purifying water, but there is controversy about the effectiveness of these approaches. Two questions exist: one has to do with individual sensitivity to the chemicals, and the other has to do with the shelf life of the products. The bottom line is that chemical purification may be more convenient, but it is never as effective as boiling. The chemicals leave an aftertaste in the water, and if you happen to be sensitive to the chemicals you might suffer some serious health problems by ingesting them. Consult your doctor to find out if you are likely to have any problems in this area.

Purification Systems

A water filter is not the same as a water purifier. Filters, as discussed above, only screen out particulates down to a certain size and may remove some chemicals. But viruses are so small that they slip right through the porous filter element. That's when you need a full-blown water purification system.

One such system is the SweetWater Guardian Purifier System. It combines a high-quality filter to screen out the particulates and a liquid chlorine-based water purification solution called ViralStop to do the actual purifying. The procedure is to filter the water first, then add five drops of ViralStop per liter of water and wait five minutes. The company claims a kill-rate of 99.99% for waterborne viruses, elimination of 99.9999% of all waterborne bacteria, and 99.9% of common protozoan parasites such as *Giardia* and *Cryptosporidium*.

MSR MIOX. A chemical approach to water purification that was developed for the military and tested by the U.S. Marines and Special Forces in Afghanistan, MIOX, made by Mountain Safety Research (also known as MSR), is unlike any other water purifier currently on the consumer market. The way it works is clever and effective. MIOX uses a small amount of untreated water, some salt, and a small electrical charge to create a chemical solution, a powerful oxidant, that, when added to untreated water, is toxic to all manner of organic pathogens (viruses, bacteria, *Giardia*, *Cryptosporidium*) but is not toxic to humans in its diluted form.

THE very compact and lightweight MIOX water purification system by MSR operates by creating its own microbe-killing cocktail to be mixed into contaminated water to kill all the pathogens.

The system is convenient, both from the standpoint of portability—it's about the size and weight of a small flashlight—and ease of operation. The only things to remember are to keep the salt chamber filled (any kind of salt will do), make sure the batteries are fresh—two CR-123A lithium camera batteries are good for purifying more than 200 liters of water—and fill the water cell before proceeding. The process is simple; with the salt chamber filled and capped, open the water cell and fill it to the brim with untreated water. The cell only holds ¼ teaspoon, so we're not talking about a lot of water here. Next, screw on the cap, shake the unit ten times, and push the button to activate the electrical charge. Pour the solution into the appropriate amount of untreated water. Mix by shaking or stirring, and allow it to stand for the specified amount of time, depending upon what type of pathogen is being eliminated. Test strips are used to make sure the solution is strong enough to kill everything.

MIOX is ideal for processing large quantities of water for a camp full of people. It works equally well for purifying small amounts for a lone hiker. What MIOX won't do is take care of particulates and inorganic contaminants such as heavy metals, chemicals, and such. It also

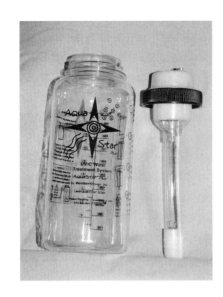

ULTRAVIOLET radiation renders waterborne organisms sterile and unable to reproduce, therefore harmless to humans. The AquaStar UV water purification bottle contains a UV light source, but being battery powered is a drawback.

won't sweeten foul-tasting water. For those operations, you still need to use a filter.

UV Purification. There is something interesting about ultraviolet light. It might seem like magic, but ultraviolet light, concentrated in the 254-nanometer range, is a light wave that is capable of disrupting the DNA of waterborne pathogens, thus rendering them unable to reproduce. If an organism is incapable of reproduction, it is harmless, even if we drink it. There are no waterborne microorganisms that are resistant to the killing effect of ultraviolet light waves, so, after treatment with a UV light source, the water is pure enough to drink. At least from the standpoint of living organisms.

A portable UV water treatment system that I have used is the AquaStar Plus (Meridian Design, Inc., www.uvaquastar.com). This unit has a UVC lamp inside a one-liter polycarbonate water bottle. After filling the water bottle with water, all it takes is a press of the button, and treatment takes 80 seconds. Because UV kills only the live organisms in water, it's a good idea to follow up with filtration to remove everything else. The one drawback to the system is that it requires battery power, so it will fail when the batteries die.

If you don't have a true purification system but you still want to ensure against viral contamination, there are three methods you can use. The first method is to pretreat the water with an iodine- or chlorine-based purification chemical to kill the organisms, and then run the water through a filter to remove the chemical taste and odor as well as the dead microbes. The second option is to filter the water and then treat with the purification chemical. The third method is to boil the water, which we're coming to next.

Thermal. The thermal approach involves cooking to death the little devils that contaminate your drinking water. This method is 100 percent effective against all three of the categories of waterborne pathogens we've discussed, but only if you do it right. To kill harmful organisms, boil water for one minute at sea level and add one minute for each additional 1,000 feet of elevation above sea level. If you're unsure of your elevation, boil the water for ten minutes just to be on the safe side. When I talk about boiling, I don't mean just making little bubbles. Bring the water to a hard rolling boil, and then keep it at that temperature for the prescribed amount of time. Boiling drives air out of the water and leaves it tasting flat, but that effect can be somewhat overcome by shaking or stirring some air back into the water.

Odor and Flavor Improvement

Boiling or chemically treating your drinking water may leave it with some foul taste or smell. Generally, those undesirable characteristics are removed by running the water through a high-quality filter. Or you can stir a bit of charcoal from you campfire into the water and then let it stand for forty-five minutes. The charcoal will help eliminate the bad smell and taste, and then you can strain out the bits of charcoal by pouring the water through a piece of cloth.

The flavor of chemically treated water can also be improved by pouring it back and forth between containers after the treatment. You might also try adding a pinch of salt per quart or flavoring the water with something like Tang or lemonade mix. Stirring about 50 mg of vitamin C into treated water helps eliminate the taste and color of iodine.

A final word about survival and water purity: If you drink impure water, illness may occur, and dehydration is one result of illness. If you refuse to drink because you believe the water is impure, dehydration is absolutely guaranteed. There are recorded incidents of people dying of dehydration at streamside because they were afraid to drink water that they couldn't purify. When it comes right down to an actual survival situation, this is a judgment call that only you can make in the given set of circumstances.

It's something to think about, and perhaps one more incentive to go prepared. All of this may sound like a pain in the neck just to get a good drink of water. But if you've ever experienced an intestinal tract ailment caused by ingesting something nasty with your water, you'd opt for a little pain in the neck rather than a pain in the gut anytime. Just ask Trudy.

SOLAR STILL AND OTHER WATER COLLECTION METHODS

Your water supply is not something you want to leave to chance, just hoping to stumble upon a way to keep yourself from succumbing to dehydration. Ideally, you should have a supply of drinking water available at all times. If you can't carry all the water you need (which you probably can't), the next best plan is to be in places where there is water that can be captured and purified for drinking. But, suppose your unexpected stay in the outback lasts longer than your water supply or takes you where there is no visible water to be gathered—then what?

This is when it is wise to have a secondary plan and the necessary equipment to make it work. One method of obtaining drinkable water from arid ground is called a solar still. Basically, this is a technique for distilling moisture that is held in the soil and collecting it for use. It works reliably, it works around the clock, and you don't have to expend energy constantly chasing a water supply. The drawback is that a solar still doesn't produce huge amounts of water. But on the plus side, every little bit helps.

The solar still was invented by a pair of American scientists, Dr. Ray D. Jackson and Dr. Cornelius H. M. Van Bavel of the U.S. Department of Agriculture. It consists of some very simple equipment that is easy to set up and use. Recommended materials include a clear sheet of thin plastic, measuring approximately six by six feet; a five-foot length of plastic tubing, about the diameter of a drinking straw; and a container in which to catch the distilled water. The only other thing you need is a piece of ground to dig in.

Setting up the solar still is relatively easy. Dig a hole three feet across at the top and three feet deep, with sloping sides. Place the container in the center of the bottom of the hole. Position the plastic tubing so one end reaches the bottom of the container and the other end is resting on the ground outside the rim of the hole. Now, stretch the plastic sheet somewhat loosely across the hole and place a small stone in the center of the sheet to weight it down, forcing the middle of the sheet down into the hole to within a few inches of the top of the container's open mouth. Make sure that the top end of the plastic tubing extends out beneath the plastic sheet and that the lower end is secure in the bottom of the container. While everything is in this position, heap dirt all around the edges of the skirt of the plastic sheet, sealing the hole completely. Cover all parts of the plastic sheet that are on the ground outside the hole, but make sure you don't cover the end of the plastic tubing.

What happens next is amazing, but the scientists who invented this thing knew exactly what to expect. As the sun shines through the clear plastic sheet, the ground inside the hole becomes warm, and water vapor is drawn out of the soil to collect on the underside of the plastic. When enough water condenses on the plastic sheet, droplets form, which then run down the cone-shaped surface and fall into the con-

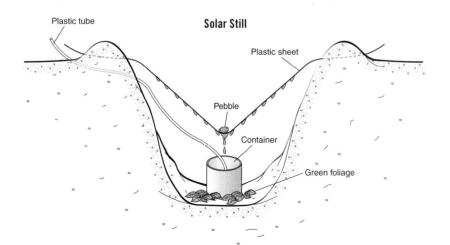

Solar Still

Plastic tube

Plastic sheet

Pebble

Container

Green foliage

WITH a sheet of plastic and a bit of tubing, a solar still can be made with little effort. Moisture condenses on the underside of the plastic sheet and drips into a container, from which it is sucked out through the plastic tube.

tainer. After a while, there is enough water in the container to allow you to drink it through the plastic tube.

Obviously, this isn't quite the same as a cool spring offering an endless supply of water. But it has been determined that even in the most arid regions, some water will be produced by a properly designed solar still. The still works around the clock as a water-gathering device, but operating efficiency diminishes by about 50 percent at night.

Water collected from a solar still is clean, as long as the components used in the collection process aren't contaminated. And because this is a distillation process, moisture drawn from the ground is pure and needs no further treatment. This means that you can actually purify water that is contaminated. For example, you can pour foul water or even urinate in the hole to add moisture to the soil, and the distillation process will deliver pure water on the underside of the plastic and in the collection container. Another way to increase the output of the solar still is to place green vegetation in the hole, where the moisture will be drawn out of the plants and deposited on the plastic sheet. At night, when efficiency has dropped, you can carefully remove the soil from one side of the plastic sheet, remove the spent vegetation, and replace it with fresh vegetation without losing too much operation time for the still.

Naturally, the quantity of water produced by a solar still depends upon the amount of water in the soil. Clay soils generally hold more water than loose sand. Low areas are likely to have a higher moisture content than higher ground. Where plant growth patterns indicate the presence of groundwater, solar still operation is more successful than in utterly barren ground. Two solar stills produce twice as much drinkable water as one, so it's a good idea to have a pair of these units working for each person in the party. Even if it won't supply all your needs (under the right conditions, it may), a solar still at least augments whatever other water supply you may find.

A couple of side benefits of such a device as this are that sometimes small animals will fall into the slick plastic depression and become trapped. Food! And, if it happens to rain, you have a ready-made basin to capture the rainwater.

Aboveground Still

An alternate way to collect water from distillation and condensation is to use what I call an aboveground solar still. This is nothing more than a plastic bag (a trash bag will do) that is filled with green vegetation, closed up tightly, and left to sit in the sun. By tightly closing all the holes in the bag, the water vapor created by the sun warming the vegetation will have no escape and will collect on the inside of the bag. Later, you can open the bag, toss out the used vegetation, drink the water, and start over again. If you had several of these bag-stills in operation, your water supply would be nicely supplemented. An advantage to this type of device over the inground solar still is that it is portable and almost immediately available without much work. In fact, you can fill a bag with vegetation, seal it up, tie it to the top of your backpack, and let it do its work while you hike.

There are a couple of ways to put this device to work—you can seal it around a bunch of leaves on a tree or bush, or you can fill it with green vegetation (grasses and leaves) that you collect in the area and just let the bag sit on the ground and soak up the sunshine. The latter method offers the advantage of total mobility. You can move the still to always be in direct sunshine and can place it on a dark boulder to absorb even more heat to increase effectiveness.

Open-Air Still

If you get up early in the morning in most parts of the country, you can collect large amounts of pure water in the form of dew. When the temperature and the humidity level cross paths, the dew point is reached, and it's either going to rain or fog will form, or heavy amounts of dew will collect on nearly every smooth surface. It's an open-air still, of sorts. Grasses, leaves, metal, glass, and plastic will all collect dew. Tent material, clothing left out overnight, nearly everything will be just waiting for you to come along and sop up the moisture. And this moisture is pure, because it was formed by the same process of distillation used by the solar still. At the seashore, all the salt and minerals from the seawater are left in the ocean as the dew condenses on shoreside plants or other objects. The caution I offer about collecting dew from plants, however, is that you should avoid contact-toxin plants such as poison ivy, poison oak, and poison sumac. While sopping up dew from those noxious plants, you would also be transferring the toxic elements that can cause you no shortage of distress when it comes in contact with your skin.

WATER CAPTURE

You never know when the sky will open up and rain will fall, so it is important to always be prepared to capture drinking water. Evaluate every piece of equipment you have to determine if it can catch and hold water. A cotton shirt that is spread out on the ground will soak up and hold rain. A poncho, laid out over rocks or bushes so it forms a natural basin, is excellent. A discarded bit of trash (cans, bottles, plastic) that you find along the way might also serve. In some areas, large leaves can be laid together like shingles of a roof to catch rain and direct the flow into a container. Rainwater is fairly pure, so every drop you can capture is ready to drink without the need for filtration, boiling, or chemical treatment. It's a free gift.

USE every opportunity to capture water as it falls as rain or collects as dew. An emergency blanket or poncho can be propped up along the edges and arranged with the center section low to form a catch basin.

DIG A HOLE

If you find some damp ground, dig a hole and then wait for groundwater to seep in. Rather than abusing your knife to dig the hole, use some other implement that you have on hand. You want to preserve the edge on your knife, so never run the blade into the ground. If you have nothing else to use as an excavation tool, use your knife to carve a digging stick, and use that as the tool to dig the hole.

After digging the hole, water will slowly seep into the depression. If you have a means of purifying the water, scoop it out with a container or simply sop it up with a piece of cloth and then squeeze it into a container for treatment. If you have no way of treating the water, but drinking is critical to avoid dehydration, drink directly from the hole. Either enlarge the hole enough to allow you to reach the water with your lips, or find a way to fashion a straw out of hollow reed grass or something that you might have scavenged such as a piece of rubber tubing from a vehicle.

Work a similar technique if you have located a slimy pool that you don't dare drink from, except that you dig the hole off to one side of the pool where the ground is only damp but not sodden. As the water moves through the soil, it will be somewhat filtered, but you can't expect that all the bad stuff will be cleaned out. This is the kind of water that you drink in case of dire circumstances when you have no way to purify it. But of course it's always best to filter, boil, or chemically treat if you can.

As with all survival techniques, it is a good idea to try them out in the backyard or someplace close to home first, so you know how to perform the task and what to expect. Nothing beats a little hands-on experience.

IN moist ground, use a digging stick to excavate a hole a foot or two deep. (Don't dig with your knife.) Allow the moisture to seep into the hole, and let it sit long enough for the particulates to settle out, leaving clear water.

WATER POCKETS

In the desert southwest there is a geologic region of Utah known as the Waterpocket Fold. It is a huge landscape of spectacular sandstone formations and is known by this name because of the numberless pockets in the top surface of the stone that capture and hold water. These water pockets are also known locally as tanks, and they range from tiny to swimming pool–size. As you might imagine, these water sources offer lifesaving moisture to any who can find them. They frequently occur on top of mesas but can also be found in the canyons where erosion has left natural depressions in the stone that capture rainwater. This type of water supply is not specific to only the desert. Anywhere you can find rocks that have depressions on their top surface, look for water that has collected. I've found these water pockets from coast to coast and from sea level to the high mountains.

I issue one caution about using these water sources. Even though the water was originally pure as it fell from the sky, it may no longer be suitable for consumption. The animals in the area know about and depend on these water pockets, and I have found rodent feces in some of them. Unless you are in such dire circumstances that you must make

WATER is sometimes caught in hollows on rock surfaces. Although the temptation is to drink this captured rainwater, it might have been polluted by animals, so it should be filtered or boiled first.

the choice to either drink now or die, I recommend that all water gathered from water pockets be filtered before drinking.

One way to drink directly from such sources is to use the Aquamira filter straw that can be poked down into any tight place to give access to the water. Suck the water directly through the straw for a quick drink. The straw filters up to 20 gallons and will stop *Giardia* and *Cryptosporidium*. The drawback to this type of product is that it doesn't filter water for storage in a container, but for a quick drink without the hassle of setting up a larger filter, it's a good way to go. (For further discussion of water-purification equipment, see Chapter 9.)

THE Aquamira Frontier is a very compact and lightweight filter device capable of filtering up to 20 gallons of water. The straw makes it easy to suck water out of otherwise inaccessible places such as crevices in rocks or small puddles.

Food

5

Food is the first thing that comes to most peoples' minds when they hear the word *survival*. It's probably because most folks are sure they will starve to death if they can't eat dinner on time tonight. The fact is, starvation is one of the least imminent threats to life under most survival conditions. But that doesn't mean food is unimportant. On the contrary, although food may not rank highest on the priority list in every situation, it is absolutely necessary and is a vital element in the long-term survival strategy. Even in the short term, food is very important when you've been on the move for hours on end and you start to run out of energy.

Obviously, not all foods are equal in nutritional value. This is especially true for handling rigorous conditions that demand a high level of calorie consumption. When you're covering a lot of ground and working hard to stay alive, fluff foods don't cut it. You need substantial nourishment, packed with beneficial carbs, protein, and good fats. And you need to drink plenty of water, so those nutrients can be processed by your body.

Ideally, you should eat at least one hot meal per day—more if possible. The thermal intake helps stave off hypothermia, which creeps up on you as your energy level diminishes because of fatigue. The side benefit of a hot meal is mostly psychological, but there is no denying that a hot meal tastes better than a cold one, and that alone gives you a strong boost to morale. Even nothing more than a cup of hot water with some pine needles or other edible leafy material steeped in it to make a wilderness tea lifts the spirits at the end of a hard day. If you're suffering through hot climate conditions, eat your meals and imbibe your drinks cold to help keep your internal temperature down.

Four major ingredients make up the recipe for our nutritional needs. The most important is water. By composition, about two-thirds of a normal human body is water. It's a resource that is being constantly reduced as it is consumed for such basic metabolic duties as transporting nutrients to every cell in the body, transporting waste products out of the cells, and promoting digestion, respiration, circulation, and excretion. One of the big problems is that you cannot continue to eat unless you have enough available drinking water or you will suffer increased dehydration. In cold weather, dehydration leads to hypothermia and frostbite. In hot weather, dehydration leads to dangerous maladies such as heat exhaustion, heat stroke, and death. That's why adequate water intake is absolutely critical to survival. One of your priorities should be to drink plenty of water to prevent dehydration. Rest during the heat of the day, and pace your activities to control your sweating. (Review Chapter 4 for information on finding water sources and water-purification techniques.)

Now let's take a look at the other three ingredients that make up our nutritional requirements—protein, carbohydrate, and fat.

Proteins supply amino acids, which are necessary for the formation and repair of muscle and other soft tissue. After a hard day that has placed a lot of stress on your muscles, it's protein that comes to the rescue and helps the rebuilding process. Amino acids are also required for the formation of hormones, natural antibodies, and enzymes. Proteins are available from eating meat, eggs, nuts, seeds, and dairy products. Energy bars also contain protein, and you can check the nutritional information label on the package to see exactly how much protein is in the bar. Depending on the intensity and duration of activity, the daily protein intake of an individual should be between 15 percent and 25 percent of their total calorie consumption.

YOU need nutrition to keep going, and there is no more convenient way to carry a supply of food than energy bars. They last a long time, are packed with calories and nutrients, and they're compact and tightly sealed for protection.

Of all the food categories, carbohydrates are perhaps the most important. That's because carbohydrates are the primary source of blood glucose, which is the most important type of fuel for all body cells. Glucose is the only fuel that powers the brain and red blood cells. Are there "good" carbs and "bad" carbs? Not if you're in a survival situation. Under those conditions, you eat everything you can get your hands on. In more civilized circumstances, the best choice is to go for the complex carbohydrates found in fruits, veggies, grains, and nuts. The carbs that come from refined sugars in candy and soft drinks lead to sugar highs, followed by energy crashes. They don't call this stuff junk food for nothing. Even so, these things can be beneficial in a survival situation because they are high in calories and fat. But a better choice would be an energy bar that offers a substantial load of complex carbohydrate calories, some protein, and fats of the unsaturated variety.

Fats—now here's a topic that raises debate. Under normal conditions, most of us try to limit the fat in our diet. But in an environment where calories are being burned at a breathtaking pace, fat consump-

CHECK nutritional information labels on food packages to make sure you're getting real nutrition and not junk food.

CARRYING lightweight foods in burnable packaging helps keep the load under control and eliminates the need to pack out a bunch of trash. The cup-o-soup concept now includes pasta meals and mashed potatoes as well as a variety of soups.

tion is necessary. Fats supply a hefty load of calories in a tiny package. Nevertheless, if you have a choice, stay away from trans fats and saturated fats. Again, study the nutritional information on the food package so you can make wise choices.

To help with meal planning, here are a few ideas.

▶ Hot drinks anytime in cool weather—My personal preference is for a cup of hot Pero, made from roasted barley and other grains. I pack the dry drink mix in zip-up baggies so I don't have to haul hard containers. Stir a tablespoon of the powder in a cup of hot water, add a bit of sweetener, and enjoy a carb drink that will help chase the morning chill away. For those who prefer tea, there are some great herb teas that will do the same job.

▶ Breakfast—You can make a special porridge out of ingredients you can carry in a plastic baggie in your pocket and two cups of water. Bring the water to a boil and add a pinch of salt, one cup of rolled oats, two tablespoons of cracked wheat, a few raisins, and some nuts. It takes only about three minutes to cook and provides a good load of carbs, some protein, and fat from the nuts. Add a little water after cooking, to loosen everything up.

▶ Lunch or dinner—On the trail, it's important to keep things light and compact. One way to do that is to carry dehydrated soup packets. For a quick lunch, all it takes is heating some water and mixing the soup in a Sierra cup. If you prefer pasta instead of soup, there are dehydrated pasta meals that are packed with carbs and protein.

MOUNTAIN House is a popular maker of dehydrated meals that are lightweight and easy to fix. MREs (meals ready to eat) are available at military surplus stores and Internet sites, and they offer plenty of nutrition without the need for much preparation.

At your outdoor store, look for meals such as macaroni and cheese that are prepared by just adding hot water and stirring. The same goes for dehydrated meals of lasagna or spaghetti and meatballs. At a military surplus store, shop for MREs, meals ready to eat that are used by the troops.

▶ Trail snacks—One of my favorite trail snacks is GORP, a homemade concoction of Good Old Raisins and Peanuts. Along with the staples, I toss in some seeds (sunflower and pumpkin) and a variety of nuts and dried fruit in a customized mix that I make myself. For a real treat, I throw in a load of M&Ms. A snack like this provides lots of carbs, protein, fat, and calories.

To maintain a steady energy level throughout the day, it is best to eat small midmorning and midafternoon snacks. Between the regular meals, nibble on foods that are easy to grab out of your pocket. This will help keep you from running out of energy or feeling famished and overeating at regular mealtimes.

In a survival incident, the rules of eating and drinking might change somewhat depending upon your situation. If you don't know when rescue will come, and your supplies are limited, do everything possible to conserve your energy by pacing your workload. Rest when you can, become efficient, and minimize struggle. That will allow you to cut back on food and, to a certain degree, your water intake and to ration your supplies so they will last longer.

BECOME A HUNTER-GATHERER

If a survival incident is not resolved quickly through rescue, food provisions will probably run out. And because you can never tell how long a survival situation will last, it's wise to include as much "wild" food in the daily menu as possible, to extend whatever "civilized" food supply you have with you. This supplementation should include both plant and animal sources, because plants are seasonal and may not be available for use when you need them.

Edible Plants

It would be great if every survival incident took place in mid-September in the Pacific Northwest where the wild blackberries are thick and ripe and sweet. But that just isn't reality. You need to be prepared to forage whatever you can find in whatever season and location you happen to be. Sometimes it's possible to make great use of plants; at other times or locations the plants won't offer much, and animals will be the only available food source.

While hiking down the trail, I am always scanning for food. I graze while I go, stopping to pluck whatever I can find that I know is edible. But here is something that is absolutely critical—never put anything in your mouth that you can't identify and know is safe to eat. It's a rule to live by. Violate that rule at your own peril, because eating the wrong thing can make you violently ill or can even kill you. Not everything that looks edible is. Not everything that tastes OK is. Not everything that you observe the animals eating is OK for human consumption. There are no reliable rules about color, leaf shape, or anything else to tell you what you can or cannot eat. The wilderness is like a grocery store with shelves filled with things in cans. If you walked into a grocery store and discovered that all the can labels were missing, it would be foolish to randomly pick out a can, open it, and eat what's inside. Drain cleaner comes in cans, and it will kill you.

The same applies to eating from the wilds. Unless you know how to read the labels presented by the plants, don't put it in your mouth. Just because a plant produces berries doesn't mean they are edible—

some are, some aren't. There are plants that faintly resemble what you are familiar with at home—some members of the parsley family, water hemlock and poison hemlock, for example—that are lethal. There are edible plants and poisonous plants that closely resemble each other, the edible camas (*Camassia quamash*) and the death camas (*Zigadenus paniculatus*) being examples. There are mushrooms that look like the ones you buy at the supermarket, but they are deadly. *Amanita virosa* is one such mushroom, and there is a reason it is called *the destroying angel*.

While I'm talking about mushrooms, I will give you one rule: No mushroom is worth eating. Some of them taste good, and they can help fill your stomach, but they provide no nutrition. Because they have nothing of value to offer, and the consequences of picking the wrong one are unacceptable, they should all be avoided.

There are hundreds of thousands of different plants on earth, but only about one-third of them have been identified as edible. That sounds like there are a lot of edible plants, and there are; but there are also a lot of inedible ones. Not every inedible plant is dangerous. Some are just absolutely unpalatable. But some are very dangerous, and unless you know how to "read the labels," you are playing a game of Russian roulette with two-thirds of the cylinder full of bullets.

What I'm getting to is that you must make a thorough study of edible plants if you intend to be able to use the wild ones as food. There are some excellent books available for this study. My library is full of many, some of which are now out of print, but new ones are being released all the time. The most useful books have illustrations that show leaf patterns, geographic location information, identification markers for all seasons of the year, and discussion of which parts are edible and how they should be prepared. Euell Gibbons wrote many books on the subject, such as *Stalking the Wild Asparagus*. It's short on illustrations but entertaining and full of good information. One of my personal favorites is *Wild Edible Plants of the Western United States*, by Donald R. Kirk. Another good one is *Eating from the Wild* by Dr. Anne Marie Stewart and Leon Kronoff. These books will give you a start on a study that can easily consume a lifetime.

When you begin eating wild plants, it's best to start with the ones you already recognize. When Becky and I began harvesting wild edible plants, we started with local varieties that were easy to identify: cattail, dandelion, thistle, stinging nettle, and wild rose. Just for fun, we even collected wild grass seeds, ground them into flour, and included them with some wild blackberries in our fourth anniversary cake. That was many years ago, and we still enjoy finding new plants to use in our foraging adventures. It's important to pick wild edibles from remote locations that have not been contaminated by weed killers, vehicle exhaust, etc.

To give a brief overview of the plants mentioned above, here are a few of the uses to which we have put them. When cooking any of these plants, don't throw away the water; drink it as a nutritious wild tea or use it for soup stock:

EATING wild foods becomes necessary in long-term survival situations when the civilized food runs out. The cattail is an easily recognizable plant that grows in moist ground. Throughout the growing season, it offers a variety of food options.

WHO doesn't recognize dandelions? These weeds are edible from root to flower, although they get bitter as they age.

▶ The cattail has an edible root system, and the lower portion of the central stalk is excellent when young, either raw or cooked like asparagus. With a little butter and salt, this is a treat! The emerging head (before it turns brown) can be eaten raw or cooked like baby corn. After the cattail heads turn brown and fluffy, they are no longer edible but make good insulation material and can be used in tinder.

▶ All parts of the young dandelion are edible; the taproot can be eaten after boiling or baking, the leaves make good salad or cooked greens (although the plant gets bitter as it ages), and the early buds remind me of brussels sprouts. I've eaten the early yellow flowers and find them not too bitter for my taste. Your mileage may vary.

THISTLES were valuable food plants for natives and pioneers alike. Use a knife to strip away the spiny outer skin, then eat the core like celery.

STINGING nettle becomes an excellent potherb after just a few minutes in boiling water to deactivate the stinging property.

▶ Young thistle stalks can be stripped of their spiny exterior and eaten almost like celery, but the stalks become woody with age. This plant was valuable for food to early western pioneers.

▶ Stinging nettle is rendered stingless by boiling the tender top leaves for about five minutes, after which they become excellent mild greens. Boiling too long makes the greens mushy. I have eaten stinging nettle raw, but the experience is not to be recommended unless you don't mind having a mouth full of prickles.

▶ Wild rose hips are high in vitamin C and taste faintly like apple. Chew off the outer pulp, and spit away the abundant seeds.

ROSE hips are the seed pods left behind after the flower falls. A pithy husk surrounds the hard seeds and can be nibbled off and the seeds discarded. These are loaded with vitamin C and other nutrients.

Start with local, familiar plants such as those, then expand your knowledge and experience one plant at a time. Pretty soon, you'll be comfortable foraging as you hike and build confidence that you will be able to survive if you're ever stranded in the outdoors. No matter where

I travel in the world, I am always on the lookout for edible plants that I already recognize. And I am always trying to learn about native varieties to add to my inventory of identifiable plants, because you just never know where you'll be when that knowledge will come in handy.

Over the long term, it's nearly impossible to survive solely on vegetation that you can forage from the wilds. Protein and fat are not available from plants, so it becomes necessary to rely on animals for survival. With some exceptions noted below, nearly all animal life is edible if it is properly prepared. The biggest problem is not what you can eat but how you can obtain it. You have two choices: hunting or trapping. Traps are preferable to active hunting because they work 24/7 and, once they are set, traps don't require continual expenditure of energy. Hunting can be successful, but it's easy to spend more energy than you get back, so you must be careful not to end up in a negative-energy-gain situation while hunting.

Birds

All birds are edible, and so are their eggs. If you observe the habits of the birds in your area, you'll see that they all come to the ground

OBSERVE the habits of the local bird population to find their nests, because these sometimes hold eggs or young chicks that can be easily taken for food. This ground nest was hidden among tall grasses.

sometimes—even if they spend most of their time in trees or flying. Eventually, they all come to the ground for water or food, and that's when you can take them. Also, by watching their patterns you can discover where they nest, and that gives you an opportunity to raid the nest for eggs or for young chicks.

It's easier to go after birds that spend a lot of time on the ground, such as quail, grouse, chukar, pheasant, ducks, and geese. One effective way to kill birds on the ground is to use a throwing stick, a primitive weapon that can be quickly and easily made from a piece of wood about two feet long and a couple of inches in diameter. A throwing stick is straight, unlike its Aussie cousin the boomerang, and you throw it at game birds (or other small animals) in sidearm fashion to get it to glance off the ground and whack the animal you're after. With a direct hit, you can knock the animal senseless and then rush in to make the kill.

Another technique that we used with success while living in the desert wilderness of southern Utah was to smoke out a small animal that had run into its burrow. A small smudge fire was built beside the entrance, and Becky fanned the smoke into the animal's hole while I stood by with the throwing stick to use as a club. After several minutes, the animal poked its head out of the hole, eyes red, choking on the smoke. Whack!

Food from the Pond and the Field

All animals need water, but some live in it almost all the time. If you come across a pond, stream, or swamp, pay attention to what's moving nearby. Depending upon where you are, you can capture frogs, crawdads, turtles, and small fish. One of my fond food memories is of a stew I made out of

SMALL game and birds on the ground can be taken by using a throwing stick. The technique is to sling the stick sidearm, skimming it along the ground to knock down the prey.

river mussels that I found among the rocks, blended with a wild assortment of edible plants that I gathered along the banks of the stream. Also good for a wild stew are insects such as ants that you can dig out of anthills (I'm partial to the large red and black wood ants because they taste like lemon drops), grub worms (these are beetle larvae that live beneath the bark of trees or in dead timber), beetles (found where you'll also find grubs), moths that are attracted to your fire, and grasshoppers (search the open fields). Watch the patterns of life to discover the active times to hunt these critters.

Caution. After capturing animals to be used as food, care must be taken to avoid potential problems with serious, even life-threatening, illness. Contact with and preparation of wild game animals can put you at risk of bacterial illnesses such as tularemia and viral diseases such as hantavirus. Tularemia (sometimes known as rabbit fever) is debilitating enough that it was reportedly used as a bioweapon by the Russians during World War II. This disease can be contracted through direct contact with openings in your skin (this includes insect bites as well as handling contaminated animals), inhalation, or consumption (eating the flesh or drinking contaminated water). To avoid tularemia, wear gloves when skinning or gutting animals, wear long sleeves and pants and apply insect repellent to protect yourself against insect bite, avoid eating undercooked game meat, and drink only purified water. Symptoms of the disease include headache, dizziness, fatigue, pain, nausea, and loss of appetite. Eyes get red, lymph nodes become inflamed, a high fever might ensue, and death is possible. There are several medications that have proven effective for tularemia infection, so before going into the backcountry, check with your doctor for treatment methods that are appropriate for you.

Hantavirus is a potentially deadly viral disease that affects the pulmonary system. It is contracted from contact with infected rodents or their droppings or urine. Eating infected rodents, handling them prior to cooking, or drinking unpurified water that has been contaminated somewhere upstream may result in contracting the disease. Early symptoms include headache, chills, dizziness, nausea, vomiting, a nonproductive cough, back pain, shortness of breath, abdominal pain, and sweats. There is no field treatment, so patients must be transported to a medical facility as soon as possible.

The death of a park ranger at Grand Canyon was attributed to plague that he contracted through contact with rodents or perhaps mountain lions. Plague is transmitted via fleas that inhabit the infected animal and then communicate the disease to humans through flea bites. Infection with plague can evolve into pneumonia that can then be transmitted to other humans as a result of coughing. This points out the risk involved in handling wild animals, especially rodents, as a potential food source. Even after the animal is dead, the fleas might be active.

When it comes to eating seafood, there are potential dangers. In the subtropics and tropics, it can be risky to eat some predatory fish such as barracuda, parrotfish, moray eel, grouper, amberjack, and other species that have become contaminated with ciguatera by eating other contaminated fish. The toxin originates with an algae that is consumed by a little fish that then gets eaten by a bigger fish that then gets eaten by you. At each stage, the ciguatoxin becomes more concentrated and dangerous through a process called biomagnification. There is no way to detect by smell, outward appearance, or taste that a fish is contaminated. The ciguatoxin is not affected by heat or cold, so the contamination cannot be removed by cooking or freezing. Anyone who eats a contaminated fish is at risk of the illness, which manifests itself through gastrointestinal and neurological symptoms such as nausea, vomiting, diarrhea, headaches, muscle ache, weakness, numbness, hallucinations, and other ailments. There is no antidote or treatment. Although many victims recover after several days, symptoms may persist for weeks or even years, with long-term disability a possibility.

At certain times of the year, shellfish (clams, mussels, oysters, and scallops) may present a serious health hazard due to paralytic shellfish poisoning (PSP) caused by the shellfish becoming contaminated by algae that contain toxin. Anyone who consumes contaminated shellfish is at risk of serious illness or death. Early symptoms include tingling of the tongue and lips, followed by similar sensations in the fingers and toes. Eventually there can be loss of control of arms and legs and difficulty breathing as chest and abdominal muscles are paralyzed. Death can follow in as little as two hours. There is no medicine to counteract the symptoms, and the only treatment is the use of a respirator and oxygen. Cooking does not eliminate the toxin. There is no visual test for PSP, because affected shellfish look no different from healthy ones. Neither is color or clarity of the water a reliable indicator. Short of receiving a warning from local authorities or being able to do your own lab tests, there is virtually no way to know if the shellfish are contaminated.

In a long-term survival situation, it becomes necessary to kill and eat animals. The fact that there are potential risks involved does not reduce or eliminate the necessity of harvesting game to keep you alive. But the risks must be recognized and every precaution taken to avoid, as much as possible, the chance of becoming infected or contaminated.

My motto is "if in doubt, leave it out." Then I go looking for something to eat that doesn't present such a high risk.

Ultimately, the decision is yours—whether to take a chance with handling and eating the animal, fish, or shellfish you have caught or to pass it up and search for something else. If you become ill from drinking contaminated water or from eating unsafe animals, your chances for survival drop precipitously. You can't afford to get sick. Nevertheless, desperate times will drive people to desperate measures, and when you get desperate enough, you'll find a way to eat things you never thought you would put in your mouth. Still, you want to do it as safely as possible, and having an understanding of the potential risks will help keep you healthy. After taking every reasonable precaution, every survivor must make the final critical choice for himself or herself—whether to eat or not.

Trail snacks

Camping, hiking, and all the other related activities that go along with life in the outdoors quickly drain us of energy. As our internal energy fires start to burn low, we get sluggish, exhausted, clumsy, and apathetic. If we let the situation go long enough, our judgment may even become impaired. Life in camp and on the trail is no place to have these things happening, because this is precisely the time when we must have all our wits about us in order to prevent accidents. The solution is to have high-energy food easily available. It's sort of like having a supply of nice dry wood to toss on the fire.

What I refer to as trail foods are best for this, because they are high energy in nature and require no effort other than to reach in a pocket, grab a handful, and toss it in your mouth. Naturally, there is some preparation required before leaving home and heading for the woods, but, once you're in camp or on the trail, have a good supply of no-fuss trail snacks close at hand all the time.

Ideal trail snacks should provide quick energy, be easy to carry without making a mess, and need no special care such as refrigeration. Most of all, they should taste good. GORP is a traditional trail snack that has fed hikers and climbers for decades, but there's a lot more you can do than just combining raisins and peanuts. Here are a few recipes for great trail foods that you can prepare yourself and package at home for your next outing.

GORP

Expanding on the concept of GORP, we come up with just about any recipe we want. There are no rules here, so feel free to experiment, but there are basically two types of GORP—sweet and salty. If you can't decide which one you want, it's even OK to mix them together.

There's nothing like a mix of chocolate, crushed cookies, nuts, and coconut. Another way to go is to mix some M&M's, a large jar of dry roasted peanuts, and some raisins (substitute dried date chunks, dried berries, or any other dried fruit you like). Toss in some pretzel pieces for a salty contrast.

For the salty side of GORP's personality, use a blend of crackers, salted peanuts, as well as other salted nuts, pretzel pieces, sesame sticks, etc. If you're in a situation that causes a lot of perspiration and subsequent loss of body salt, this is a good way to add the much needed sodium into your diet, but you should also drink plenty of water when nibbling a salty snack. My favorite recipe is a blend of whole almonds, soy nuts, pumpkin seeds, raw sunflower seeds, and raisins, as well as dried cranberries or dried date pellets.

Crackers and Cheese

Sometimes, I love to carry a sandwich baggie full of Ritz crackers or tortilla chips and another baggie full of pre-sliced bits of sharp cheddar cheese and make little hors d'oeuvres as I go. You can buy snack packs of crackers and cheese, but the issue I have with that kind of product is the package disposal problem. Empty plastic zip baggies are easy to stow in a pocket when the meal is over. When I'm in the mood for meat, I add a bite of jerky or slices of thin-cut pepperoni that I keep in a separate baggie.

Pemmican

Traditional pemmican was a method used by some North American Indians and mountain men for preserving a tasty high-energy food without the need for refrigeration. Think of it as the earliest known energy bar. Originally, it called for the use of melted suet, a hard, crumbly fat that surrounds the internal organs of animals, as a binding agent to hold the ingredients together in a small ball. Lucky for our taste buds, this recipe replaces melted suet with peanut butter and honey. The use of cayenne is optional, depending upon individual taste:

  1 cup jerky
  1 cup dried berries
  1 cup raw sunflower seeds or any type of crushed nuts
  2 teaspoons honey
  ¼ cup peanut butter
  ½ teaspoon cayenne (optional)

Grind or pound the dried meat until it is reduced to a mealy powder. Mix the meat with the dried berries, seeds, and nuts. Warm up the honey and peanut butter until they are soft, then blend in cayenne to taste. Pour all the ingredients together and mix. Separate small portions into golf-ball-size batches and allow to cool. After the pemmican has cooled, store it in plastic bags in a cool, dry place until you're ready to use it.

FOOD SAFETY: BEARS, BACTERIA, AND MORE

Nobody wants to have a big predator wander into camp and tear everything apart while looking for a quick meal. Most campers are familiar

TO protect your camp from predators that are looking for a meal, stash all food in an animal-proof locker.

BEARS aren't the only animals that will raid your food; raccoons, jays, eagles, squirrels, and other varmints are also a concern.

with the cautions about how to keep the campsite and the food supply safe from bears. But to reiterate the rules, here's a quick review of the major points.

▶ Don't leave food lying around camp because it will attract bears. That goes not only for human food, but for pet food and livestock feed as well.
▶ Store double-wrapped and tightly sealed food in a bear-proof container, available for rent or loan at some national park headquarters or for purchase at some sporting goods outlets. If a bear-proof container is not available, place food in a backpack or other container and suspend it from a tree limb at least 10 feet above the ground and 4 feet away from the trunk.
▶ Be strict about maintaining your tent and sleeping bag as a zero-food zone. That means never take food (not even midnight snacks) into your tent. And never sleep in the clothes you wore while cooking.

USE a bear wire or simply hang your food bag from a tree limb at least 10 feet off the ground and 4 feet away from the trunk.

GARBAGE must be treated the same as food. Protect it inside secure bins or hang it high above the ground some distance away from camp.

▶ Keep a clean camp to eliminate odors that attract small animals like raccoons, which in turn attract big animals like bears. Don't cook smelly or greasy foods. Maintain the cooking and food storage area at least one hundred yards from your campsite, preferably downwind. If you barbecue dinner, wash the grill immediately after use. For that matter, wash all the dishes immediately after use, and do this cleanup away from camp.

▶ Store garbage, fish parts, and meat waste in double-sealed plastic bags that are placed in bear-proof trash containers (where available) or containers with tight-fitting lids. Keep the containers well away from camp and suspended from a bear wire or tree limb.

▶ Pack everything out in double plastic bags. Do not bury or burn garbage—bears will be attracted to the residual odor. (For more tips on animal safety, see Chapter 10.)

It Isn't Only the Bears

When it comes to keeping food in camp, bears can be a hazard. But big hungry beasts aren't the only danger. Even in parts of the country where there are no bears, camp food is at risk. And unlike bears, this threat doesn't stomp around camp tearing things up and making noise. This menace to camp food is bacteria that cause illness to those who eat infected food.

Preventing food-borne illness, also known as food poisoning, should be as high on the priority list as taking steps to keep bears from invading your camp. Not to minimize the seriousness of a bear invasion, but just look at the numbers. Statistics indicate that from 2000 to 2007, there were only nine fatal bear attacks on humans in the United States (according to answers.com), and three of those occurred in Alaska. But every year, according to the Centers for Disease Control, food poisoning causes approximately 76 million illnesses, puts 325,000 people in the hospital, and kills more than 5,000. It's a serious issue, and campers are definitely at risk.

Prevention. The best way to prevent *food poisoning* is to control the temperature of the food. If you keep the food out of the danger zone (40°F to 140°F), harmful bacteria won't grow. In two hours' time in the danger zone, the bacteria can grow enough to make food hazardous to your health. If you are doubtful about whether or not any of the food has become infected, throw the stuff out. Replacing food is far less expensive than a trip to the hospital.

In a serious survival situation, however, you are probably going to be reluctant to discard any potential food source. The good news is that the bacteria can be killed by cooking the food. A good policy is to subject the suspect food to a rolling boil and then let it simmer for five minutes. If you aren't able to boil the food, place it in the fire and cook it until you are sure no bacteria could possibly survive.

If you're taking precooked food to your campsite, unless you can manage to keep it hotter than 140°F, it's best to cool the food and then keep it below 40°F while you travel. Then rewarm it for your meal.

To help your camp cooler be more efficient, follow these recommendations:

▶ Prechill the camp cooler for several hours before packing the cold food inside. Rather than using loose ice blocks or cubes, freeze water in sanitized old plastic milk jugs that can be sealed. Another solution is to use sealed freezer packs that you can buy. These methods will keep meltwater from sloshing and cross contaminating the food.

▶ The day before your camping trip, freeze those food items that can be frozen, then seal them in plastic bags and pack them in the cooler just before your trip. Precool in the refrigerator all the rest of the food items before pulling them in the cooler.

▶ While traveling, keep the cooler in the coldest part of the vehicle, out of the sun. If you can't keep it out of the sun, throw a blanket or sleeping bag over the cooler to insulate it. You can also use a reflective emergency blanket to protect the cooler.

▶ Keep the lid closed to maintain the cold temperature inside. If you need to get something out of the cooler, do it quickly and get everything you need at once. Then shut the lid tightly.

▶ Organize the cooler—place raw meat, poultry, and fish in sealed containers, packed in the bottom of the cooler where the temperature is lowest.

Another step you can take to prevent food poisoning is to keep everything clean.

▶ Before and after using the camp cooler, wash it thoroughly.

▶ While in camp, wash utensils, plates, drinkware, and cookware after each use.

▶ Use a good camp soap to wash your hands before and after touching meats, seafood, vegetables, and fruits. Also wash your hands after touching pets, changing diapers, using the bathroom, or touching anything else that is dirty. Good camp hygiene is one of the best ways to prevent illness.

And finally, cook your food thoroughly. By bringing the internal temperature up to a safe level, you can destroy any harmful bacteria that are present. Use a food thermometer to make sure the inside of the food is hot enough. Reheat precooked meats to at least 165°F. Chickens and turkeys (whole birds) should be heated to 185°F. If you can't verify those internal temperatures, it's risky to eat the meat. In an emergency, cook the food until there is no doubt that it is thoroughly heated beyond the recommended temperatures. It might not be soft and tender when you're done, but at least it won't make you sick. (For information on trail stoves and other methods of camp cooking, see Chapter 9, which covers outdoor equipment and survival gear.)

If you follow all of these recommendations, chances are the bears and the bacteria will leave you and your food alone to enjoy safe camp meals.

Signaling

6

Escaping to the wilderness is a great way to leave civilization behind for a while, but there are times when having other people around is exactly what you need. In an emergency, your ability to summon the assistance of others may make the difference between getting rescued or not. In some cases, it can literally separate life from death. Using some type of signaling technique or device is the best way to call for help.

The whole subject of signaling can be boiled down to two simple concepts: calling attention to yourself and making your message understood. To accomplish this, you have three methods at your disposal—visible signals (things that can be seen), audible signals (things that can be heard), and electronics such as cell phones, radios, and personal locator beacons.

Let's examine this subject from the standpoint of the searchers, and then later we'll look at it from the standpoint of the victim in an emergency situation. First, imagine that you are part of a search team in a light, fixed-wing aircraft or a helicopter. Let's further imagine that the lost party doesn't have, or isn't capable of using, electronic signaling methods. It's noisy in small aircraft, so you're not going to hear any audible signals. In spite of the apparently arbitrary limitations of this scenario, this is actually a very common situation, so, as a searcher, you're now limited to visual recognition of the victim.

Searching from the air is the quickest way to cover a lot of ground, hoping to spot something that looks unnatural or out of place—the flash of a shiny object, some movement, an unusual shape or color. However, searching from the air isn't necessarily easy. Unless there's some effort on the part of the person on the ground trying to attract attention, it is nearly impossible to see through a forest canopy while flying several hundred feet overhead and scanning the huge picture puzzle of colors, contrasts, and textures on the earth's surface.

The only alternative to an air search is to put boots on the ground, perhaps dozens of searchers combing tough terrain, looking behind every rock and under every bush, scouring the landscape inch by inch. Ground search parties have the benefit of being able to pick up audible signals in addition to visible signals, but the progress over the terrain is painfully slow and tedious.

Each type of search offers specific benefits and drawbacks. Both are necessary, and there is nearly always a marriage of the two at some point in a prolonged search. By understanding how to use a few simple signaling techniques, the searchee (victim) makes the whole process much more effective.

In an emergency situation, one of the important things a person can do is to employ all three modes of signaling to attract the attention of anyone in the vicinity. Keep in mind that "in the vicinity" may be a very large area when search aircraft are involved. Searchers in an aircraft can spot a column of smoke or the flash of reflected sunlight on a mirror from miles away. And in the realm of electronic signaling, the vicinity can be effectively the whole world, depending upon the type of signaling technology.

VISIBLE SIGNALS

If you're fortunate enough to catch the attention of a search aircraft, you can communicate with those in the aircraft by using standard body signals and ground symbols. Body signals are sent by positioning your body where it can be seen by someone in the aircraft. Ground symbols are laid out on the ground using whatever you have at hand. These signals and symbols are standard among search organizations the world over. In order for them to be effective, the signals and symbols must be out in the open where they can be seen easily.

Bright colors or exceptionally contrasting materials are the easiest to see from the air or from a distance. Make the symbols as large as possible—at least 2 to 3 feet wide and 6 to 12 feet long. Use whatever materials are available, such as brightly colored fabric, wood, brush, rocks, wreckage, trampled snow, etc. Be creative. Bark slabs laid out against light-colored ground or light-colored stones laid out on a dark green mossy surface will offer great contrast. Use dark brush piles arranged on the blank sheet of a snowy meadow. Dig a shallow trench in the sand (shade in the trench will appear as a dark contrast from the air). Constantly think of new ways to call attention to yourself.

If you are using body signals, perform them slowly and repeatedly. Don't quit just because the plane passes you by. The aircraft might make a sudden turn that allows an observer to spot you even though the aircraft is heading away. Body

AN emergency blanket can be used to make a large and easily visible distress signal to attract the attention of searchers.

signals are easier to see if you hold colorful cloth or something flashy in your hands.

Body signals are simple. A person standing erect and waving one hand overhead indicates that everything is OK and that no help is needed. So if you need help, don't just stand there and wave pleasantly at the airplane as it flies over. If someone is injured, that message is communicated by lying down with arms above the head and legs extended. Waving a cloth up and down to the side of the body means "yes"—kind of like nodding your head. The signal for "no" is shown, as you might logically expect, by swinging the cloth side to side in front of the body below the waist. These signals are useful in situations where the search team in the aircraft is able to communicate with you via megaphone, dropped message, or other means and you need a way to respond.

Multiple signals are more effective than one. In addition to the standard ground symbols that you can set up as permanent signals, add a variety of other signals as well. Use a combination of every available visible signal you can think of.

Reflected Light

It's nice if you are always equipped with your survival kit, complete with a signal mirror. But if you have to improvise, take inventory of everything around you and look for all the possibilities. If you are near your vehicle and it has a CD player and a collection of music, you're in luck. A CD can be used as an excellent signal mirror. You might have to resort to removing a side-view mirror or other shiny components from your vehicle. If the vehicle is not available, use a metal canteen cup or a tin plate to reflect sunlight. You can even use a belt buckle, a pair of glasses, binoculars, a camera lens, or anything else that is reflective.

The purpose of using a reflective signaling device is to aim the flash at every passing airplane, car, or truck that you see. However, it is probably not going to do any good to aim your flash at commercial aircraft that are 30,000 feet up and flying on cruise control. But certainly do not pass up any opportunity to signal low-flying aircraft, even if you don't think they are part of a search effort.

The technique for using a signal mirror is to extend one arm and hold up two fingers at arm's length and, holding the mirror in the other hand with the shiny side facing away from you, shine the light toward its destination, allowing the reflected light to play through your fingers as if

A signal mirror can be seen over a distance of many miles. Aim the mirror by holding up fingers to serve as sights through which to flash the beam.

they were a gunsight. If the target vehicle or aircraft turns toward you, continue your efforts so they can get a fix on your position. Keep in mind that you do not want to blind the driver or the pilot by focusing your beam steadily at them. Rather, sweep the beam of light back and forth across the plane or vehicle. Even if you can see no vehicles or aircraft in your vicinity, beam the reflected light at distant ridges, down into valleys, toward peaks. It is possible that there are people hiking, camping, hunting, or fishing in those places, and they might notice your signal and either investigate or notify authorities.

Direct Light

One of the easiest and best ways to use direct light as a signal is to use a fire. (For various fire-starting techniques, review Chapter 3.) There is nothing so visible from a distance at night in the wildlands as a bright flame illuminating the trees. The rule is to keep a signal fire going all night, every night, until you are rescued. A triangle of fires or three blazes arranged in a straight line has always been a recognized distress signal. If someone sees fires arranged in that type of pattern, they will probably know it is not just somebody's campfire but is a distress signal.

You increase the chances of the signal fire being seen if you place it out in the open, in a clearing, or on a bare ridge where it is visible from a great distance. It is possible to increase the effectiveness of the firelight by positioning a reflective emergency blanket, stretched over a framework of branches, and using it as a large signal mirror.

The direct light cast by lanterns and flashlights can be helpful when trying to signal rescuers. But recognize the limitations—these tools depend on fuel or batteries for power, and that eventually runs out. Save the lantern fuel or flashlight battery power until you are certain that searchers are nearby.

Signal flares are effective in some situations such as water rescues or in the desert when searchers are near enough to see the flares during their brief life. But in a forest or on open grasslands, flares are a fire hazard, as they are shot into the air. Nobody can predict or control where the wind will carry them.

Smoke

A bright blaze at night is the best use of a signal fire, but during the day it's the smoke from your fire that brings help. A column of smoke is visible for miles and generally attracts the attention of anyone in the area. White smoke is made by feeding bits of green or damp foliage into the fire, being careful not to kill the fire. Black smoke is such an anomaly in the wilderness that it sends a particularly loud visual message that help is needed. Make black smoke by burning oil, rubber, or plastic cannibalized from the vehicle. If you choose to burn tires, deflate them first.

A smoky fire may attract the attention of searchers during daylight hours. Create smoke by adding green foliage to the blaze.

Motion

Second only to light and smoke, it is motion that attracts the eye of searchers. If you can set up a system of flags, colorful pieces of cloth tied to limber branches, that flap in the breeze, that is a perfect way to passively create motion. As with fire, place your motion-signaling devices out in the open where they are easy to spot from a distance. You can also create motion actively by waving your arms or a flag of colorful cloth. But don't wear yourself out when there is nobody around to see you. Save your energy until searchers are near, then wave and swing your flag like crazy.

Pattern

Almost as good a signal as motion is a static pattern that appears to be unnatural. A giant SOS made of logs or stones, laid out in a clearing, will catch the eye of a search party. The more colorful the pattern is, the better. On a ridge or in a clearing, design a totally unnatural pattern of colorful or contrasting items such as a tent, sleeping bag, articles of clothing, backpack, etc. You can make a contrasting pattern by using stones or logs, scooping out a system of trenches, or stomping down dry grass. Create a large pattern, much larger than you think you need, so it is visible from a great distance. Although "SOS" or "HELP" is effective, it isn't necessary to write such a long message. The shape of a V says, "I need help." A large X means medical help is needed. The letter *Y* indicates yes, and the letter *N* means no. A large arrow indicates the direction you took when you left the area.

MOTION and visual contrast are effective for attracting attention. Tie a white or brightly colored shirt to a stick and wave it as a flag.

Ground Symbols

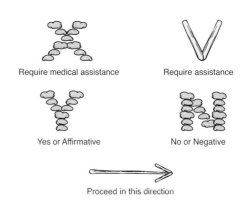

Require medical assistance

Require assistance

Yes or Affirmative

No or Negative

Proceed in this direction

TO make these ground symbols that are recognized by aerial search teams, use contrasting patterns in an open area that is easily seen from the air.

AUDIBLE SIGNALS

Sound doesn't travel very far compared to visible signals, which can catch someone's attention from miles away. But there are times when, for one reason or another, visible signals are not available and the only thing you're left with is noise. That's OK. There have been many lives saved by audible signals. One thing to keep in mind, though, is that in order for audible signals to be heard, searchers must be close by.

Anything that makes noise should be considered a possible candidate for an audible signal device. Use whatever you have available, but only when you have reason to believe that there is someone within earshot. You must weigh the possibilities—if you're near a populated campground, it is far different from being seventeen miles back on a lonely road with no evidence of anyone being around. It makes little sense to deplete the vehicle's battery by blowing the horn, wear yourself out banging on the hood of your truck as if it were a primitive drum, or wasting your ammunition firing shots in groups of three when there is no chance anyone will hear the signal.

Sound signals, no matter how you make them, in groupings of three are recognized as distress signals. Even something as primitive as beating a stick against a hollow log—three beats, silence, then three more beats—is an unusual sound in the wilderness and will attract the attention of anyone close enough to hear.

Gunshots, fired in sets of three, are effective and recognized as signaling distress. The problem is that you eventually run out of ammunition. If you know other people are nearby and you want to alert them that you're in need of help, firing three rounds might do the job. But don't go shooting all your ammo into the night sky simply because you're desperate to attract help. Even if the effort attracts the attention of rescuers, save some ammo until they are close enough to be able to zero in on your position by hearing more shots. Consider saving some ammo for food gathering in the event you are there for a while. While we're talking about shooting as a signal technique, it's a better idea to fire rounds into a stump rather than shooting into the sky, because those rounds have to come down somewhere and there's no sense endangering other people while you're trying to get yourself rescued.

One valuable signal device is a survival whistle. The piercing sound of a whistle carries a long distance, and there is nothing natural about it, so it immediately attracts attention. The best whistles are compact, light-weight, and durable and can be used when wet. Mine is a JetScream from Ultimate Survival Technologies (www.ultimatesurvival.com), but another good one is the Storm Safety Whistle from West Marine (www.westmarine.com).

THE most effective low-tech audible distress signal is a whistle. It's easy to use, and the shrill sound carries over a long distance.

Live noisy. Hang a metal plate and spoon together from a tree branch, so they will bang together in the breeze. Thump a walking stick against trees and logs as you hike. Sing your favorite song out loud. Not only will that help lift your spirits, but you never know when you might have an unexpected audience walk out of the woods after hearing your performance, wanting to see what's up.

The general concept is to do almost everything you can think of to make noise. The one thing you don't want to do is yell for help. Not only will the effort exhaust you, but listening to the sound of your own desperate voice screaming for help can unhinge you psychologically. Take a steady approach to signaling. Always be inventing new ways to make yourself obvious to the world. Think clearly, proceed in a logical fashion, and conserve your energy.

ELECTRONIC SIGNALS

Remember the James Kim family? Stranded in a lonely canyon in the mountains of Oregon, Mrs. Kim used her cell phone to summon help. Of course it wasn't as simple as making a phone call and waiting for rescue. Unable to make solid contact with a cell tower, her phone left only a faint "ping" signal, but rescuers were able to track that signal to her location. That signal saved three lives that day.

Another related technology is a two-way radio. This device came in handy one day in the Teton Mountains when I ended up injured after an unfortunate cataclysmic act on my part. My mountain biking buddy, Steve, was riding some distance behind me, as we headed down a fairly steep single-track trail that was a minefield of sharp rocks and tree roots. At speed, I made a move to jump a root, and as my front tire made contact with the ground, I heard an explosion. Steve later told me that he thought I had been shot with a 30.06 rifle, because the explosion sounded exactly like a rifle shot. He looked around to see if he could spot any hunters, but there were none. Meanwhile, my flat tire tangled up in the front brakes and came to an immediate stop. That sent me soaring over the handlebars, and, according to Steve, I did a graceful three-quarter flip before landing on the point of my shoulder and then on my rib cage ten feet down the trail. My helmet never touched the ground, but lots of body parts did. I knew I was injured badly, and Steve said I looked like a wounded animal as I came to my knees, hugged the left side of my rib cage, and crawled off into the bushes groaning. Fortunately, Steve had his two-way radio with him. He called his wife and asked her to come and meet us at the nearest access road. Then he hid my bike in the bushes so it would be safe until we could come back for it and helped me to my feet. Together, we slowly made our way the last couple of miles down the trail to find Steve's wife, Dana, waiting for us with the truck. Then it was a quick trip to the emergency room.

I'm happy to report that I once again cheated death and lived through that one. Had I been in more serious condition, the two-way would have been used to contact local authorities higher up the chain of command than Steve's wife. The authorities could then initiate a full-blown rescue operation. In the case of a lost individual who is able to make a call on a radio, it might be possible for authorities to "triangulate" on the signal by using RDF (radio direction finding) equipment (if available), effectively zeroing in on the signal sent by the lost person.

High-tech electronic equipment can be extremely helpful in survival situations, but only if you have it available when you need it. Satellite phones, portable ham radios, marine band VHF radios, and other types of communication devices are available to the general public these days, and they can help save lives in an emergency.

When it comes to serious situations, one of the most effective and positive emergency signal devices is a PLB (personal locator beacon). These are related to maritime distress signal devices called EPIRBs (emergency position-indicating radio beacons) that automatically or manually send distress messages via a satellite system to activate search-and-rescue efforts. PLBs are the little brothers to the EPIRBs, but

ELECTRONIC methods for signaling your distress situation might include cell phones, short-range walkie-talkies (FRS radios), or even a portable ham radio that can communicate over a longer distance.

they do the same powerful job, alerting search-and-rescue personnel and sending GPS coordinates that lead rescuers directly to the individual in distress. Because they employ a system of satellites to communicate distress signals, they are not limited as to range of operation. I am comfortable saying that if the climbers on Mt. Hood who were trapped by storms in December 2006 and eventually perished before rescuers could find them had been equipped with PLBs, they would probably be alive today. The climbers called for help by using a cell phone, but that accomplished only half of what was needed—it did not help rescuers zero in the exact location of the victims the way a PLB would.

It's the same story for countless others who perish because nobody knows they are in trouble, or where to find them. So, why doesn't everyone carry a PLB? My hunch is that it is a matter of money. Depending on which unit you buy, these devices cost between $450 and $650, and most people are unwilling to shell out that much. The good news is that less costly satellite distress signal devices are rapidly making inroads to the market, so the "too expensive" excuse is not as strong as it once

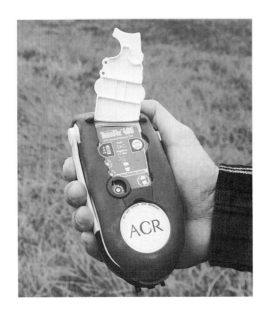

A PERSONAL locator beacon (PLB) is for use in life-and-death situations when you absolutely must contact the outside world to come and rescue you.

was. The other excuse for not buying a PLB is that none of us think we will ever need such a device because we're not going to need to be rescued. We tell ourselves that disasters happen only to other people; that is the common human belief.

Fortunately, on June 8, 2004, Bob Williams didn't follow that kind of thinking. If he had, it would have been the last day of his life. As he prepared to fulfill his lifelong dream of paddling a canoe solo the length of the Yukon River, he decided to buy a PLB. A few days into the trip, Bob, who suffers from narcolepsy, fell asleep while drifting down the river and capsized the canoe. The frigid water immediately woke him, but he instantly started feeling the effects of hypothermia. Soon, he was confused and cold, exhausted, and spitting up blood. After half an hour, he managed to drag himself and the canoe up on a mid-river island. He was totally exhausted, cold, and unable to get dry or warm. That's when he decided that unless he got help, he was going to die. He activated his PLB, then collapsed. Four and a half hours later, rescuers found Bob.

How does the system work? The best way to explain it is to tell the story of some hikers in the Olympic National Forest who found themselves in need of rescue. It was May 29, 2006, when two of the four nineteen-year-old friends hiking along the Washington coast got into trouble by falling in the swift current of a frigid stream. The two who remained on dry land managed to rescue their wet friends, but the deteriorating weather was cold, rainy, and getting worse. Soon some members of the party were showing signs of hypothermia, so the group decided to activate the ACR Terrafix PLB that the father of one of the boys had rented from PLB Rentals, LLC (www.plbrentals.com or 425-299-5662) and insisted be carried on this trip. As soon as the system was activated, Search and Rescue Satellite-Aided Tracking (SARSAT) satellites detected the distress signal. The PLB transmitted the GPS coordinates, and the Air Force Coordination Center in Langley, Virginia,

SPOT is a personal satellite tracker that has the capability to call in rescue teams, contact friends and loved ones back home to request help, or just let them know that you are OK and allow them to track your progress on a computerized map.

contacted authorities at Olympic National Forest and told them about the distress signal coming from their area. They then contacted other emergency service providers in the region, and a U.S. Coast Guard helicopter was dispatched from Port Angeles, Washington. With exact coordinates provided by the PLB's internal GPS system, the helicopter crew was able to locate the hikers. But due to high wind conditions, the helicopter couldn't land, so national park rangers were directed to the location, where the young men were rescued and treated for hypothermia.

Another approach to this same type of electronic signaling is a product called SPOT. It is similar to a PLB, but the company, SPOT Inc., calls it a satellite personal tracker, and it also has a satellite message function. It operates on a different satellite system than is used by PLBs and costs about one-third the price of the least expensive non-GPS-integrated PLB. SPOT has a GPS built in that delivers precise coordinates to rescuers or friends, depending upon which button you push. If it's a life-or-death emergency, push the "911" button, and the GEOS satellite system that it operates on will activate a search-and-rescue effort in much the same manner as the PLB. But one of the differences in operation is that if the situation calls for a level of help that is less than a full-on search-and-rescue effort, the user can push the "Help" button, and a prerecorded message is transmitted via e-mail or cell phone text message to those people you want to notify about your need for assistance. The system allows those receiving your messages to track your progress with GPS waypoints that show up on a Google map.

PLBs and systems like SPOT work no matter where you are and are by far the best personal rescue assist devices that have ever been invented. And the day you find yourself in need of rescue, you would gladly pay ten times the asking price of one of these units, because it would bring rescuers to your aid with greater speed and precision than any other method. Fortunately, this is a growing market that will see advancement in technology and reduction in price as time goes on. (For further discussion of signaling gear, see Chapter 9.)

Do I advocate that everyone carry a PLB or a personal tracking device? Let me answer by saying I believe that if James Kim had been equipped with one of these, he and his family would have been rescued the first day, and he would be alive today. This kind of equipment isn't only for extreme outdoor enthusiasts, but is for anyone who travels into areas where they might become stranded, lost, or end up in a situation from which they need to be rescued.

Never give up hope. Someone out there may be watching or listening. Do something to catch their attention.

Medical Emergencies

7

Only once in my life have I felt the deadly grip of hypothermia begin to embrace me, but once was enough. It was during military training maneuvers in the Rocky Mountains of Utah during the dead of winter. I was wearing standard Army-issue clothing of the Vietnam era and was sent to recon an area that required lengthy, motionless exposure to the cold and damp and the ceaseless wind. There I was to stay, lying in the snow watching the target of our training mission until another soldier came to relieve me. Time seems to stop in those conditions, and my relief took an eternity before coming to replace me. By then I was already in trouble.

The progression of symptoms was classic—after a few hours I began to shiver, as my body attempted to overcome my inactivity by creating its own heat-producing exercise. Not long afterward, I became lethargic, weary, sleepy. I felt the numbing cold invade my very center. Then the intense shivering died off, and I honestly didn't care much about the situation anymore.

When my relief arrived, he recognized the symptoms, initiated the proper actions, and the short version is that I lived to tell about it. Many are not so fortunate.

HYPOTHERMIA: DEATH FROM THE INSIDE

Hypothermia moves quickly and without mercy against the unprotected and unprepared. Succumbing to hypothermia used to be referred to as dying of exposure. It is the chilling of the body's core, the gradual extinguishing of the inner fire that keeps the individual alive. During the process, the victim passes through a series of dangerous physiological and mental stages that diminish his ability to survive, unless the process is stopped and then reversed. If the situation goes too far, it becomes impossible to reverse the relentless decline toward coma and death. (See Table 7-1.) Obviously, it is better to prevent hypothermia than to have to treat the problem in the field.

Preventing the onset of hypothermia is not complex, but it does require an understanding of the problem, followed by careful planning and then constant vigilance against this subtle enemy. First, an understanding—hypothermia is not necessarily a cold-weather problem, nor even a cool-weather problem. Swimmers in 80-degree Caribbean water can become hypothermic after a lengthy stay in the water because even 80-degree water that feels comfortably warm is cooler than the body's core temperature. Any condition that drains away the body's core tem-

Table 7–1   Hypothermia

Body Core Temperature	Hypothermia Level	Signs and Symptoms	Cardiac and Respiratory Response	Consciousness and Behavior
95°F	Mild	Shivering, chattering jaw	No change	Quiet and withdrawn
90°F	Mild	Loss of coordination	No change	Confusion of thought
85°F	Moderate	Stupor or exhaustion	Slow pulse	Lethargic and sleepy
80°F	Severe	Possible coma	Weak pulse and respiration; possible arrhythmia	From irrational to unconscious
78°F	Severe	Coma to death	Ventricular fibrillation; cardiac arrest	From unconscious to dead

perature can bring on hypothermia. So vigilance is necessary during all seasons and in every situation.

Preparation includes being in good physical condition. That is not to say you must be an athlete—ironically, a little flab on the body serves as insulation—but the more efficient the body is at maintaining its vital processes, the better off you are. People in poor health are more prone to develop problems with hypothermia. If you know you are going to be engaging in activities such as a cool-season hunting or fishing trip that could possibly lead to hypothermia, get yourself into as good health and physical condition as possible beforehand.

Begin the trip well rested and well nourished. Then, during the outing, maintain a continual intake of high-energy foods and drinks. Hot meals and warm drinks help keep the inner furnace blazing. Snacking on cold food and iced beverages may add caloric energy to your system, but hot meals and warm drinks are better by far.

Continually hydrate your body by maintaining a steady intake of fluids to stave off dehydration. Dehydration thickens the blood, slows circulation, and promotes the onset of hypothermia. The very best fluid to drink is water. The very worst fluids are any that contain alcohol. Alcohol is a dehydrator. It is also a vasodilator, so it speeds hypothermia by flooding the core of the body with chilled blood from the extremities.

Advanced planning also includes making sure you're wearing the proper type of clothing. In the military, I had no choice in the matter of my wardrobe, and the thin cotton Army fatigues were a poor excuse for winter clothing. Cotton soaks up moisture like a sponge and does little to provide insulation or turn the wind. A body loses a lot of heat through convection (air movement), evaporation, and conduction (direct contact with cold objects). Proper clothing plays an important role in reducing these factors. If your outer shell is windproof and waterproof, and if you wear insulation layers beneath that shell that resist soaking up body moisture, you have a much better chance of avoiding hypothermia.

Staying warm in cold weather is nice but, from a survival standpoint, staying dry is even better. All other factors being equal, the difference between life and death may be decided by how dry you stay. Hypothermia loves wet clothing and a damp body, so of all the factors involved in hypothermia, one of the most deadly is getting wet. The problem with getting wet is that moisture transfers body heat into the atmosphere at a perilous rate, so saturated clothing removes warmth from your body like an evaporative air conditioner.

Learning to survive in extreme conditions challenges you to develop an instinct for avoiding hazards. This can be a problem for people who are accustomed to living in cold climates, because familiarity breeds complacency and carelessness. A tragic example of this involved the son of our friends who live in a high mountain valley at the foot of the Teton Range in Idaho. The son grew up where the 6,200-foot elevation of the valley floor promised long, cold, deep winters. These conditions prompted him to become an avid snowmobiler who often went out riding on the foothills and low mountains rising from the valley floor right out his back door. After being away from home for a couple of years, he returned one winter and asked his dad if he could borrow the snowmobile for a few hours so he could ride in the hills behind their property. Off he went, alone. But he was familiar with the terrain, the weather, and the sport, so his folks didn't worry too much. A few hours went by, then a few more, then a few more, and soon it was night. The son didn't return home. The parents stood outside in the growing darkness, listening for the sound of the snowmobile, but they heard nothing. Finally, they called the local search-and-rescue squad. The next day, the young man was found. He was dead. And he was nearly naked. The trail to his stranded snowmobile told the story—after the machine got stuck in a deep drift, he had apparently decided to abandon the machine and walk out of the mountains through waist-deep powder snow. Along the way, he became hypothermic and then delusional, imagined himself to be overheated, and started removing items of clothing that he left scattered along the trail. This is not unusual behavior for hypothermia victims. At some point in the lonely darkness on the side of the forested mountain, he died—virtually in his own backyard.

The lesson for us is that we should never become complacent because we are intimately familiar with the surroundings. Familiarity does not reduce the danger but, in fact, may increase it if we become overconfident and either ignore the hazards or treat the risks lightly.

To live with the cold, learn to constantly analyze every move and avoid situations with the potential to leave you wet. For example, avoid brushing up against anything wet. Don't sit on the snow or a damp log. When you pause for a rest, squat so that only the soles of your boots touch the ground. Avoid overhead drips. Don't wade through deep snow or wet foliage in absorbent clothing.

Staying dry requires that you pace your activity level to avoid perspiration. As far as hypothermia is concerned, it doesn't really matter whether the dampness comes as a result of a soaking rain, falling through the ice, or excessive perspiration. The point is, you're wet, and that's all that counts. Staying dry is among your highest priorities, and that means paying attention to your own level of perspiration. The rule is, don't work yourself into a sweat.

The way you dress can help reduce excess perspiration. It's easier to avoid sweating if you dress in layers that are easy to open or remove.

IT'S important to protect against the dangerous buildup of perspiration inside clothing. These pit zips help ventilate the shell layer, removing unwanted moist air.

Yes, it's OK to remove whatever clothing is necessary to let your body vent and dry out rather than confine the moisture inside your clothing. Once the clothing is wet, you're in trouble, so pay close attention and vent early.

Carry heavy outer layers of clothing in a waterproof bag or backpack, and put them on when needed. The insulating layers of clothing do three things—help retain body heat, quickly move dampness away from the skin, and refuse to hold moisture in the fibers. When it comes to natural fibers, cotton absorbs moisture like a sponge and holds it next to your body, where it can do the most damage. Wool, on the other hand, tends to wick moisture away from your skin, reducing the effect of evaporative cooling even when wet. If you don't like the feel of wool, technology has come to your rescue in the form of synthetic fibers such as polyester or polypropylene. These materials do not absorb water; they transfer moisture away from your skin and dry quickly.

Outer shell layers should be waterproof yet breathable. Breathability allows perspiration to escape, while waterproofness prevents outside moisture from entering. That's the beauty of Gore-Tex and similar fabrics; they keep all the wet on the outside and all the dry on the inside. This kind of clothing is expensive, but your life is worth it. Some of these shell garments have underarm zips that can be opened to speed the escape of perspiration.

The most functional layers are those that can be unzipped, as opposed to pullovers, to regulate body heat and moisture during periods of hard labor. Each item of clothing should be thought of as an individual component in a system, beginning with the underwear and working all the way to the outer shell.

When you're wet, the wind is your worst enemy, so windproof clothing is a high priority. Ideally, a windproof shelter should be available so you can escape the elements and maintain body heat. Natural resources might offer some shelter that will turn the wind. This can be something as simple as a boulder, a dense cluster of trees, or an embankment made of dirt or blocks of snow you can hide behind. Or it may be a more elaborate shelter constructed of available materials such as tree limbs, slabs of bark, etc. Each situation and geographic area offers different natural resources, and you must train your mind to be constantly aware of what's around you and how you can use it to your benefit.

At all costs, avoid working yourself to exhaustion. A little exercise to keep the circulation moving and to generate body warmth is fine, but don't overdo it. Performing labor is like running an engine, and unless you can replace the fuel, it eventually runs out. Work only as hard as your food and fluid supply will comfortably allow without exhausting your body or mind and without producing sweat.

If you're traveling on foot, pace yourself to avoid fatigue. Make camp early so you can prepare adequate shelter, build a fire, and have hot food ready several hours before sundown. If you are overcome by a storm, stop immediately and take shelter to protect yourself from precipitation and wind.

Expeditioneers and adventurers all over the world live outdoors in extreme conditions for long periods. The only way they successfully do this is through meticulous preparation and by strictly adhering to the rules of survival.

In the end, it isn't the environment that kills us—it's ignorance or lack of preparation—failing to do what must be done in order to stay alive. In a survival situation, you're in a battle for your life. And most of the time, hypothermia takes no prisoners. (For additional tips on preventing hypothermia, refer to the section "Surviving Cold Weather" in Chapter 2.)

FROSTBITE: DEATH ON THE OUTSIDE

Whoever invented the word *frostbite* chose the term well. This cold-weather injury bites hard and destroys the flesh. Exposed skin is most vulnerable to flash freezing from a cold wind and frigid temperature, but even tissue that is protected inside mittens or thick socks and sturdy boots can eventually fall victim. Frostbite can happen whenever the body is exposed to temperature below 32°F. Depending upon conditions, this can sometimes happen very quickly. For example, you grasp a frozen bit of metal with a bare hand, or worse yet, you splash some intensely cold gasoline, which won't freeze until far below zero, on your hands or feet while refueling a vehicle—instant severe frostbite injury.

As long as the body is protected against the chill, all is well. But when the body begins to feel the impact of the cold, it automatically shuts down some blood flow to the extremities in an effort to preserve core temperature (a survival strategy to avoid hypothermia). Cutting off the flow of warm blood leaves the extremities without the very thing needed for protection against frostbite. Unable to stay warm, these parts of the body gradually chill, loose sensation, and the fluid in the cells starts to freeze, forming ice crystals that can slice through the cell membranes, causing deep and serious damage.

How Serious Is It?

The first stage of frostbite is sometimes referred to as *frostnip* and affects only the outermost layer of tissue. Many winter enthusiasts have suffered mild frostnip and felt the pinpricks and numbing of the skin as it becomes slightly stiff. At this stage, evidence of freezing is the appearance of white or gray areas on the skin, but the deeper tissue is still warm and pliable. This degree of frostbite is not extremely serious, as long as it is recognized early and steps are taken to reverse the situation.

To catch frostbite in its earliest stage, the best practice is to establish a buddy system in which you watch each other for telltale signs of frostnip: patches of white or yellowish-gray on exposed skin. If you're by yourself, use a small mirror to check the condition of your cheeks, chin, forehead, nose, and ears. Flex fingers and toes, wriggle your face to encourage blood flow, and periodically place a warm hand over those parts of your face to warm them and feel for frozen spots or stiff flesh. If any problems are detected, immediately cover the affected areas to protect against exposure to cold and wind and get to a warmer environment. Then gently rewarm the injured area by applying warm—not hot—moist compresses or submerging in warm water.

The second stage is called *superficial frostbite*. The freezing reaches deeper tissue. Ice crystals form in the cells, making the skin feel waxy or leathery, and the flesh becomes more rigid. Discoloration ranges from white to yellowish-gray or even slightly blue. Blisters are likely to form. This is a serious medical problem, and the victim should be taken as quickly as possible to a medical facility for professional treatment in order to prevent permanent injury.

If exposure continues or treatment is not obtained, superficial frostbite will probably advance to the third stage—*deep frostbite*. The skin appears blotchy white or gray-blue. The deeper flesh becomes hard and cold to the touch. Permanent injury, blood clots, gangrene, or loss of the limb is likely. Total death of the flesh is the worst case, with black fingers and toes that have exploded by the bursting of swollen blisters. This is a very serious condition. Professional medical attention must be sought as quickly as possible.

Prevention

Prevention is far better than a painful cure:

▶ Dress in layers that trap air inside. Wear clothing that is waterproof and breathable to allow perspiration to escape. Keep head, neck, and wrists covered to preserve core temperature. Mittens are often better than gloves because fingers can keep each other warm. Make sure mittens, socks, and boots are not so tight that they restrict circulation

A neoprene face mask, mittens, and a winter cap with earmuffs help protect the extremities from frostbite.

Table 7–2 Wind Chill

		Actual Thermometer Reading (°F)											
		50	40	30	20	10	0	–10	–20	–30	–40	–50	–60
		Equivalent Temperature (°F)											
	Calm	50	40	30	20	10	0	–10	–20	–30	–40	–50	–60
	5	48	37	27	16	6	–5	–15	–26	–36	–47	–57	–68
Wind Speed (mph)	10	40	28	16	4	–9	–21	–33	–46	–58	–70	–83	–95
	15	36	22	9	–5	–18	–36	–45	–58	–72	–85	–99	–112
	20	32	18	4	–10	–25	–39	–53	–67	–82	–96	–110	–124
	25	30	16	0	–15	–29	–44	–59	–74	–88	–104	–118	–133
	30	28	13	–2	–18	–33	–48	–63	–79	–94	–109	–125	–140
	35	27	11	–4	–20	–35	–49	–67	–82	–98	–113	–129	–145
	40	26	10	–6	–21	–37	–53	–69	–85	–100	–116	–132	–148

Potential for freezing exposed flesh:

☐ Little danger   ☐ Increased danger   ▨ Great danger

to fingers and toes. Wear gaiters to keep snow out of boots. In extreme cold, wear a neoprene face mask.

▶ Stay dry. Pace activities to avoid perspiration and exhaustion. Becoming wet or exhausted is asking for trouble.

▶ Limit exposure to wind and cold. Take breaks from exposure by periodically coming indoors or getting in the vehicle. If no building or vehicle is available, find or improvise a shelter to protect yourself. (See "Surviving Cold Weather" in Chapter 2 for tips on improvising cold-weather shelters.)

▶ Avoid use of alcohol and tobacco. Alcohol dilates blood vessels, resulting in loss of body core temperature. Tobacco constricts blood flow to extremities, increasing risk of frostbite.

▶ If your hands are affected, pull off your gloves and insert your hands under your bare armpits.

▶ If your buddy has cold feet, you may have to take shelter, pull off his boots, and hold his chilled feet against your warm stomach. This is where you learn who your true friends are.

▶ Get out of the cold as soon as possible. Then get out of your cold clothing and into something warmer. Frozen boots are like an icebox, and your feet just get colder if you leave them inside. You must start working on creating a warmer environment for yourself.

Treatment

When it comes to treatment of deeply frozen flesh, the very best course of action is to get to a medical facility as quickly as possible. If a seriously frozen area is thawed and then allowed to freeze again, extreme damage results. Treatment of profound frostbite is best left to the professionals. In cases of solidly frozen feet or hands, do not attempt to remove boots or gloves. Just transport the victim as fast and safely as you can.

While waiting to get the victim to a medical facility, field treatment will help prevent further damage.

▶ Move the victim out of the cold and into a warm, protected place.

▶ Do not thaw frostbite unless you can guarantee that the flesh will not be refrozen.

▶ To thaw the flesh, either immerse the affected part of the body in warm—not hot—water or soak a cloth in warm—not hot—water and gently lay it on the affected area. Do not massage or rub the frozen flesh. Leave blisters intact.

▶ Avoid exposing the affected area to sharp objects or dry heat (fire, hot pads, etc.) because the flesh is numb and might, due to this lack of feeling, unknowingly be burned or otherwise injured.

▶ Expect the thawing process to be painful—continue with treatment in spite of anguished protest. After thawing, carefully wrap the affected area with clean bandaging material. Keep fingers and toes separated. Caregivers might need to feed and clothe the victim to prevent use of the injured limb.

▶ Keep the injury clean.

SURVIVING COLD-WATER IMMERSION

For as long as I can remember, one of the great fears related to falling into cold water has been death by hypothermia. And that is a legitimate concern if you fall into a shallow creek. But fall out of a boat into cold water or go through the ice in a frozen lake—we call this *cold-water immersion*—and the threat posed by hypothermia changes positions with other, more immediate dangers.

There is no doubt that hypothermia is a killer, and if you are able to drag yourself up on the shore or back into the boat, hypothermia is the greatest concern. But if you can't make it to safety in a hurry, you are faced with three extremely serious problems that are likely to kill you before hypothermia has a chance to become an issue. Your first dilemma is surviving long enough to even worry about hypothermia.

A friend of mine who was a dentist had a nice, large, safe fishing vessel that he used for catching salmon and halibut in the cold waters off the Washington coast. One day, a few years ago, he cast off the dock lines and headed out from La Push for an afternoon of fishing. That was the last time anybody ever saw him. Several days later, his boat was discovered washed up on a remote beach, the engine control still in gear. There was no sign of my friend. His body was never found, despite extensive ground, water, and air searches conducted by numerous volunteers, sheriff's personnel, national park rangers, and the Coast Guard. What happened to this man is a matter of speculation, but I have my theories, and they fall in line with what we're talking about here.

Your personal physiology plays a role in the risk you face in an incident involving cold-water immersion. Some people are more hardy, others more fragile. But as a generality, the immediate lethal effect impacts anyone who falls into water colder than 59°F (15°C).

In order of priority, the steps in the process of dying from cold-water immersion include:

1. Instant death from coronary failure
2. Cold shock

3. Swimming failure

4. Hypothermia

5. Post-rescue collapse

Keep in mind that these things are sometimes hard to separate because they overlap and work together to kill the victim.

Cardiac Arrest

A person who falls into cold water suffers a significant increase in heart rate and blood pressure. The shock of immersion in cold water can be so severe that it causes sudden cardiac arrest. If that happens and the victim is recovered from the water quickly, he will be a PNB (pulseless non-breather) and will require CPR (cardiopulmonary resuscitation). Assuming coronary failure doesn't take place, the following threats line up and take their positions as the next greatest concerns.

Cold Shock

A natural human response to cold-water immersion is to suddenly gasp. The problem is that this response doesn't necessarily wait until the victim's face is clear of the water. Often, the person has his face underwater when the sudden involuntary gasp occurs. When that happens, he inhales water and begins the drowning process.

Even if the individual doesn't drown right away, a further problem exists with cold shock. If the victim is lucky enough to have his face up and no water is inhaled, his breathing will be erratic. Cold shock causes the victim's breathing rate to increase, while the ability to hold his breath disappears. At the same time, the victim loses his ability to move hands and feet. This makes it almost impossible to do such simple tasks as fastening a life jacket buckle or gripping a rescue rope or flotation device that is thrown to him.

Swimming Failure

Along with loss of ability to manipulate the hands and arms comes a loss of muscle coordination that leads to swimming failure. Arms and legs flap ineffectively, and no swimming progress is made. The attempt to breathe and swim becomes uncoordinated, and the victim has difficulty keeping his head above water. Very quickly, the victim of cold-water immersion finds that he cannot swim very far before lapsing into total swimming failure. Drowning soon follows. I remember the video footage of victims struggling to survive in the frozen Potomac River after a Boeing 737 crashed into the 14th Street bridge in Washington, D.C., in 1982. Some crash survivors who were only several feet from the riverbank couldn't swim even that far. They were basically power-less to save themselves because they couldn't hold onto flotation devices or ropes that were lowered to them from a hovering helicopter. Heroic efforts saved five people that day, out of seventy-nine passengers and crew on board.

Hypothermia

If the victim does not suffer cardiac arrest and survives cold shock and swimming failure, perhaps because he is wearing a life jacket that keeps him afloat with his head above water, the next threat is hypo-thermia. Depending upon the temperature of the water and the cloth-ing being worn by the victim, serious hypothermia can set in within thirty minutes. In an effort to save itself, the body shuts off the flow of blood to and from the extremities. This physiological tactic keeps cold blood from returning to the body core from cold arms, hands, legs, and feet. The result is a progressive loss of dexterity in the extremities fol-lowed by severe shivering, which eventually stops as the body's systems begin to fail. Then comes loss of consciousness and heart failure or lethal heart arrhythmia.

Post-Rescue Collapse

One of the problems with cold-water immersion is that, even if the victim is rescued alive, he is not necessarily home free. As circulation is restored to the extremities, blood pressure can drop to a critically low level, throwing the victim into shock. And as chilled blood returns to the body core from the extremities, severe heart problems develop. If water was inhaled, there can be damage to the lungs, rendering them incapable of processing oxygen. All of these things contribute to a syndrome known as post-rescue collapse. If they are to survive,

Table 7–3 Immersion Hypothermia

Water temperature	Time to exhaustion or unconsciousness	Expected time of survival
32.5°F	Less than 15 minutes	Less than 15 to 45 minutes
32.5° to 40°F	15 to 30 minutes	30 to 90 minutes
40° to 50°F	30 to 60 minutes	1 to 3 hours
50° to 60°F	1 to 2 hours	1 to 6 hours
60° to 70°F	2 to 7 hours	2 to 40 hours
70° to 80°F	3 to 12 hours	3 hours to indefinitely
More than 80°F	Indefinitely	Indefinitely

cold-water-immersion hypothermia victims must be handled with the utmost care, preferably by emergency medical care professionals.

Your Best Chance

A very high percentage of those who fall into cold water drown from a combination of cold shock and swimming failure. It doesn't matter how physically fit they are; it doesn't matter how good they are at swimming. Cold shock and subsequent swimming failure are physiological reactions that cannot be defied any more than you can defy gravity.

The best chance for survival is to wear a PFD (personal flotation device, a.k.a. a life jacket) that is capable of keeping your head face up and above water. Then, even if you lose muscle coordination and can only float helplessly, at least you won't drown. Everyone aboard a boat should wear a PFD whenever the boat is under way on cold water. Just having one nearby is not good enough. Demonstrations prove that even if a person hits the water with a PFD in hand, the nearly instantaneous loss of coordination and dexterity prevents him from being able to put it on. But those who fall in the water while wearing a proper PFD remain afloat and upright, even if they experience swimming failure from cold shock. Not only does the PFD provide flotation, but it also adds insulation to slow the onset of hypothermia.

Rescue

Rescue rule #1 is "Don't go in the water to save someone else." I know that heroic efforts sometimes work and are tempting, but think about it this way—if you hit the water and become a cold-shock and swimming-failure victim yourself, you can help nobody and have only added to the number of victims in the water. To keep from making the problem worse, stay on the boat or onshore and do all you can from there to help rescue those in the water.

If you are called upon to help rescue a person who has fallen into cold water, expect that he will suffer the nearly total loss of strength and dexterity. His hands will be all but useless, and he will not be able to grasp anything. Using a boat hook to snag and pull him to safety is probably the best option.

To prevent the rapid loss of body warmth, get the victim out of the water as soon as possible. If a capsized boat can be righted, it floats high enough to support the occupants, even if it is flooded. If the boat cannot be righted, climb on top of the overturned hull. Even though hypothermia is a distinct hazard, at least the risk of drowning is decreased. And drowning is the most immediate threat.

Stay with the boat. Do not give in to the temptation to swim toward a distant shore. The odds are stacked against you being able to swim even a hundred yards before succumbing to cold shock, swimming failure, and drowning. Swimming actually hastens the onset of hypothermia, because flailing your arms and legs causes increased loss of body heat as cold water circulates around you, and the exertion causes warm blood to be pumped to the extremities, where it becomes chilled.

If you fall into cold water, assume the HELP (heat escape lessening position) posture, which gives you the best chance of survival. To do this, pull your knees up toward your chest and hug them with your arms. If you are wearing a PFD, this position rolls you slightly back, faceup, and out of the water and helps preserve your body heat. If you are part of a group in the water, gather together in groups of two or more and huddle with arms over each others' shoulders. The water in the center of the huddle will be warmed by body heat, so place children or elderly people in the center of the circle. If everyone is wearing

HELP Position

Huddle Position

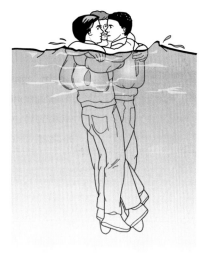

TO prolong survival time in cold water, assume the HELP position by drawing your knees up to your chest and hugging them with your arms. This assumes you are wearing a life jacket and can float without using your arms and legs to tread water.

a PFD, there is no need to move about and tread water. Being quiet in the water lengthens survival time about 50 percent. Do all you can to calm and reassure the others in the group and get everyone to agree to stay together.

Keep your clothes and shoes on. Air trapped inside clothing helps with flotation. Water next to your skin warms to body temperature and helps prevent hypothermia. Unless your footwear is unusually heavy and threatens to drag you down, keep your footwear on. You'll need it later to prevent foot injuries after you reach shore and need to move around to build shelter and fire. An exception is if you fall into a swift current while wearing hip or chest waders. Get out of those as quickly as possible, because waders filled with flowing water will pull you down. After removing the waders, empty them of water and fill them with air to use them as a flotation device. Later, after reaching safety, wear them to help protect against hypothermia and/or frostbite.

Cold-water immersion is one of the most challenging survival situations. But survival is possible, if you do everything right.

▶ To help prevent post-rescue collapse, transport the victim to the nearest emergency room as quickly as possible.

▶ Rewarming the victim must be done properly. The key is to proceed gently and gradually. Begin by providing warmth to the neck, underarms, and groin, but do not use heat that will burn the skin. Heat only the trunk of the body to guard against core temperature afterdrop, which occurs when extremities warm faster than the trunk, forcing cold blood to reenter the circulatory system.

▶ Do not give alcohol to a victim of hypothermia. Alcohol is a vasodilator that opens the vascular system, flooding the core of the body with chilled blood from the extremities. This can prove fatal.

Hot-weather injury

Here's the scenario—the weather is beautiful, and you're outside in the sunshine having a great time. The next thing you know, you're on the ground, staring at the sky, feeling sick, and wondering what happened. It's a problem that hits a large number of people every year from coast to coast, from mountains to seashore, and sometimes even indoors. I call it hot-weather injury.

In hot weather, there are several levels of illness that affect active people. As the temperature goes up, it's necessary to increase water intake, reduce the amount of activity, and get out of the heat or some type of heat overload injury is likely.

The first level of illness caused by dehydration is heat cramps. If you don't take care of the problem at that level, it quickly escalates to heat exhaustion and then progresses to deadly heat stroke. These heat-related problems are so serious that it's possible to go from feeling perfectly fine to being dead within a couple of hours.

You're more likely to fall victim to heat overload if you hike, hunt, and fish where temperature and humidity are high. It's a two-edged sword. One edge is the heat index factor, which calculates effective heat load when humidity is added. You've heard the old saying, "It isn't the heat, it's the humidity." It's true that humidity is part of the problem. Under high temperature conditions, when humidity is added, the apparent temperature, the temperature we feel, is higher than the thermometer indicates. Use the heat index chart (see Table 7-4) to calculate apparent

Table 7–4 Heat Index

		Temperature (°F)														
		80	82	84	86	88	90	92	94	96	98	100	102	104	106	108	110
Relative Humidity (%)	40	80	81	83	85	88	91	94	97	101	105	109	114	119	124	130	136
	45	80	82	84	87	89	93	96	100	104	109	114	119	124	130	137	
	50	81	83	85	88	91	95	99	103	108	113	118	124	131	137		
	55	81	84	86	89	93	97	101	106	112	117	124	130	137			
	60	82	84	88	91	95	100	105	110	116	123	129	137				
	65	82	85	89	93	98	103	108	114	121	128	136					
	70	83	86	90	95	100	105	112	119	126	134						
	75	84	88	92	97	103	109	116	124	132							
	80	84	89	94	100	106	113	121	129								
	85	85	90	96	102	110	117	126	135								
	90	86	91	98	105	113	122	131									
	95	86	93	100	108	117	127										
	100	87	95	103	112	121	132										

Potential for heat-related illness due to prolonged exposure or strenuous activity:

☐ Caution   ☐ Extreme Caution   ☐ Danger   ☐ Extreme Danger

Source: National Oceanic and Atmospheric Administration

heat for a variety of temperature and humidity conditions. Locate the row showing the air temperature and follow it across until it intersects with the column for the relative humidity. The box at the intersection indicates the heat index. These heat index numbers are for conditions of open shade and light wind. If we are exposed to full sunlight, the heat index values increase by as much as 15°F. In the heat index range from 90 to 104°F, heat cramps, heat exhaustion, and heat stroke are listed as "possible," if exposure and/or physical activity are prolonged. From 105 to 129°F, those problems move up the ranking and are listed as "likely" to occur. When the heat factor rises to 130°F or above, heat stroke is "highly likely" with continued exposure.

The other edge of this two-edged sword is the fact that high humidity decreases your body's ability to cool itself through perspiration and evaporation. When the humidity is high, evaporation doesn't work effectively, so the body keeps pumping out sweat in a futile effort to cool itself, and before long your body is out of water, and you're in a world of hurt.

The onset of heat-related illness is a result of excessive body fluid loss, as well as the loss of important minerals. As the minerals are depleted, you suffer an electrolyte imbalance that drops you into the early stages of heat-related illness. To replace the lost minerals, there are sport drinks that are meant to restore the electrolytes. These work well for athletes who have an unlimited amount of water to drink because these sport drinks must be matched by an equal amount of water. If you drink 12 ounces of sport drink, you should also drink 12 ounces of water. In addition to ready-made sport drinks, there are powders that are added to water to make an electrolyte-replacement drink. The problem is that in an outdoor survival situation where drinking water may be limited, you should not add a lot of electrolytes to your body without sufficient water intake. Loss of electrolytes leads to heat cramps and other problems, but if you allow your body to rest and you drink enough water, the body is designed to eventually return to the proper electrolyte balance on its own. The best course of action is to drink water, rest, and pace activities to limit internal heat production and fluid loss through sweating.

As we examine the problems related to heat overload, remember, the victim may be you. Be aware of what's happening inside your own body, and remember that prevention is better than treatment.

It's important to realize that heat-related illnesses are not always associated with being out in the sunshine. Working hard in a hot garage can bring about everything from heat cramps to heat exhaustion to heat stroke (also known as *sunstroke*). These maladies are both physical and chemical in nature and can occur in any location where heat and exertion are combined.

Too much exposure to heat, whether it be in the mountains, jungle, or desert, and a lot of exercise can drop you in your tracks if you're not careful. If you are out of condition or if you have not acclimatized to the area's warm weather or to the workload, you are especially vulnerable.

Be familiar with the causes, signs, and symptoms of hot-weather illness and understand how to treat a victim. Hot-weather injury can result in fatality if treatment isn't immediate and proper.

Heat Cramps

The lowest level of heat-related illness is known as *heat cramps*, so named because the primary symptom is painful muscle cramping. This is a result of an imbalance between electrolytes (body salts) and water within the body brought about by excessive sweating, which causes a loss of body fluids and body salts. Sweating is one of the body's mechanisms for lowering temperature by evaporation during hot weather or when the system begins to overheat as a result of exertion. Sweat carries body salts to the surface of the skin, where they are deposited as the sweat evaporates. Because far more water than salt is lost from the body by sweating, the recommended remedy for heat cramps is to have the victim rest in a cool place and drink water. The body naturally and gradually brings the electrolyte-to-water ratio back into balance.

Heat cramps are most frequently brought on by heavy exertion during hot weather, which causes excessive sweating. One way to avoid heat cramps is to nibble on some salty trail snacks, such as pretzels, salted nuts, etc., throughout the period of exertion, making sure to also drink lots of water. But if someone is experiencing heat cramps, the treatment is to have the victim (remember, it may be you) stop all activity, get out of the sun, rest in a cool place, and drink lots of water. After a while, the victim should start to feel better. Do not resume heavy activity. Let the victim rest and allow his body to recover and come back into balance.

Heat Exhaustion

This is the second level of hot-weather illness, although it is actually the most frequent malady suffered as a result of heat. Heat exhaustion, also known as *heat prostration* or *heat collapse*, is, oddly enough, more prevalent among spectators of an activity in a hot, humid climate than among the participants. Presumably, this is because the participants are drinking plenty of water, while the spectators are not.

A victim of heat exhaustion sweats profusely and has cool and clammy skin. Body temperature is normal or even slightly below normal. He typically exhibits pale skin color and rapid pulse and feels dizzy, nauseated, and faint (and may pass out). This victim is actually going into hypovolemic shock, a form of shock caused by low blood volume in the important parts of the body.

What's happening here is that the body is trying desperately to cool itself through evaporation by means of sweating profusely. High humidity is an enemy in hot weather, because evaporation slows in the humid environment and prevents the body from cooling. In response, the body tries even harder to get rid of the heat. In another attempt to cool the inner body, blood vessels near the surface of the skin load up with warm blood that is being sent from the core of the body to the surface in an effort to get rid of some of the heat by radiation and convection. That leaves the heart, lungs, and brain short of sufficient blood volume, and shock ensues.

Because this is a heat-related condition, get the victim out of the sun and into a cool place. Treatment for this individual is the traditional treatment for shock: lay the victim down, elevate the feet slightly, and administer cool water to drink if the patient is conscious. Although this is not an extremely serious condition, it can worsen. Keep the victim at rest and under observation, and if improvement is not apparent in a short time, take him to an emergency medical facility for further treatment.

Heat Stroke

This is the most dangerous of the bunch. It is deadly. Heat stroke is always fatal unless proper treatment is administered immediately. This is a condition in which the body can no longer counteract its own rising temperature. Think of it as nuclear meltdown. The only way to stop it is to take immediate action. Even then, there could be permanent cell damage. In the case of heat stroke, the damage extends to the brain cells. Time is of the essence.

A victim of heat stroke may or may not be sweating. As the condition advances, the body quits sacrificing its water supply for sweat, and the victim becomes dry and hot and has a red skin color. Body temperature rises to extremely dangerous levels, and brain cells begin to die. Coma and death can result.

Step one is to get the victim out of the heat and sun. It is critically important to get him cooled down immediately by any way possible. Generally, don't apply ice directly to the skin because of the potential for inducing frostbite. Of course you shouldn't throw an unconscious person in a cold stream and leave him to flounder. But, if the individual is conscious, submerge and support him in cool water and sponge cool water over his body or wrap him in a cold, wet cloth, then get a breeze moving past him to increase the cooling effects of evaporation. If the person is conscious, you may administer cool water by mouth.

The next vital step is getting this victim to an emergency medical facility as swiftly as possible, all the while continuing the cooling process. Death or permanent disability is always possible with heat stroke, so don't mess around with it.

Prevention

All of these problems are preventable. Drink lots of water and pace yourself to limit perspiration in hot, humid weather. Become a "lizard" by seeking the shade and limiting your activity to the cool part of the day. Don't allow the fear of looking weak keep you from taking a break. This is a time to be smart, not macho. Wear lightweight, light-colored clothing that covers the body and protects against the sun. (For additional tips on preventing heat-related illness, see "Surviving Hot Weather" in Chapter 2.)

Don't wait until you feel thirsty before taking a drink. Although it's OK to drink electrolyte drinks, these should be taken in addition to water. Water is the fluid of choice, because it is the only drink that doesn't fool the body into thinking it is ingesting food. When it comes to hydration, you can't replace water with pop, beer, coffee, and other liquids, though they have water in them. The body considers these fluids to be food that requires digestion, and digestion speeds the metabolic rate, which heats the body and increases the need for water.

It is every bit as important to reduce the need to drink water as it is to increase the intake. By slowing your pace, hiding out in the shade during the heat of the day, and keeping yourself protected from the dry wind, you'll extend your endurance and reduce the potential for heat-related illness and injuries.

STOP THE BLEEDING!

In the world of medical emergencies, there is almost nothing that takes precedence over bleeding. This is because it is possible for a human being to die in a matter of only a few minutes, if he is bleeding seriously enough. Delaying treatment or failing to take the proper action when a wound is bleeding can lead to dire consequences. When dealing with a medical emergency that involves bleeding, you must be able to assess the injury accurately and quickly take the appropriate action.

In the circulatory system, there are three categories of blood vessels. With one exception, arteries send oxygen-rich blood from the heart all throughout the body, while veins are the return conduits that bring oxygen-poor blood back toward the heart from the extremities. The technical exception is that when blood begins its voyage at the right side of the heart, it is the pulmonary artery that carries the oxygen-poor blood to the lungs, where it drops off carbon dioxide and picks up oxygen. Then the pulmonary vein carries oxygen-rich blood back to the left side of the heart, from which it is pumped to the rest of the body. As the blood travels on its outbound journey, it enters smaller vessels, the capillaries, the conduits through which oxygen-rich blood and nutrients are delivered to every cell. Understanding the distinctions between these vessels is the key to making a proper assessment of a bleeding trauma.

There are several types of injury that cause bleeding. Among these are scrapes (abrasions), slice-type cuts (incisions), ragged gashes (lacerations), puncture wounds, and amputations.

Abrasions are common causes of capillary bleeding. The injury is not deep enough to open a vein or artery but is serious enough to damage the capillaries and result in a slowly oozing wound that should be treated as follows:

▶ Inspect the wound for the presence of foreign matter (dirt, leaves, slivers, pebbles, etc.) and gently remove.

▶ Clean the injury with cotton swabs and a diluted antiseptic solution. Check with your doctor for advice about which antiseptic solution is recommended for you.

▶ If it is necessary to cover the wound, use a dry, nonadherent dressing (find these at your local pharmacy, and keep them in your first-aid kit).

Injuries that involve punctures, gashes, and lacerations often result in bleeding from veins. You can tell if a vein has been opened by the dark red blood that pours from the wound in a slow and steady fashion.

▶ As with abrasions, first inspect the injury for foreign matter and remove any that is found.

▶ Stop the bleeding by applying direct pressure over the wound.

▶ Cover the wound with a dry, nonadherent dressing that is appropriate for the size of the injury.

▶ Secure the dressing by wrapping with a roller bandage.

▶ If the wound is to a limb, immobilize the afflicted area and elevate it above the level of the heart to help slow the loss of blood. Do this by laying the patient down to treat for shock and elevating the wounded limb.

If a puncture is caused by an impaled object, this type of wound must be treated with special care.

▶ Calm the victim, and encourage him to be as still as possible.

▶ Do not attempt to remove the impaled object. In fact, be careful to avoid disturbing it at all, as that may increase bleeding.

▶ To stop the bleeding, apply direct pressure around the wound or indirect pressure on a pressure point between the wound and the heart (see the Illustration on page 195), if possible.

▶ To prevent movement of the impaled object, stabilize it the best you can, perhaps by using a roller bandage.

▶ If possible, immobilize and elevate the injury to a level above the heart.

▶ Call an ambulance, or transport the victim yourself to an emergency medical facility as gently but as quickly as you can.

The same type of injuries that cause venous bleeding can also result in arterial bleeding. A deep laceration, gash, puncture, or amputation that breaches an artery produces powerful spurts of bright red blood, making it fairly easy to distinguish from the dark red, slow bleeding that comes from veins. Each heartbeat generates a lively spurt from the wound, and the victim loses a lot of blood in a hurry. This is the most dangerous type of bleeding and must be considered life threatening.

▶ Quickly remove foreign matter from the wound, but waste no time being too fastidious. The victim's life is rapidly draining away.

▶ Immediately apply direct pressure to stop bleeding. Use whatever you have available to plug the wound, even the bare heel of your hand if necessary.

▶ Ideally, apply a nonadherent dressing directly on the wound, followed by one or more sterile pads. When possible, apply a roller bandage to secure the dressings, but stand by to reapply more vigorous direct pressure if the bleeding resumes.

▶ Help the victim into a horizontal position to prevent further injury from fainting and to treat for shock.

▶ Immobilize the injury and elevate it to a level above the heart to help slow the bleeding.

▶ If possible, call for emergency medical assistance. If that is not possible, use your own vehicle to transport the victim to a hospital.

In the care of doctors or other professional emergency medical care providers, the victim will be treated with specialized equipment. But in the field, where that equipment is not available, there are four very effective emergency techniques to stop external bleeding.

▶ Direct pressure is applied on top of the wound itself. When possible, use direct pressure on top of sterile dressings that are applied directly on the injury. If you have no sterile dressing, place the heel of your hand directly on the wound and apply enough pressure to stop the bleeding. If bleeding

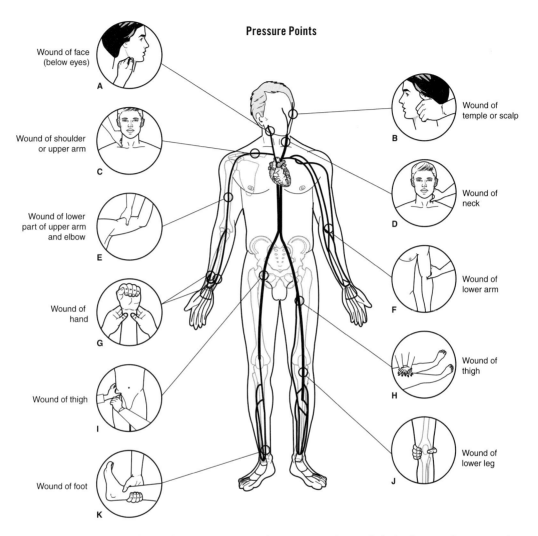

Pressure Points

Wound of face (below eyes) — A

Wound of temple or scalp — B

Wound of shoulder or upper arm — C

Wound of neck — D

Wound of lower part of upper arm and elbow — E

Wound of lower arm — F

Wound of hand — G

Wound of thigh — H

Wound of thigh — I

Wound of lower leg — J

Wound of foot — K

TO stop aggressive bleeding, it is sometimes necessary to apply pressure to points on the body where arteries are near the surface. Pressing on these pressure points may slow the flow of blood to the wound and allow you to get the bleeding under control.

is extreme, you may need to insert your fingers directly into the wound to stop the flow of blood. After the bleeding has subsided, maintain pressure and add dressings as you withdraw your fingers. While keeping the pressure on the wound, add more sterile dressings and apply a roller bandage, but watch the injury closely and be prepared to resume direct pressure if bleeding starts again.

▶ If direct pressure alone isn't enough to stop the bleeding, use your fingers to apply pressure to the pressure point along the artery between the wound and the heart. This will help slow the pulsing flow of blood. You may add pressure point control as well as direct pressure to slow the flow of blood to a severe injury. Apply pressure between the wound and the heart over the artery that feeds the bleeding.

▶ To help slow the flow of blood to the wound, elevate the injured area to a level above the heart. Depending upon the part of the body that is injured, this may not be possible, but if the injury is to a limb, it usually can be done to great benefit.

▶ A constricting bandage, or tourniquet, is used as a last resort, when all else has failed and the situation is life threatening. Using a tourniquet is a trade-off—you are sacrificing a limb to save a life, because it is almost certain that the limb will be lost due to tissue damage from the crushing pressure and the total loss of circulation to the tissue downstream of the constricting band. Tourniquets are not recommended except in the most extreme cases, when the victim will die unless the device is used. If you use one, take note of the time when it was applied, because the doctors need that information as they continue treatment.

External bleeding can be a serious medical emergency, and every outdoor enthusiast should be prepared with both the knowledge and the first-aid equipment to handle these situations. A life may depend on it.

Shock

Injuries that involve the loss of blood, either externally or internally, can result in the patient going into shock. There are several versions of shock, but the one that is most commonly caused by excessive blood or fluid loss is called hypovolemic shock. This occurs when there is insufficient blood volume in the circulatory system to allow the heart to effectively deliver a full load of blood to the brain. Symptoms can include any or all of the following: low blood pressure, rapid and weak pulse, sweating, rapid breathing, dizziness, anxiety, pale/cool/clammy skin, nausea, weakness, fainting, and death.

Hypovolemic shock is always a serious matter, and professional medical attention should be sought as quickly as possible. Complications for this type of situation can include kidney damage and brain damage. Be aware that, even with professional treatment, it is possible for a shock victim to die. The more serious the injury, the greater the blood loss, the longer it takes to reach an emergency room, and the weaker the patient, the more likely the outcome will be worse. That said, there are some steps that can be taken in the field while awaiting transport to an emergency medical facility.

▶ Unless the victim has suffered head, neck, back, or leg injury that would preclude readjusting his body position, have the patient lie down on his back. However, if there are injuries to those parts of the body, keep the victim in the position in which he was found, unless the victim must be moved because he is in a precarious position and leaving him there would present a risk.

▶ Avoid moving an injured person who has suspected spinal injury, but if it must be done, stabilize the head and neck.

▶ If the victim can be placed horizontal, elevate the legs and feet slightly (about 12 inches) to help retain blood volume in the upper body. If the victim must be carried to another location, maintain him in this position during transport.

▶ Keep the victim comfortable. If necessary, use a blanket to prevent body heat loss that may lead to hypothermia.

▶ Do not administer fluids by mouth.

▶ Hypovolemic shock may be caused by allergic reaction to a bee sting. If that is the cause, and you have a bee sting kit available (this is a prescription item, so consult with your doctor), administer treatment for the allergic reaction. (For information on the field treatment of snakebites, scorpion stings, and venomous spider bites, see Chapter 10.)

SPRAINS AND BREAKS

All it takes is one misstep, and down you go with a bad injury that might be a sprain or a broken bone. If it happens in the wrong place and the wrong time, you might be disabled in the wilderness and not be able to make it back to camp or to your vehicle. Something as simple as a twisted ankle can quickly turn into a survival situation.

These injuries happen in all sorts of ways. Perhaps you step on a rock and your ankle rolls painfully to one side. Or maybe you catch a foot on a snag, or your boot slips on moss, or you lose your balance and take a slide, or you fall off a horse. Hundreds of injuries like these occur every year while folks are hiking, camping, hunting, or fishing. The law of gravity doesn't care how it happens; the pain is about to begin. The fact that these injuries are so common makes it important to be able to distinguish between a sprain and a fracture and know what to do about them.

Sprains

Sprains are caused by overstretched or torn ligaments, the tissue that connects bones together at a joint. This happens when a joint is suddenly overextended beyond the range of movement normally permitted by the ligaments. It's the ligaments that stabilize and support the joints, so a sprain results in the joint losing stability. Not only that, but the injury itself can be wildly painful, causing the victim to stop using that joint and place no pressure on it, leaving the victim lame.

It's a common saying that a bad sprain can be as serious as a break. Actually, it can be even worse. The pain can be as bad. The debilitation can be as bad. The recovery time can be as bad. And if proper treatment isn't applied, the aftermath of a sprain can be worse than a fracture. A joint that has once suffered a sprain is prone to future injury. If proper rehabilitation is not performed, the joint may become permanently weakened and susceptible to reinjury.

A mild sprain causes only short-term pain and loss of joint function, but a serious sprain can make you think a bone has been fractured. There is pain, bruising, inflammation, swelling, and loss of ability to use the joint. There may be the sound and sensation of a "pop" or "snap" that makes the victim believe something is broken. In fact, fractures sometimes occur along with a severe sprain. Without an x-ray, it is often impossible to know whether the injury is a sprain, a fracture, or both.

Since without an x-ray you can't make an accurate diagnosis, the rule is to automatically treat the injury as if it were a fracture. Immobilize the bones and joints involved and elevate the injured limb. Then take the patient to a medical facility. In all but the mildest cases, a doctor should treat the patient and establish a rehabilitation routine.

If you are certain that the injury is nothing more serious than a mild sprain, field treatment follows the RICE method: rest, ice, compression, elevation. Do all four parts of this treatment at the same time.

▶ Rest: The injury must be protected against movement as much as possible to allow healing to begin.
▶ Ice: Wrap a cold pack in a layer of damp cloth to avoid direct contact with the skin and apply it to the injury to help slow the swelling and reduce inflammation. After the first 48 to 72 hours after the injury, apply the cold pack intermittently for up to 20 minutes at a time.
▶ Compression: Lightly wrap the injured area with an elastic bandage (like an Ace bandage) to help reduce swelling. Take care to not wrap the bandage so tightly that it cuts off circulation.
▶ Elevation: To further reduce swelling, raise the injured part of the body above the level of the heart. The patient may need to lie down to accomplish this.

Fractures

Treatment of broken bones can be tricky. A skull fracture, for example, doesn't manifest the same as a broken arm. A fracture of the long bones in a leg or arm is somewhat easier to diagnose and treat than other types of fractures (hips, for example) that are buried deep inside the body tissue.

There are two types of fractures to long bones: simple and compound. In a simple fracture, the bone either splits or breaks all the way through, but the bones remain in place and the jagged ends don't exit the skin. Compound fractures, on the other hand, are nasty injuries. The broken bone is bent at an angle, and the sharp ends penetrate the skin, sometimes opening a bloody, ugly wound.

The standard rule of treatment for all fractures is to stabilize the patient (stop the bleeding, treat for shock) then immobilize by splinting the fracture exactly as it is. In other words, don't try to reduce the fracture by straightening the limb. Just splint the injury and transport the victim to a medical facility.

A word about splinting—to splint a joint, immobilize it by placing rigid splints on both sides of the joint and using gauze roller bandages to secure the splints to the limb both above and below the joint. The point is to prevent the joint from moving. Don't try to straighten the joint; just leave it in the position you find it and secure the splint to keep it that way.

To splint a mid-bone break, use rigid splints on both sides of the limb, attaching them both above and below the break. The object of splinting is not to get the patient back on his feet again but to immobilize the fractured part of the body so no further damage will be done while you're transporting the patient. Be careful not to attach the splints so tightly that circulation is cut off.

There are inflatable splints that are lightweight and compact and fit almost every part of the body that is likely to need a splint. These are excellent and make the whole process easier. But if inflatable splints are not available, use whatever rigid materials and cloth strips you have at hand.

ALTITUDE SICKNESS

I don't know about you, but I'm an air breather. My favorite air has plenty of oxygen in it, because that's what feeds every cell in my body. As much as I like oxygen-rich air, I also like to go way up high in the mountains where the air is thin. That's OK, as long as I do it the right way, but if I mess up I can fall victim to altitude sickness. It's not my fault, it's just physiology.

I'm not alone in this. Under the right conditions, everybody is vulnerable to altitude sickness. It isn't a matter of how old you are, except that young children tend to be at increased risk. It doesn't matter how many muscles you have. It doesn't matter that you have been up high in the mountains in the past and never had a problem. It doesn't matter that you're an excellent hiker. Actually, it is even possible for altitude sickness to strike a person who is riding in a vehicle.

This condition we call altitude sickness is the way the body responds when it is suddenly subjected to a low-oxygen environment. It's the "suddenly" part that is most important. Acclimatization to high altitude is a slow process but can be done. The problem is that most of us don't take the time to do it right. In our impatience, we want to be at the top of the mountain right now, so off we go. And that's when problems strike.

In a nutshell, altitude sickness results from going too high too fast. Approximately 20 percent of those ascending from sea level to 8,000 feet in less than one day develop some form of altitude sickness. On the other hand, if the climb to high elevation is taken over the course of a couple of days, most people are able to acclimatize to 10,000 feet. The laws of physiology dictate that the greater the elevation, the longer it takes to reach full acclimatization. Above 10,000 feet, about 75 percent of people feel some symptoms. The factors that determine whether or not you'll be hit with altitude sickness are the elevation, your rate of ascent, and your particular susceptibility. Those who have suffered altitude sickness in the past are slightly more at risk of recurrence.

If you gain altitude slowly, gradually acclimatizing over a period of time, you may never experience an altitude-related medical problem. Ascending beyond 8,000 feet should be done at a rate of no more than 1,500 feet per day. To assist the body in acclimatizing after reaching altitude, avoid strenuous exertion for a period of 24 to 36 hours.

At high altitude, the air is not only thin and oxygen-poor, it is also very dry. This makes it especially important to drink more water than you are accustomed to at lower elevation. As you exert yourself at high altitude, the tendency is to over-breathe the exceptionally dry air, and this accelerates dehydration. As dehydration increases, blood volume is reduced, and that intensifies altitude sickness.

There are three acronyms related to altitude sickness. The first is AMS, which stands for acute mountain sickness. This is the first stage of a three-stage assault on your body by the low-oxygen environment that exists at high elevation. AMS presents the following symptoms:

- Headache
- Loss of appetite
- Nausea or vomiting
- Fatigue or weakness
- Dizziness or light-headedness
- Difficulty sleeping
- Confusion
- Staggering

If you neglect AMS, it will progress from a mild condition to more severe, with increasingly intense symptoms.

If you think that sounds bad, wait until you read what comes next. If you allow AMS to continue without taking proper steps to reverse the condition, it will advance into the next stage—HAPE (high-altitude pulmonary edema) or HACE (high-altitude cerebral edema). These are conditions in which lack of oxygen at high elevation results in fluid leakage through the capillary walls into the lungs or the brain. The only good news about these illnesses is that they are more rare than AMS. The bad news is that those who choose to ignore the early symptoms are in life-threatening trouble. HAPE and HACE strike those who fail to acclimatize slowly, choosing rather to ascend too quickly to an elevation that is too high. The trouble with these conditions is that, even if you acclimatize properly, HAPE and HACE are serious risks to those who remain for too long high on a mountain.

Pulmonary edema is a very serious situation and should be treated without delay. HAPE symptoms include the following:

- Shortness of breath even while resting
- A sensation of tightness in the chest
- Exhaustion or deep fatigue
- Nocturnal feelings that you are about to suffocate
- Weakness
- A persistent cough that brings up fluid
- Confusion
- Irrational behavior

The immediate lifesaving step for HAPE victims is to descend at least 2,000 to 4,000 feet without delay. Following the descent, the victim must be evacuated as soon as possible to a medical facility for follow-up treatment.

HACE attacks brain tissue, flooding it with fluid that leaks from capillaries, resulting in swelling. Symptoms include:

▶ Headache

▶ Loss of coordination

▶ Weakness

▶ Gradual decreasing levels of consciousness

▶ Disorientation

▶ Loss of memory

▶ Hallucinations

▶ Psychotic behavior

▶ Coma and death

To save a HACE victim's life, get the patient down to an elevation that is 2,000 to 4,000 feet lower. Then evacuate to a medical facility for follow-up treatment.

One of the keys to survival at altitude is to acclimatize for several days before ascending. Then go slow and easy. During the ascent, constantly observe your own condition and that of others in the party. If you suspect that symptoms of altitude sickness are appearing, change your plans and cancel the high-elevation excursion. It's a matter of survival.

HEART ATTACK

There is something about the outdoors that inspires vigor in your step. You feel more alive, as if you were inhaling fresh energy in every breath. It makes you want to get up early so you can watch the sunrise and climb to the distant ridge where the view promises to be exceptional. And with this newfound enthusiasm, sometimes you overdo it. The next thing you know, you don't feel well. Tightness constricts your chest, and your forehead is bathed in sweat. Nausea and dizziness sweep over you, and you can't catch your breath. The question looms in your mind—is this a heart attack?

The answer to that question is not always easy to find, because some of the same symptoms that signal a heart attack are mimicked by disorders no more serious than indigestion. But the consequences of dismissing the possibility of a heart attack and trying to convince yourself that the symptoms are not *that* serious can be fatal. If what you're feeling is a heart attack, every second counts. Consider this advice from the National Heart, Lung, and Blood Institute: "Coronary heart disease (CHD) is the leading cause of death for both men and women in the United States. CHD is caused by a narrowing of the coronary arteries that supply blood to the heart, and often results in a heart attack. Each year, about 1.1 million Americans suffer a heart attack. About 460,000 of those heart attacks are fatal. About half of those deaths occur within one hour of the start of symptoms and before the person reaches the hospital."

The American Heart Association echoes the advice that time is of the essence. "Today heart attack and stroke victims can benefit from new medications and treatments unavailable to patients in years past. . . . But to be effective, these drugs must be given relatively quickly after heart attack or stroke symptoms first appear."

From those statements, it becomes obvious that when it's a heart attack, timely treatment gives the best chance of survival. Understanding the symptoms of heart attack is critical to knowing how to respond when someone in camp becomes ill.

As you examine the symptoms for heart attack, here's what to look for:

▶ **Chest discomfort.** Heart attack survivors report the presence of chest discomfort that may feel like pressure or squeezing, a sensation of fullness, or outright pain. This discomfort can continue for several minutes, or it might reduce for a time and return later.

▶ **Discomfort elsewhere in the upper body.** A heart attack victim might experience discomfort or pain in one or both arms, in the back, neck, jaw, or abdomen.

▶ **Shortness of breath.** Difficulty drawing a full breath sometimes happens along with discomfort in the chest, but it might also occur in advance of chest discomfort.

▶ **Additional symptoms.** Other symptoms to watch for include nausea, dizziness, or light-headedness, and the victim breaking into a cold sweat.

The key to making a safe decision for the patient is to observe his symptoms and determine how many of them are occurring together. For example, if the patient complains of chest discomfort together with one or more of the other symptoms listed here, get the victim to an emergency medical facility as soon as possible.

Heart attacks do not always show the same symptoms. A friend told me one day that he had been to the doctor for a comprehensive physical examination. He was stunned when the doctor asked him, "When did you have your heart attack?" To my friend's knowledge, he had never had a heart attack, but the damage was clearly there. Perhaps we've been conditioned by what we see in movies to expect that all heart attack victims suddenly clutch their chests in pain, then collapse. My friend is evidence that heart attacks don't always happen that way. Some begin slowly, with nothing more than mild discomfort. If symptoms are mild, it's easy for the seriousness of the situation to be played down, leading to potentially deadly delay in seeking treatment.

No matter how mild the symptoms, the safest thing to do is to summon the assistance of emergency medical services (EMS) personnel. These people are trained and fully equipped to handle heart attacks in a manner that will give the greatest possibility of survival and recovery. If you are far from civilization, a satellite phone or a ham radio can be a lifesaver at times like this, allowing you to call for a medevac. But if it's impossible to make contact with the outside world, you must handle the crisis the best you can on your own.

If you are the victim and no one else in camp knows how to handle a heart attack, you must direct the others who are trying to help you. Tell them what is happening to you and that they need to follow the procedures outlined below. If possible, send somebody to contact local authorities who can commence a medical rescue. That includes sheriff's personnel, park rangers, the nearest hospital, the closest 911 service, and sources of rescue.

If you are not the victim but are on the scene, and the victim is still conscious:

▶ Ask if he uses heart medication (nitroglycerin). If so, locate the meds and place one tablet under the victim's tongue. It's OK to administer up to three tablets in a ten-minute period, if necessary.

▶ To make the patient more comfortable and to promote ease of breathing and circulation, loosen the clothing around his neck, chest, and waist.

▶ Move the person into a comfortable half-sitting position. This is especially helpful if there is trouble breathing. Use a pillow, blanket, or rolled towel to lend support and comfort to the patient's back and head. Bring his legs up, slightly bent at the knees, and support the knees with a pillow or something soft.

▶ Speak calmly to the victim, giving reassurance that help is on the way.

▶ Continually monitor the patient's pulse and respiration. Prepare yourself to perform either CPR or rescue breathing, if those interventions become necessary. For the record, CPR (cardiopulmonary resuscitation) is performed only on victims who have no pulse or respiration. Never perform CPR on a patient who is still breathing, even if he is unconscious. CPR is only for patients who are PNB (pulseless non-breathers). Rescue breathing is similar to CPR but involves only the breathing assistance, not the chest compressions, and is performed on patients who still have a pulse but need assistance with breathing.

There is the question about administering aspirin to someone displaying symptoms of heart attack. Here's what the American Heart Association recommends. (I include this bit of information with the understanding that calling 911 might not be possible.)

"The more important thing to do if any heart attack warning signs occur is to call 9-1-1 immediately. Don't do anything before calling

9-1-1. In particular, don't take an aspirin, then wait for it to relieve your pain. Don't postpone calling 9-1-1. Aspirin won't treat your heart attack by itself. After you call 9-1-1, the 9-1-1 operator may recommend that you take an aspirin. He or she can make sure that you don't have an allergy to aspirin or a condition that makes using it too risky. If the 9-1-1 operator doesn't talk to you about taking an aspirin, the emergency medical technicians or the physician in the Emergency Department will give you an aspirin if it's right for you. Research shows that getting an aspirin early in the treatment of a heart attack, along with other treatments EMTs and Emergency Department physicians provide, can significantly improve your chances of survival."

Rescue Breathing on Adults

▶ Lay the patient comfortably on his back.

▶ Tilt the victim's head back by lifting the chin. This opens the airway that might be pinched closed by a chin-down position.

▶ Pinch the victim's nose shut to prevent the escape of air as you breathe.

▶ Take a deep breath, then open the victim's mouth and seal your mouth around his mouth and deliver a slow but full breath into the victim's lungs. Pull back only long enough to take another full breath, and then repeat the procedure for the second breath. While you are breathing into the victim's mouth, observe his chest, and continue blowing until his chest rises.

▶ Check for a pulse. If the victim has a pulse but is still not breathing, continue delivering one slow breath every five seconds for a minute—twelve breaths in all.

▶ After delivering the first set of twelve breaths, check again for pulse and respiration. Do this again after every set of twelve breaths, at the end of each minute.

▶ Continue rescue breathing as long as a pulse is present but the person is not breathing. Keep this going until natural respiration is restored.

CPR

Rather than try to explain the technique of CPR here, I suggest you contact your local fire department, ambulance service, or hospital and arrange to be professionally trained in the administration of this lifesaving technique. This is a technique that cannot be learned by reading a book, and by taking the course you will become certified and possess a level of experience that will allow you to actually perform CPR when you need to.

CARBON MONOXIDE: THE SILENT KILLER

You could tell scary stories around the campfire about this invisible killer. It creeps into camp entirely undetectable by your natural senses—you can't smell it, taste it, feel it, hear it, or see it. But when it arrives in your camp, at the very least it makes you sick; at the worst it quietly kills you and everyone with you in a matter of minutes.

Unfortunately, this isn't just a scary campfire story. The culprit is carbon monoxide (CO), a common by-product of the combustion process. Carbon monoxide is a poisonous gas that is a hazard to campers, regardless of the kind of shelter they use.

Hard-wall shelters such as cabins, truck campers, motor homes, or camping trailers seal tightly, providing a perfect environment for carbon monoxide to accumulate. But even a tent, which you might logically think would allow plenty of ventilation to pass through the fabric, may become a death trap. If the tent is tightly zipped shut, and if any heating or cooking is done inside, carbon monoxide can build to dangerous concentrations. This is especially true if the tent fabric is wet, because moisture seals the pores that air might otherwise pass through.

Because carbon monoxide is a by-product of incomplete combustion, anything that involves the burning of fuel in an area that is not properly ventilated can potentially result in illness or death caused by carbon monoxide poisoning.

I mention ventilation because that is one of the most critical factors in preventing a carbon monoxide problem. Whenever fuel-consuming appliances, such as heaters, stoves, and lanterns, are used inside an enclosure, it is vital that adequate fresh-air ventilation is provided. The best ventilation arrangement involves two openings to fresh air, one high and one low, on opposite sides of the enclosure, because this helps establish natural convection currents to move air through the shelter. Many fuel-burning appliances include instructions in the owner's manual, spelling out the number of square inches of ventilation that are required for safe use in an enclosure. An example is the Coleman propane catalytic heater (variable 2,000–4,000 Btu) we use for camping. The instructions call for 48 square inches of total ventilation, equally divided into two openings, one high and one low, on opposite walls of the structure. The warning goes on to say that the operator should provide additional ventilation of at least 2 square inches for every 1,000 Btu per hour of input for any additional fuel-burning appliances.

With an understanding of how carbon monoxide attacks the human body, the importance of adequate ventilation becomes apparent. Carbon monoxide attacks without warning because it is virtually undetectable by human senses. The deadly gas accumulates in enclosed places, often while the victims are asleep and the heater is still burning. But carbon monoxide is not a threat only to the sleeping. It will literally plunge a fully conscious person into a sleep from which he may never awaken.

Carbon monoxide gas prevents the hemoglobin in blood from delivering oxygen to the cells of the body. Shortage of oxygen to the cells gradually weakens the body and eventually results in unconsciousness. By the time the victim realizes there is a problem, he or she may be too weak to open a door or window or move outside to fresh air. Of course, as the process continues to deny oxygen to the cells, the victim dies.

Symptoms of carbon monoxide poisoning range from having a slight headache to nausea, weakness, vomiting, drowsiness, and heart palpitations. Unless the conditions that caused the symptoms are reversed, eventually the victim falls into a coma and dies. Those with preexisting respiratory or cardiac conditions are at greatest risk. The heart is a primary target of CO poisoning, so it is no surprise that carbon monoxide–related heart attacks are prevalent among victims.

Unfortunately, CO poisoning is cumulative. Small doses accumulate in the tissues of the body, and further exposure adds to the already toxic level. Gradually, the level increases until symptoms begin to show up. Another unhappy aspect of CO poisoning is that, even after the victim is removed from exposure to excess carbon monoxide in the atmosphere, it takes longer to purge the body of the toxin than it took to arrive at a dangerous level in the first place. It's kind of like getting fat—seems like you can gain weight overnight, but it takes forever to get rid of it. That's the way it is with carbon monoxide poisoning; you can be poisoned quickly, but it takes a long time to get it out of your system.

To help prevent excessive contact with this lethal gas, include a high-quality carbon monoxide detector as part of your camping safety equipment. Monitors are small and should be placed inside a shelter about midway between the floor and ceiling, where they will most effectively detect the presence of the dangerous gas as it circulates freely in the air.

There are important differences between detectors. Some are totally portable because they are powered by a 9-volt battery, but others are intended to be permanently hardwired into a 12-volt electrical system, such as that found in an RV. Some of the units feature sensors that must be replaced annually, while other detectors are rated for as many as ten years of service. Some detectors are calibrated to trigger an alarm at lower levels of CO than other units. Certain detectors activate the alarm any time a preestablished level of carbon monoxide gas is discovered. Other systems operate on a time-weighted averaging system in which the level of gas is factored in with the duration of time the gas has been in the atmosphere to determine if the condition is worthy of an alarm.

The detector you choose depends upon your individual situation, but the important thing is to have a detector and use it. For our personal camping style, we use a portable unit with a replaceable sensor/power pack. For years, the thing was silent, except when I pushed the test button or when the battery was low, and then it would beep to alert me to replace the power pack. Other than that, it never made a peep, and I sometimes wondered if it was really working. Then one cold day, with things buttoned up too tight and the single-burner camp stove working on heating up our dinner, the carbon monoxide alarm started screaming its head off. I immediately opened the shelter so we had a large amount of cross-ventilation, and we stepped outside into the fresh air until the alarm went silent. Ever since then, I've slept with a greater degree of confidence that the alarm will wake me up if the CO level climbs too high.

CARBON monoxide is virtually impossible for human senses to detect, so a CO alarm is necessary to protect against this unseen killer whenever you are in an enclosure near any form of combustion, such as a stove, heater, lantern, or gas-powered generator.

Carbon monoxide poisoning originates in many places—a leaky vehicle exhaust system, poorly operating camp appliances, and a portable power generator, to name a few. In some situations, problem levels of carbon monoxide may not come from your own camp. If you are surrounded by other campers, you may suffer the effects of carbon monoxide originating from activities taking place in another camp, especially if the breeze blows in your direction.

Here are some tips for preventing a carbon monoxide problem.

Before You Leave Home

▶ Inspect the exhaust systems of your vehicle and portable generator to make sure there are no leaks. Make repairs, if necessary.

▶ If you have a camping trailer or motor home equipped with a power generator, make sure the tip of the generator exhaust pipe extends beyond the RV's exterior wall. Exhaust fumes expelled directly below the floor may find a way inside.

▶ Inspect propane appliances to see that combustion is efficient. Flames should burn bright blue. Yellow or reddish flames indicate inefficient combustion, resulting in higher levels of carbon monoxide.

▶ If you use an RV (even a tent trailer) equipped with a furnace, make sure the outside exhaust system is unobstructed and is sealed off from the interior of the RV.

In Camp

▶ If you use a camper, trailer, or motor home, close windows that are near the generator or furnace exhaust outlets when operating these accessories. Inspect window and door seals to make sure they are in good condition.

▶ If possible, position yourself so the prevailing wind blows smoke and fumes away from your camp. This applies to your position relative to neighboring campers as well as to the position of your own sources of exhaust fumes.

▶ When operating a heater, stove, or lantern that burns liquid fuel, pressurized fuel, or solid fuel, provide for adequate cross-ventilation.

▶ Make sure there is adequate ventilation while you are cooking.

▶ Never use the stove as the primary source of heat for the interior of the shelter.

▶ To prevent accidental poisoning with carbon monoxide gas, don't run a power generator at night while you are asleep.

▶ Never go to bed with a combustible-fuel heater, stove, or lantern burning.

▶ If anyone in the shelter begins to feel a headache or onset of nausea, get outside into the fresh air as quickly as possible. Seek medical attention as soon as possible, so professional detoxification procedures can be initiated.

With attention to safe use of fuel-burning camp appliances, carbon monoxide poisoning can be prevented. Avoid this potentially tragic medical problem with proper installation, use, and maintenance of fuel-burning appliances and engine exhaust systems. Do periodic inspections to make sure there is no damage or deterioration that could result in exhaust leaks or inefficient combustion. During operation of any of these appliances or engines, follow the commonsense rules outlined here. And finally, always use a high-quality carbon monoxide detector.

Doing all of these things is your best defense against the silent killer. Then you can spend time telling campfire stories about other scary monsters that lurk just beyond the shadows in the forest.

Navigation

8

I'll never forget the moment I realized that the scene before me was identical to the one I saw only half an hour earlier, as I tromped through the Louisiana woodlands. Not similar—identical—right down to the armadillo scurrying through the underbrush. Undeniably, I had circled back on my own earlier trail. The concept that I might actually be doing such a stupid thing assaulted my ego and shook me to the core. I never get lost. I always feel very secure in my ability to navigate by dead reckoning. But here I was—in a moment of slack attention,

I lost my way. The incident was sharply humbling and would have been embarrassing if anyone else had been there to witness it other than that armadillo. And he wasn't talking.

THE ART OF NOT GETTING LOST

In reality, embarrassment is the least concern when it comes to being lost. Losing one's way in the wilds is not a joke. It is not the least bit funny, and when it happens to you there is a sudden and stunning sense that all is wrong with the world. Your confidence is shattered, as you spin and stare at the scene around you, utterly confused and disoriented. Which way is the right way? You have no clue. You're lost.

Beyond doubt, it is better to avoid getting lost than it is to struggle with getting found. Knowing how to become rescued is important, but prevention is better than the cure any day. So on these pages I present my top ten list of ways to avoid getting lost. We aren't going to worry about the numbers too much, just the concepts. If it works out to ten, enjoy the miracle of it all.

1. **Plan your movements.** Before you hike away from camp, paddle across the lake, or use whatever means you have to wander around the countryside, develop a detailed plan of where you're going. Do your planning with a map of the area spread out on the table, and try to visualize what the country looks like—where the peaks are, the tilt of the land, which direction the rivers flow, stuff like that. Decide ahead of time which trails to follow, which destinations to reach. Write it all down. Make an extra copy, and give it to someone who can share these plans with a search team if you fail to show up on schedule.

2. **Resist the temptation to deviate from your plan.** This is a difficult concept to sell, when all that glorious outdoor scenery beckons. There's always another meandering trail to follow, or the surprise of a tiny creek that tumbles out of a side canyon. Something always comes along and begs you to deviate from your plan. As you give in to those temptations, the assurance

of always knowing where you are diminishes. I know what you're going to say—you go outdoors to explore, to be surprised by what you discover, to break away from the boring assurances of always following a plan and coloring within the lines. I understand perfectly. At the same time, I am here to let you know that exploration sometimes leads to getting lost. It was ever so, it will ever be. Explore at your own risk.

3. **Use dead reckoning.** What if something goes wrong with your plan—like the dog eats all that nice homework just as you begin the trip? Or maybe you decide to explore and wander, and you stray from the original plan. Moving about without the plan simply requires that you put all your senses into service to keep you from getting lost. In a way, this actually heightens the whole experience of being outdoors, because you must pay close attention to everything around you. Dead reckoning is the name of the technique, and done properly this becomes a very close companion to overall land navigation. By dead reckoning, you maintain constant awareness of your position in relation to the landscape around you. Every step you take, you pay close attention to every feature and its relationship to the others, thereby maintaining a mental fix of your position.

   To take it one step further, once you identify your position, you keep track of your direction and time of travel and estimate your speed. Then, by using a simple time-speed-distance formula, you can make a fairly accurate estimate of your location. The formula is $60D = S \times T$, in which D is distance, S is speed, and T is time. If you know the value for any two of the three factors, you can calculate the third one by working the formula.

4. **Study the lay of the land.** Before walking away from camp, look around and memorize relative positions of the most notable terrain features—the major peaks, the old snag of a tree that stands above all the rest, how the canyon gapes open between two ridges, stuff like that. Turn all the way around and look in every direction, picking out landmarks that stand out around camp. By doing this, when you approach camp from a distance later on, you are more likely to recognize the natural signposts that lead you back.

5. **Pay attention to drainages.** If your camp or the place you parked your vehicle is near a river of any size, take note of the general direction of flow of water in relation to your camp or parking area. As you hike, pay attention

to whether you walked upstream or downstream. Later on, when it's time to return, if you can locate that same river, all you have to do is follow the flow of water back in the opposite direction and it will lead you to your starting point.

6. **Make a mental note of roads and trails.** A technique that is closely related to the previous one is used when there is no river but perhaps a road or significant trail. As you leave camp, take note of which side of the road or trail you are staying on. Let's say a forest road wanders generally east to west, and you hike away to the south of the road. Hours later, after having followed every dead-end game trail in the woods, you want to return to your vehicle, but it's useless to try to backtrack your bewildering route. Knowing that you are somewhere south of the road, all you have to do is go north until you intersect the road. You have only two choices to make when you get to the road: go left or go right. Somewhere on that road is your vehicle. Using the best logic you have available, make your choice. If nothing looks familiar, you are probably up-canyon of where you parked, so you've never seen this part of the canyon. If you recognize landmarks, you are probably down-canyon of the vehicle.

7. **Preview the map.** Be aware that a road may take a dynamic turn and not always go east-west or north-south. Preplanning is the most important part of dead reckoning. Know the nature of the road from studying it on the map ahead of time. Be constantly aware of the amount of time you are traveling and the estimated speed of travel. Then when you turn back, if you maintain the same speed for the same amount of time, you should cover the same distance. If after using this technique you come to the conclusion that you hiked too long in a direction you think is back toward the road and still have not found it, you may have missed it where it takes a giant turn. Only knowing the nature of the road in advance will help you figure out what to do next—i.e., swing left or right to try to intersect the road after the turn.

8. **As you follow a trail, turn around often and study your backtrail.** Things look very different on the way back. The back side of trees may be more lush than you remember them from the opposite direction. There may be brightly colored moss or lichens growing on the boulders that are invisible from the other angle. Where you were nose-to-the-trail while hiking uphill

on the way in, the return trip may display an open sky and distant peaks as the land falls away down the slope. Everything looks different when viewed from the opposite direction, so turn around and study your backtrail very often.

9. **When you are studying your surroundings, triangulate your position.** Use prominent landmarks, whether they are trees, peaks, boulders, firebreaks, power lines, or anything else that presents itself as a noticeable monument. Memorize the positional relationships between these natural guide marks, so that on the return trip you will know that this tree is supposed to be left of that boulder, and the far peak should be directly off your right shoulder when facing the direction you want to travel.

10. **Count.** Keep track of the number of times you crossed the creek, or the number of ridges you topped and canyons you dropped into, or the number of saguaros you passed along your way. The old joke about going to the eleventh bush and turning left has some merit, as long as you are sure they are the same bushes you passed on your way in.

PERIODICALLY turn around and study the trail behind you, because that is the view you will have as you return along the same path. Memorize specific features such as trees, rocks, stream crossings, or distant peaks.

OK, I lied—there are more than ten top ideas, but I'm on a roll, so hang in there with me.

11. **Keep track of time and try to relate it to distance.** This isn't always easy. The lay of the land, the condition of the trail and foliage, the weather, as well as your own physical condition all play a major role in determining how much ground you can cover in an hour. Before the trip, try to figure out how fast you normally hike under varying conditions. Then, as you travel, try to determine how many miles there are between you and your camp. This helps you know when it's time to turn around and head back, so you aren't caught in darkness.

12. **Leave your own signs.** As you hike, take note of the natural signs you create as you use the trail. Boots will leave tracks. Be familiar with the pat-

BE aware of the pattern of your own boot tracks, so you can follow them as you return along a previously used trail. Because of the way the shadows fall, tracks are easier to see if you are looking at them toward the sun.

tern of your own tracks so you won't confuse them with those of another. When you are trying to make your way back to camp, if you come to an embankment that doesn't show any sign of your prior passing, you know that this is not where you crossed the creek earlier, and you have to go in search of the place along the creek where you did cross.

13. **Play Hansel and Gretel.** Remember the story about the two children who were led off into the woods to become lost? One of the kids was smart enough to drop pebbles to mark the trail back home. You can do the same thing, but use brightly colored surveyor's tape instead. This is particularly important where trails come together or fork, leaving a possibility of confusion about which trail is the correct trail. Pluck off a six-inch ribbon and attach it to a twig at eye level. In dense conditions, you may need to do this quite often. The rule is to always drop a new pebble while you're still able to see the last one, so attach the markers so they are visible from both a front and backtrail perspective. Unless you are leaving the trail markers to help rescuers find you, remove all the trail markers you have placed before you leave the area. Don't remove markers that have been set by other people, because you don't know why those were put in place.

14. **GPS is the ultimate trail of pebbles.** If you have a GPS, use it to mark waypoints as you hike. When it's time to turn around and head back to camp, you simply follow the return route. The GPS tells you which direction to go and how far you have to travel as you retrace your steps from waypoint to waypoint. The nice thing about GPS is that it works in the fog or the dark when surveyor's ribbon is not visible. On the downside, the batteries are the weak link. Always carry spares.

PLAY Hansel and Gretel by marking your trail with colorful surveyor's tape. Keep the trail markers at eye level and arranged so you can spot them from any angle. To preserve the environment, remove the markers when you leave the area.

15. **Trust your instruments, and use them.** Everyone who goes into the backcountry should have a map and compass. The map should be the most detailed USGS (U.S. Geological Survey) topographic map you can obtain,

so you are able to read terrain steepness, water, forest, open areas, swamps, trails, drainages, and every other important feature. Learn to read the map, and use it for your initial planning. Learn to use the compass in relation to the map, properly orienting the map to north, and be able to recognize terrain features that appear in front of your eyes and identify them on the map.

Navigators have always been regarded as a magical breed who, through some mystical methods, seem to know exactly where they are on planet Earth. Using these techniques, you may join their ranks. At least you'll never have to stare at the same armadillo you just saw half an hour earlier and realize that he knows more than you do.

A GPS unit is the best electronic tool for keeping from getting lost. It can be used to establish waypoints at critical places along your route, allowing you to retrace your steps from point to point until you return to camp.

Finding Your Way Without a Compass

Moss grows on the north side of trees. You've heard that before, but did you know that this bit of old-timer's woodlore is wrong? Actually, moss does grow on the north side of trees—but it will also grow on the west, east, and south sides, depending upon where you are. So, if you can't believe the moss thing, what can you believe about determining which direction is north?

First, let's debunk the mysticism about the value of finding north. Having the ability to determine which direction is north is useless, unless you also know which direction you need to go in relation to north. If you wandered away and got lost in the middle of nowhere, and you had no idea which way it was to reach camp, just knowing the cardinal directions would not get you back to camp. Even if you have a compass, you're stuck, unless you also have a map and the expertise to use it properly.

The only value in being able to determine which way is north (or any other direction, for that matter) is if you know which direction you need to travel in order to reach safety. However, the ability to determine direction so you can continue to travel in a relatively straight line toward a known destination is valuable, because it keeps you from wandering in circles. You need a reliable way to find a foundation direction.

So, let's see how this works in a practical situation. Let's say that early one morning you wander out of camp, heading generally in the direction of the sunrise. That's east, because everywhere on earth, the sun rises in the east. Depending upon latitude and seasons, the sun may appear on the horizon more nearly northeast or southeast, but at least it is always easterly. Early in the afternoon, you get hungry and want to return to camp, but by now you're confused about which way to go. Everything looks the same in every direction. So, what do you do?

Here's the problem. Early in the morning when the sun is low on the horizon, it is easy to know which way is generally east. Now, with the sun high overhead, it's hard to tell. You don't want to wait until the sun is low in the west to show you the way back to camp, because that will leave you out on the trail after dark. What you need to do is allow the sun to move a little bit to reveal its east-west path. If you watch the way the shadows move as the sun courses across the sky, the direction becomes clear. Make a shadow by thrusting a stick in the ground at an angle, then observe the way the tip of the shadow moves as the sun travels. The taller the stick, the faster the shadow moves across the ground.

When you begin, use a small rock to mark the position of the tip of the shadow. Then wait a while and observe the way the shadow moves. After the shadow moves far enough to give a clear indication (give it twenty minutes or more), use a second stone to mark the new position of the shadow's tip. Draw a straight line between the two stones. This line points generally east and west. The first stone is to the west of the second. Take a sighting along your east-west line, spot a distant landmark, and head out.

By using succeeding landmarks and perhaps repeating the shadow-stick method another time or two, you should be able to walk a fairly straight course in your desired direction. Eventually, the sun will drop low enough to give a clear indication of west.

Maybe that was too simple. So, what if you want to hold a course to the southeast? It really doesn't matter which direction you want to go—the technique is still the same. Once you have established your east-west line, it's a simple process to use that line as a foundation, draw a compass face in the dirt, list all the directions, and head out to the southeast.

The hands of an analog wristwatch can be used to indicate direction. In the Northern Hemisphere, hold the watch horizontal and, using the current time, point the hour hand toward the direction of the sun. Bisect the angle between the hour hand and the twelve o'clock mark on the watch face, and that bisecting line will point south. In the Southern Hemisphere, the procedure is to aim the noon mark toward the sun. The midpoint between 12 and the hour hand indicates north.

If you wear a digital watch, no problem. See what time it is, then draw the face of an analog watch on a piece of paper, with the hands

TO determine direction without a compass, use a stick and mark the end of its shadow with a pebble. Every twenty minutes or so, mark the new end of the shadow with another pebble. The line between the pebbles will run east to west, with the first pebble being to the west of the last one.

South

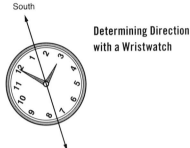

Determining Direction with a Wristwatch

AN analog wristwatch can be used to determine direction. In the Northern Hemisphere, aim the hour hand at the sun. Bisect the angle between the hour hand and the noon mark, and that line will point roughly southward. In the Southern Hemisphere, aim the noon mark at the sun. The midpoint between 12 and the hour hand will indicate north.

showing the correct current time. Hold the paper horizontal, and rotate it to point the hour hand toward the sun, as if you were using a real watch. Then just follow the same procedure as if you were dealing with a real analog watch. No paper and pencil? Draw the face of the clock on the ground with the numbers and hands in the proper relationships with the sun. If you're clever, you can even do this in your head, imagining the face of an analog watch.

There are other methods of making a rude compass—like magnetizing a needle and floating it on a chip of wood. Yes, it can be done, and if you were a POW escaping into unknown territory with only crude implements, maybe you would use something like that. But in the real world, it's much easier to carry a compass and a map than to carry a magnet and a needle.

Have I ever been lost? Yes, and it confused the daylights out of me. I always thought I was immune. Nobody's immune. So keep your eyes open, pay attention to what's around you, and watch your backtrail to identify landmarks you'll see coming back toward camp. In a perfect world you would always be prepared to navigate your way back to camp—hopefully with your trusty map and compass. But in an emergency, remember the tips you've read here.

Also remember that navigating after dark is not a good idea. It's too easy to get injured by stumbling over stuff in the dark. If you're caught away from camp at night, hunker down in a makeshift shelter, start a fire, and wait until morning to continue.

MAP AND COMPASS

The whole point of navigation is to move from one place to another safely. That applies to land navigation every bit as much as it does to aircraft or ships. If you are to move from one place to another safely, the first principle of navigation is that you must know where you are.

I can almost hear you shout, "What if I'm lost?" Yes, that does present a problem, but it doesn't diminish the absolute necessity of knowing where you are. I understand how contradictory this sounds, but the truth remains that if you don't know where you are, you don't know which way to go. Maybe this sounds like a chicken-and-egg conundrum, but the reality is that the first step in getting un-lost is to discover where you are. Until you know that, nothing else matters. When you do know that, the good news is that you're not quite as lost as you think you are.

Let's work from the top down. Unless you've been abducted by aliens, you're still on Earth. You also know what country you're in; you know which state or province; more than likely you know which county or parish. See, we're already zeroing in on your precise location. Let's take it a step farther. You probably know what little corner of real estate you're in—be it a national park, a particular forest, or land administered by the BLM (Bureau of Land Management). By now, you almost know where you are. The next trick is to pinpoint your location, so you can figure out where to go next.

Taking that next step requires that you have two pieces of equipment: a map of the area and a compass. Hopefully, the map is a highly detailed topographic one. Just having these things is no guarantee that you won't get lost. Unless you've been keeping a close eye on where you've been going, it is possible that even with a map and compass in your pocket you might not be able to pinpoint your location on the map. When that happens, you are lost, and we're back to the concept that if you don't know where you are, you don't know which way to go to get out of this situation. For the map and compass to be useful, you must determine your position on the map. To do this, you establish a "fix" on your position.

Step one in the process of obtaining a fix is to orient the map so the graphic representations of the landscape agree with what is actually on the ground. To do this, spread the map on the ground and place the compass on it. Now rotate the map until the top of it faces north, because maps are printed with north at the top. What you're trying to do is get both the map and the compass to agree on where north is.

MAP and compass are essential tools of navigation. Learn how to use them, and take them with you.

Once this has been done, the mountains, rivers, lakes, and other topographic features shown on the map will be properly oriented with the real mountains, rivers, and lakes around you.

Now that the map is oriented, look around and see if you can spot some prominent terrain features that are on the map. Depending upon where you are, you might not be able to spot the water of a river or lake, but a close study of the terrain might give you some clues such as dense foliage that grows near water.

If you are working with a topographic map, study the brown contour lines that indicate elevation changes that shape the terrain. Where the contour lines are close, the land is steep—where they are far apart, the landscape is relatively flat.

If you can see prominent terrain features, use them to get a fix on your position. Usable landmarks include peaks, a bend in the river, a lake cove, a unique ridge, or other easily identifiable features.

With a few terrain features identified, it's time to shoot some bearings with the compass. Begin by facing north so you are oriented with the map. This will help eliminate confusion as you spot distant landmarks. You must be oriented with the map in order for anything to make sense around you. Let's say, for example, that you see a peak in the distance to your right as you face north. Study the map to identify a prominent peak in the same general direction. If you think the real peak and the one on the map are the same, use the compass to shoot a bearing to the mountain. To shoot a bearing, hold the compass with the magnetic needle oriented to the 0-degree mark on the dial and then aim your eye across the compass at the landmark in question. Note the degrees on the dial corresponding to the direction you are looking. For the sake of argument, let's say the compass shows a bearing of 105 degrees to the peak. Draw a line on the map beginning at the peak and running a back azimuth (a back azimuth is the direction

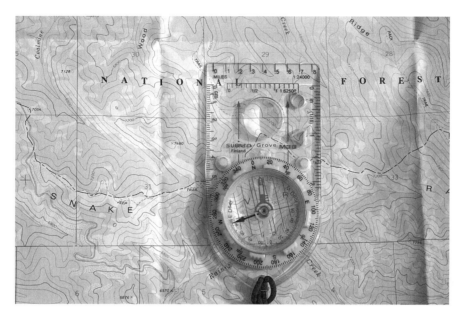

BECAUSE map grid lines are oriented toward grid north, and the compass indicates magnetic north, the map and compass must be oriented properly to each other to compensate for the difference.

exactly opposite) of 285 degrees (105 plus 180). In other words, draw a line on the map beginning at the peak and running in a direction of 285 degrees. In navigation terms, this line is called a *line of position*, or LOP, and you are somewhere on that line.

That's better than being totally lost, but it still doesn't pinpoint your location. The next step is to find out exactly where you are on that line. You do this by shooting one more bearing and drawing another LOP. To obtain the most accurate fix, shoot your second bearing at a terrain feature that lies between 60 and 120 degrees from the first one. Follow the same procedure to draw the second LOP, extending it far enough to intersect the first one. You are at the intersection of the two LOPs. At least it gives you a reasonable proximity of your location. If you can shoot more bearings, the accuracy of the fix increases.

All of the foregoing assumes that you are in terrain that allows you to see a great distance. The process is more difficult if you're deep in the woods and can't see distant landmarks. This is when you are forced to use less obvious terrain features. The brown contour lines on a topographic map indicate elevation changes, and these show the direction of water flow, hills, ridges, valleys, and other features. If you locate a swamp, a river, or lake, study the map, looking for those features. Then orient the map and try to get a fix on your location.

Even with all the foregoing accomplished, you still can't navigate with a high degree of precision unless you first factor in the difference between your local magnetic north variation and the true north grid that is depicted on the map. So that brings us to the next step. After you understand what is presented in the next discussion, take that information and insert it into the process of obtaining a fix. This is a chicken-and-egg thing, but you needed to understand the fundamental concept of obtaining a fix before you could know the value of calculating variation. So here goes.

Variation/Declination

OK, now for that word *variation*, which is also sometimes referred to as *declination*. It all begins with an explanation of true north and magnetic north and the way maps are drawn.

Because the world is a weird-shaped spheroid, it's impossible to make a map on flat paper that accurately represents the surface of the earth. A long time ago, two types of maps were created—one is called *polyconic*, because it slices up the sphere into many cone-shaped pieces of paper, which are then laid out next to each other to make a flat map. Problem is that, using polyconic projection, there are gaps between the slices at the north and south ends of the map.

The second is called *Mercator projection*, named after its inventor. Mercator maps are the most popular, but the problem with this type of map is that it projects the sphere onto a cylinder that is then opened up to make a flat map. The distortion at the north and south ends of the map is enormous. So you end up with a grid of longitude lines that run to true north (and south), and they're all parallel. In real life, the meridians become closer together the closer to the poles you get.

But that's only half the problem. The other half is that your compass doesn't care about true north; it only responds to magnetic north. And the magnetic force that attracts your compass needle is hundreds of miles from the geographic North Pole. To complicate matters, the magnetic pole moves a little bit every year.

What all of this means is that when you are using your map and compass, it is necessary to compensate for the variation (or declination; the terms are absolutely interchangeable) in magnetic north vs. true north. On topographic maps there is an information block showing the number of degrees of variation to use for calculations. The 0-degree meridian for variation in North America is on a line that runs roughly north and south through Chicago. This is where true north and magnetic north line up. If you are west of this meridian, the variation is easterly—if you are east of this line, the variation is westerly.

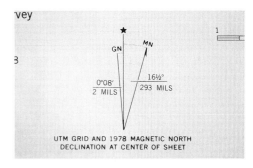

UTM GRID AND 1978 MAGNETIC NORTH DECLINATION AT CENTER OF SHEET

THE declination diagram on the map indicates how much variation there is between grid north (GN), true north (the star), and magnetic north (MN). The map and compass must be rotated until the compass needle matches the MN on the declination diagram.

So, what do you do with variation? When you used the compass to orient your map to magnetic north with the longitude grid lines in perfect agreement with the needle on your compass, the map was actually in error by the amount of variation. To correct for that error, rotate the map and compass (at the same time) either east or west to adjust for variation. Rotate until the compass needle points the proper number of degrees in the direction of the stated variation when viewed in relation to the grid lines on the map. Let me give an example: If I'm camping in the Olympic Mountains in Washington State, the map indicates a variation of approximately 20 degrees east. To compensate for variation and get the most accurate orientation, I rotate the map and compass counterclockwise until the compass needle is showing an angle 20 degrees to the east of the true north grid lines. Reverse the process if the variation is westerly.

If your compass features a rotating bezel, turn the bezel to match the variation for your location. A compass needle always points toward magnetic north, so it's impossible to adjust the needle. But by adjusting the bezel, you have a proper relationship between the map and compass.

Calculating for variation is important. If you depend on your compass to lead you to camp, you don't want to be off by 20 degrees. A navigation error of that magnitude, continued for a distance of five miles, would mean you miss camp by a mile and three-quarters.

Life in the electronic age makes the whole thing a lot easier. If you carry a GPS unit, you can continually fix your position with latitude and longitude readings, then transfer those to the map and see exactly where you are. We talk about GPS in length below and in Chapter 9 as well.

Only after you know your location can you use the map and compass to plan where you want to go. 'Cause, if you don't know where you are now, nothing else matters.

GPS: The Eye in the Sky

Outer space is keeping track of your every move. That might sound like the intro to a sci-fi B movie, but it's real. The eye in the sky is a constellation of satellites that keep in touch with your GPS, no matter where you wander.

GPS is the acronym that refers to the Global Positioning Satellite system—a cluster of twenty-four non-geosynchronous orbiting satellites that tell you where you are when you're wandering around, whether it's in an unfamiliar city or deep in the backcountry. The term *non-geosynchronous* indicates that the satellites do not maintain a constant position above the earth. Each satellite flies its own unique orbit about 11,000 miles high. With a total of twenty-four satellites in the network, and following their pattern of orbits as they do, there are always at least 6 satellites overhead to communicate with your GPS, no matter where you are on the planet.

GPS is a wonderful navigation tool, but it has its limitations. It's best to consider GPS as an additional tool to be used along with a map and compass—not as a replacement for a map and compass.

Surprise—you cannot use most GPS units as a compass. Even though they feature a "compass" page, they don't operate as real magnetic compasses, because they don't tell you what direction you are facing when you're standing still in the middle of Elk Meadow trying to decide which direction to go. The only time the compass function operates is while you are moving. There are a few high-dollar GPS units on the market that do include a fluxgate compass, but chances are the one you own now isn't one of those. If you think that owning a GPS allows you to get rid of the old map-and-compass techniques, I have news for you. An important reason to hang onto your maps and compass is that the GPS goes dead when the batteries are drained. But the batteries never die in a map and compass. Think of the GPS as a backup to the old reliable navigation equipment.

There are other good reasons why you still need to use a map, even if you have a GPS unit. A good topographic map is a detailed graphic representation of the earth's surface. If you transfer the coordinate information supplied by the GPS to your map, it's possible to pinpoint your position on the map. With your position identified, the next step is to study the map to see where you are in relation to other things—like the water source you need so you can keep from dying of thirst, or the dark and dismal swamp you heard old-timers warn against, or the end of the forest road where you intend to meet your buddy after the hunt. All that stuff (and more) is shown on the map, but not on the GPS. Even GPS units with downloadable maps do not show the detail you need to be able to make critical land navigation decisions, such as the steepness of the terrain and the locations of canyons, waterfalls, cliffs, swamps, and other topographic information that is vital to your route planning. All this is visible on the map, but not on the GPS unit.

While it's true that there are topographic map programs for GPS units, if you think that is an excuse to leave your paper map and your old-fashioned compass at home in the drawer while you head out into the backcountry, please back up and read what I said about electronic equipment taking a vacation when the batteries die. OK, you say, so I'll carry spare batteries instead of carrying my paper map and the clunky old compass. And my answer to that is, "What good will fresh batteries do if something else goes wrong with the electronic brains?" Hey, it happens all the time. Like the old saying goes, hydraulics are made to leak, and electronics are made to fail. OK, so I just made that up, but it's true nonetheless.

In order for the GPS to deliver coordinate information that is accurate for use with your topographic map, you must set the GPS datum to agree with the map datum. This is one of those easily resettable operations that takes only a few moments once you're in the "setup" mode of your GPS unit. The map datum information is found in a block of writing, usually in the lower left-hand corner of the map. It will say something like, "1927 North American datum." Here's where you check the GPS owner's manual. My Garmin datum menu lists "NAD27 CONUS" as the match for my topographic map's 1927 North American datum for the lower forty-eight states. Once you program your GPS unit to match the datum of the map, the GPS coordinate readout will be accurate for your map.

One of the most valuable functions of GPS is the waypoint. Waypoints are positions along the route that, for one reason or another, are important enough to mark on your virtual map. They are starting points (your camp), destinations you want to reach, and critical points in between where you might turn in another direction. A series of waypoints forms a route. The convenient aspect of GPS route planning is that you can sit at the dining room table at home and program waypoints before the trip begins. This is when the topographic map comes in handy, because if you mark waypoints without consulting the map, you invariably make serious navigational errors. The GPS does not know what type of terrain lies between one waypoint and another. You might plan a route that takes you directly across the Grand Canyon, and the GPS will obediently lay out the route without indicating the impossibility of the route. You must consult the map to avoid pitfalls along each leg of the route (the span between waypoints).

What if you are caught without a map—is a GPS unit any good to you? The answer is yes. If the GPS is switched on while you travel, it keeps track of your every turn. In a sense, it leaves an electronic trail of crumbs that you can backtrack to return to camp. As an example, while in camp you create a waypoint and name it "camp." When you leave camp, the GPS will keep track of your movements. Every now and then you can create and name new waypoints as you reach things like a fork in the trail, a river crossing, or some other important spot. Then, when you want to return to camp or to any other waypoints along the route, all you have to do is choose the name of the waypoint from the menu and follow the directions displayed on the GPS unit.

Never forget that a GPS unit is an electronic device that depends on battery power, so you should always carry spare batteries. If you're really paranoid (not necessarily a bad thing), carry a backup GPS unit in your pack. Of course, that one won't track your path unless it's turned on while you're on the move.

If you're serious about knowing where you are in the backcountry, always carry a detailed map of the area, a compass, and a GPS unit with spare batteries. Then practice using these tools, so they will work for you when you need them.

Buying a Compass and a GPS Unit

Get a compass with a rotating bezel that you can set up to compensate for local variation (also known as *declination*). Mine is a Suunto M-3G, and it features a magnifying glass (handy for reading tiny print as well as for starting a fire under bright sun), four different scales for calculating distances, and a lanyard so it doesn't get lost. How bad is that—a compass getting lost!

Now for the GPS. Mine is a Garmin GPS 76, nothing fancy. It's kind of big and clunky by today's standards, but it works marvelously. My backup is a compact and waterproof Garmin Geko 201. It doesn't matter whether you buy a Magellan or a Garmin or some other brand; this is a very competitive industry, and the technology is moving quickly toward smaller, lighter, and more feature-packed units. But you don't necessarily need lots of bells and whistles. Even the simplest late-model GPS does everything you need, and then some. WAAS (Wide Area Augmentation System) is the latest upgrade to accuracy of locating your position. Read the manual and practice the basic functions, so you know how to use the GPS when you need it most. (For further discussion of navigation equipment, see Chapter 9.)

A compass has the advantage of not needing batteries, but it does require skill to use. A GPS unit delivers unequalled precision of location and ease of operation, but it requires good batteries. It's best to have both in your survival gear.

RULES OF LAND NAVIGATION

On a faint trail in the Sierra Mountains, I learned an important lesson. We were a group of Boy Scouts on a campout that was led by a crusty old outdoorsman. We were hiking along a trail, when suddenly our leader held up one hand and pulled us to a halt. Then he pointed at something. There, in the shadow of the next log we were about to jump over, was a rattlesnake. I spent the rest of the hike carefully investigating every shadow and walking circumspectly around every obstacle. Believe it or not, that was a lesson in land navigation.

The aspect of land navigation we're going to discuss here is not about map and compass work—it's about the techniques that expert outdoorsmen use for moving over the ground efficiently with economy of energy and with minimal injury. Following are a few of the most important rules to this game.

Rule #1: Never Step on Anything You Can Step Over

This rule helps you avoid planting your foot on a moss-covered rock or the loose bark on a log, which might place your life and limb in danger when the ground underfoot suddenly slips. You avoid stepping on a boulder that may roll from underfoot. You avoid stepping on dry twigs that snap and spook the game you've been tracking or dead limbs that can twist your ankle. Trust me—it's a good rule.

Because it prevents so many problems, stepping over trail obstacles sounds like the ultimate land nav technique. But stepping over that log on the Sierra trail would have put us directly on top of a rattlesnake. When stepping over, it is vital to look at where your feet are going to come down and what's going to reach up and bite you in a tender spot. And that brings us to the second rule.

Rule #2: Never Step over Anything You Can Step Around

In every case, it's better to find a way around obstacles rather than to step over them. If you walk around rather than stepping over, you avoid the danger of losing your balance and taking a fall as you stretch your stride too far, or your foot comes down on something unstable.

NEVER step on anything you can step over. If you place your weight on the log, the bark might slip. If you step on a large rock, it might roll underfoot and throw you.

NEVER step over anything you can step around. Stepping over might throw you off balance or put you in danger of snakebite from an unseen serpent resting just beyond the log.

Stepping around allows you to walk naturally, so it minimizes the strain on muscles, joints, and tendons. And that translates to fewer sprains, pulls, tumbles, and other injuries. Besides, you look so much more cool still standing on your feet than lying flat on your back and writhing in agony.

Rule #3: Give Up Your Elevation Grudgingly

Relinquish your position on the high ground reluctantly. You worked hard to attain the elevation where you're standing, partway up the side of a mountain, and you don't want to give that up. Sometimes it is better to follow the contour of the earth when trying to maneuver to a new location than to go down and then back up. Think of it as walking around an object (in this case a dip in the earth's surface), rather than trying to walk across the decline and up the other side. It's true that you cover more distance staying on the high ground, but you actually expend less energy than by descending and then having to climb to the high ground again.

Rule #4: Mind Your Feet

It's easy to end up in a wreck if you don't pay attention to your footing. Watch out for loose sand or pebbles on a hard surface, because they act like ball bearings underfoot and can leave you on your back staring up through the trees, wondering what happened. And then there are the burrowing animals that create tunnels that break through and trap your foot, perhaps causing a stumble. Be cautious of puddles, because they can be deeper than they appear. Another hazard to be avoided is the moist surface along a riverbank that can actually be a quicksand bog.

When the surface is suspect, either take another route to avoid the danger altogether or at least step lightly to test the footing. If you don't trust the footing, don't commit all your weight to the next step until you are confident the surface is secure.

Rule #5: Look Up

We've been giving a lot of attention to our feet, but we also need to keep our eyes on the way ahead (and overhead) so we don't bang into anything. If we are too focused on the trail, it's easy to run headlong into overhanging branches or a rock outcropping suspended over the trail. These can pose a hazard to eyes and brain cells, depending upon how hard you whack into them.

Rule #6: Beware of Shadows

Since my episode in the Sierra Mountains as a boy, I'm always especially wary in snake country. To be safe, always inspect shaded areas around bushes and trees where the serpents are likely to hide out during the heat of the day. Snakes seek the shadows to stay cool when the sun is high, and those shadows might be under a log or beneath the shelf of a rock ledge. Be particularly careful where you put your hands while climbing around boulders. And for heaven's sake, watch where you sit down. You don't need any more holes in your backside.

Rule #7: About Glissading on the Scree . . .

Hiking across a sidehill can be dangerous. Gravity and loose soil or rocks conspire to bring you down (really). You have two choices when faced with having to cross a sidehill where there is no firm trail or where the trail is covered by a landslide. The first choice is to look around to see if there is an alternate route.

The second choice is to make a slide area work to your advantage. The technique is called *glissading on the scree* and is somewhat like skiing on the loose soil or shale. If you start high on the hillside, you can slide-step your way across, moving diagonally downslope as you go. With a little practice, this can be a fun (albeit risky) way to navigate a tough spot. The danger is that you may lose your balance, blow out an ankle, or trip and end up glissading on your head. Be forewarned. Your mileage may vary.

Crossing water

If we believe what is recorded in holy writ, by the ninth verse in the first chapter of Genesis, the water and land were divided. And before the end of the chapter, man showed up—who knows, perhaps with a fishing rod. It takes about seven chapters before we read anything about boats, and back in those days a chapter took a long, long time. So we might presume that people were wading across rivers since the beginning of history because they simply had no other way of making it across.

Not much has changed. We still find ourselves struggling, sometimes successfully, to get to the other bank for one reason or another. Every fisherman knows that the big ones live over there, just out of reach of the purest fly cast. Which is why we see men (most women seem to be too smart for this) standing anywhere from knee-deep to waist-deep in the middle of rivers. Every now and then, one of these *sapiens* disappears momentarily only to resurface somewhere downstream, refreshed, enlightened about something to do with the lubricity of mossy rocks, and trying for all he's worth to pretend that the maneuver was intentional and for the purpose of scouting the underwater pools for fish.

Well, we are not fooled. We all know the truth, and the truth is that wandering afoot in a river is asking for trouble. It can be such big trouble, in fact, that sometimes it leads to an unfortunate decline in the human population. So on these pages we want to talk about how to survive a river crossing.

The surest way to survive a river crossing is to do it in an airplane, or drive across a bridge, or something like that. But even I, supposedly an expert on such things, refuse to stay out of the water. You'll find me, fly rod in hand, gingerly making my way into the deeper and swifter water. And I have to confess that I've spent my share of time underwater—scouting the pools for fish, of course.

Not every river crossing is for fishing. Sometimes it's a matter of survival in an emergency situation when you really must get to the other side. Regardless of the reason, the proper techniques need to be employed. Perhaps the most important technique is to get an accurate assessment of the river. This makes all the difference. Don't underestimate the importance of water temperature, because extremely cold water causes such a shock to the system that it paralyzes you, leaving you unable to swim or grip things that might save your life. (For information on the dangers, prevention, and field treatment of cold-water immersion, review "Surviving Cold-Water Immersion" in Chapter 7.)

Next consider route. If possible, hike up and down the stream a ways and look for natural aids to crossing, such as shallows, a broad stretch that breaks the stream into several small channels, a fallen log that reaches bank to bank, or calm areas. On the same river, you may find a place that's so wide and shallow that you can walk across easily and another place where the water rages through rapids and tumbles over falls, so it pays to study the river before selecting a crossing site. If necessary, climb a hill that gives you a view up- and downriver so you can pick your spot. Avoid crossing where the current is strong and the water is above your knees.

It's possible that you will find a place where there are stepping stones that lead partway across. The temptation is strong to stay dry by using the stones, but there is the danger of slipping off a rock and taking a fall that will leave you injured. Sometimes it's best to just step into the water and wade across rather than risk the tumble.

Of particular importance are the entry and exit points. Make sure you pick a crossing spot that allows you to climb out of the water easily after you reach the other side. You don't want to find yourself in a deep cutbank that looks calm on the surface but is bottomless and swept by a strong current.

Study the crossing before entering the water, so you can pick your route across to avoid hazards such as a large rock with a powerful eddy on the downstream side that can suck you under. Try to identify underwater snags that might grab you and pull you down.

Once you've picked the perfect fording location, it's time to get yourself ready. If you're going to be able to wade across, consider removing your clothing and carrying it above your head so you'll have dry clothes to get into once you reach the other side. At the very least, remove your socks and put your boots back on so you don't risk injuring your feet on sharp rocks and snags. The dry socks will be welcome on the other bank when you pour out the water and hike the boots dry. If you are carrying a pack, as a matter of safety, unbuckle the waistband and loosen the shoulder straps so you can ditch the bag quickly if you get swept off your feet by the current. If you do take a fall, try to hold onto the pack, if it floats, and use it to stabilize yourself, but don't die trying to save your gear; let go of it if it threatens to drag you down. After your crossing, you might find the bag snagged in the brush along the bank downstream and be able to recover your equipment.

Wading across is easier if you use a long pole to help stabilize yourself as the current is trying to sweep your feet and legs from under you. Probe the water ahead for solid footing, holes, snags, or hidden boulders. Face toward the current and keep the pole on the upstream side (in the direction opposite to the flow of the stream), because in this position the current helps hold you down rather than lifting weight off your feet.

If possible, select a route that leads at an angle upstream to an ideal exit point, because you have less tendency to be swept off your feet if you wade while facing the flow of current. Make sure each step is steady before taking the next. Shuffle your feet, rather than taking strides; try to keep your feet always in contact with the streambed. If you lose your footing and get swept away by the current, chances of regaining your feet are slim. If that happens, consider yourself to be

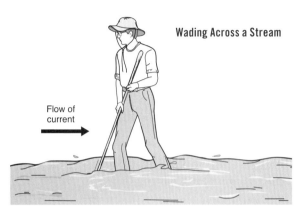

Wading Across a Stream

Flow of current

TO wade across a swift stream, use a pole on the up-current side. By planting the pole on the stream bottom, you help maintain balance and actually increase the weight on your feet, thus keeping them more firmly planted and less likely to be swept out from under you.

swimming. If you find yourself in this situation, position yourself on your back with your feet going downstream first. This helps protect you against impacts with rocks and submerged snags. Use your hands to try to paddle and guide yourself toward the far bank. In deeper rapids, swim more aggressively on your stomach and try to guide yourself into currents that help carry you to the chosen exit point.

If several people are crossing, and if there is a rope of sufficient length available, secure one end on the near bank, then have the first person swim or wade the rope across and secure it to the far side. If he loses his footing, pull him back to the near shore with the rope. With the rope all the way across the river, use it as a safety line for the rest to hold onto while crossing. The last one across releases the rope from his side, and if he loses his footing, the others can pull him across while he holds onto the rope.

If you need to cross a small lake—with emphasis on *small*—or a narrow river in which there is little to no current and the water is deep, there is a way to cross with relative safety as long as the water is not too cold and as long as you are equipped with some kind of flotation device. I'm not talking about swimming across; most people think they can swim a lot farther than they can, but by the time they discover the truth, it's too late. Don't even consider swimming. I'm talking about making a crossing with the aid of a flotation device.

NOTE OF CAUTION: Under no condition should you attempt to cross a large lake or a wide river, because the risk of drowning is extremely high. Review the information in Chapter 7 about cold-water-immersion hypothermia if you think I'm being overly cautious. This stuff is a killer. It is always better to search for an alternate route that doesn't force you to cross a body of water. But, if you have no other options and the situ-

ation demands that you *do* cross, you must utilize the safest technique possible.

To make the crossing easier, remove your clothes so you don't have to fight the weight of sodden clothing. Not only that, but clothing creates a lot of drag in the water and will slow your progress. You want to be sleek and hydrodynamic so you can move through the water with minimal effort.

If you have a plastic bag, an emergency blanket, or a rain poncho, use it to tightly wrap your clothes and other equipment to keep everything dry while you cross. As you seal up the package, leave some air inside, but then double the open edges over and over again on themselves to create a watertight seal. With some air inside, the bundle will become your flotation device. If you decide to swim on your back, wrap one arm over the bundle and hold it tight to your chest to keep yourself afloat while you kick with your legs and stroke with your free arm. If you cross on your stomach, hold the bundle ahead of you with one hand and use the other one for stroking. Kicking adds minimal propulsion, but because it uses the large muscles of the legs, it tires you out quickly. Protect the integrity of the bundle with your life, because without it you may lose your life.

When you reach the far shore, be careful to avoid injuring your bare feet as you scramble onto dry ground. Dry off quickly, get back into your clothes, and you're on your way.

Equipment

9

In any discussion about outdoor gear, the question naturally arises about what constitutes a suitable survival kit. What should be included? What is most likely to be needed in any given situation, and what items are mostly just gimmicks? To answer these questions, let's use our imaginations in an attempt to foresee what conditions are like when the survival kit is used. This helps us understand what kit items are actually useful.

SURVIVAL KITS

A survival kit is assembled with one thought in mind—if I have to spend the night in the woods with nothing but this stuff, what do I need? Obviously, one kit does not fit all situations. I have one for my backcountry skiing adventures, a completely different one for summer

A fanny pack is an excellent way to carry a comprehensive survival kit. The water bottle holders on each side give the user a convenient way to carry the day's ration of water, and a couple of straps make it possible to lash on a jacket.

hiking, and yet another one for mountain biking. The differences between these kits are reflections of the seasons when these activities take place and the space available. The winter kit requires a larger fanny pack than the summer hiking kit because of the additional clothing and food items carried. And the backcountry biking kit includes things like tubes, patch kits, and tools that are specific to the bike.

But regardless of the specific differences, the overall similarity between the kits is striking. Each has something that can be used to make a shelter—a shiny foil Space Blanket, pocket poncho, some heavy-duty twine. Each has fire starters. Each has a signal mirror and whistle. Each has emergency food rations in the form of GORP or granola bars. Each has a small LED flashlight and extra batteries. Each has a folding knife. Each has a first-aid kit.

When it comes to specific differences, the summer kit has a small container of bug repellent, which is unnecessary baggage in the winter kit. The winter kit, on the other hand, has spare socks, a neoprene face mask, spare glove liners, and more high-calorie food.

As we go through the process of analyzing what needs to be included in a survival kit, it becomes obvious that a homemade kit can be far superior to a store-bought one, if for no other reason than that the individual who is assembling the kit becomes familiar with everything that is inside. Too often, people who buy ready-made kits assume that because it was assembled by "professionals" it must be perfect. They never look through its contents until an emergency situation arises. How disappointing it would be to sit huddled against a relentless freezing wind on the exposed face of a mountainside, only to discover that whoever assembled your survival kit didn't think to include an emergency blanket to help ward off hypothermia.

While certain items in a kit can be shared among a group, each person in the party should carry other pieces of equipment. How many people can really take advantage of one Space Blanket, for example? Every person should carry his or her own personal survival kit, and every person should know exactly what is in the kit and how to use the equipment. Don't leave children out of the equation. Familiarize them with their own kits, and train them in the use of every item in the kit.

Assembling a survival kit is a project that requires your personal attention. There's no such thing as a perfect kit that you can buy off the shelf with everything in it you need. On the other hand, there are some store-bought kits that make a nice addition to the rest of the stuff you pack into your personalized survival gear. Some of the items in my own kit came as component parts of the Ultimate Survival Deluxe Tool Kit marketed by Ultimate Survival Technologies (www.ultimatesurvival .com). The kit includes a BlastMatch Fire Starter, WetFire Tinder, a StarFlash Signal Mirror, a JetScream Whistle, and a SaberCut Saw. But other than this, I assembled the rest of my kit one item at a time.

My kits have evolved over time, and so has the way I carry them. One of my favorite methods of carry is in a fanny pack that's flanked by two water bottle holders. Attached to the wide waist belt are two net pockets that zip closed. Across the back is a compression strap that also serves as a place to tie a vest, and beneath the pack are two straps where I can tie a jacket. But I also have a kit that is spread out among the many pockets of a great hiking vest made by Filson. And there are times when I stuff everything into the pockets of my zip-off cargo pants. How you carry your gear is less important than the fact that you actually do carry it. Just make sure you always remember to take the essentials.

Now, let's take a look inside. Here's what I carry.

A vest or jacket with multiple pockets will carry a limited inventory of survival equipment. Essential gear, such as fire starters, should be carried in every item of clothing so you're never without.

A lightweight cable saw is a nice addition to a survival kit, because it allows you to cut wood that is too large to handle with a knife. This is especially useful for cutting poles for a shelter.

FIXED-BLADE and folding knives are among the most important items of survival gear. With a good knife, you can fashion materials and tools to start a fire, build a shelter, make traps, dig for water, and do many other critical chores.

Knife

On my belt, I hang a sturdy fixed-blade knife. I don't count that as part of my survival kit, but rather part of my normal outdoor equipment. For the kit, my preference is a folding knife with a blade that is strong enough to cut small saplings that can be used in shelter construction and sharp enough to whittle fuzz sticks for building a fire. Look for a folding model that is compact yet sturdy. For more serious woodcutting chores, I have a cable saw that consists of a short length of saw cable with hand grips at each end. I use this for cutting wood that is too large to be handled by the knife.

Multitool

In addition to my knife, I have a multitool that also offers a knife as part of its collection of handy tools. You can never have too many knives; that's my theory. The multitool I carry on my belt is a Leatherman Surge, which features four useful tools that can be accessed without even opening the handles: a razor-edge knife, a serrated knife, a saw, and a scissor. After opening the handles, the remaining tools include needle-nose pliers, wire cutters, can opener, awl, and a variety of screwdrivers. The reason a multitool is so important is that if I had to disassemble parts of a vehicle to scavenge items that could be used in a survival situation, this is the tool that would be most useful. The same would hold true if I happened upon some trash (discarded metal items) that could be fashioned into useful implements for catching and boiling water, among other uses.

A multitool with a knife blade, saw, pliers, scissors, and a variety of other tools can be handy in a survival situation.

For the record, my wife carries a SwissTool Spirit by Victorinox. She likes it because it's compact, lightweight, and smooth as silk but still offers all the benefits of a heavier unit. It fits her hand better than my big Leatherman. In addition to these, we also have multitools in each of our vehicles; one is the Diesel model made by Gerber and the other is the PowerLock made by SOG. Why so many different kinds? We collected them over the years and they are all excellent, so we put them where we can always have access to one.

Signaling

No matter which kit I'm carrying, I always have a signal mirror and a whistle. To determine the long-range effectiveness of the mirror, I conducted some field tests in which I used it to beam a signal from a mountaintop and across a wide valley, a distance of several miles. At a predetermined time of day, a buddy looked toward the mountain I was climbing, caught my signal, and signaled back, so I knew the message was received. The mirror is so effective that a search-and-rescue airplane would be within range of the reflected signal all the way to the horizon. There isn't another type of daylight-visible signal that would carry as far and be so lightweight or inexpensive. Some mirrors

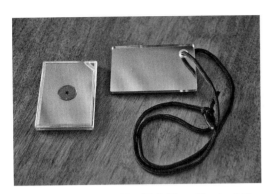

SIGNAL mirrors are available with (left) or without a sighting hole in the center. Some have a red reflective surface on the back, so you can use a flashlight against it at night to beam a red flash that can be seen for miles.

have a sighting hole in the middle that aids sighting on the target. There are mirrors that have a normal reflective surface on one side and a red reflective surface on the opposite side. By shining a flashlight at the red surface at night, you can beam a very noticeable red flash at the target.

The whistle I keep in my kit is functional whether it is wet or dry and creates a far better audible alarm than can be delivered by yelling for help. The piercing cry of the whistle will carry farther, and it is less fatiguing to blow the whistle than to shout for help. Not only that, but the sound of one's own voice screaming in desperation is enough to drive some people into a panic.

A cell phone works in some hunting and fishing locations, but it is not reliable under all conditions, especially in remote areas. A cell phone or FRS/GMRS radio—these two-way handheld radios use the radio frequency bands allocated for Family Radio Service/General Mobile Radio Service and have a range of up to 5 to 10 miles or so, depending upon terrain—or my handheld ham radio may find its way into my pocket, but these items are not carried as a routine component of my survival kit. The stuff that is in the kit stays in the fanny pack 24/7. I can't leave the phone or radio in the fanny pack indefinitely without the batteries going bad. So the electronic signaling devices are carried separately.

In a life-or-death emergency, there is nothing to compare with a personal locator beacon (PLB) when you need to call in the search-and-rescue teams to save your life. With the ability to transmit your exact GPS coordinates to rescuers via a satellite system, the PLB is one item that should (in my opinion) be in every survival kit. Always make sure the batteries are in good condition before leaving for the backcountry. Have the unit serviced, if necessary, before the trip. (Review Chapter 6 for in-depth discussion of signaling techniques.)

WATERPROOF/WINDPROOF matches in a sealed case and an inexpensive lighter are easy to stow in shirts and pants pockets, so you are never without a means of starting a fire. Tear off the striker panel from the matchbox and keep it in the container, because the striker on the bottom of the match case won't work with these special matches.

IN another pocket, carry a flint and steel set like this BlastMatch and some accelerant-type tinder material such as WetFire. With this equipment, you'll always be able to get a fire going, even in foul weather.

Fire Gear

Because the ability to start a fire is so important in a survival situation, I carry redundant systems and spread them throughout my clothing so I'll always have at least one with me no matter how I'm dressed. In my pack are an inexpensive Scripto Piezo lighter (look for this at the checkout of your local grocery store) and a small container filled with water- and windproof matches. What I like about this lighter is its range of adjustability, from a wee little flame to an outright flame-thrower. And the Piezo igniter is easy to operate, even with stiff, cold fingers. The water- and windproof matches are carried in a waterproof container. In a pants pocket I carry a BlastMatch Fire Starter and some WetFire Tinder fire-starting cubes that (as their name indicates) burn even when wet. Call me paranoid, but I *do* like to be able to start a fire when I need one! So in a shirt pocket is a Brunton Helios windproof butane lighter. (Chapter 3 provides a thorough overview of many methods of fire starting, with and without store-bought equipment.)

Shelter

Shelter is an absolute necessity. As with some other aspects of my kit, I carry redundant shelter items: a Heatsheets Emergency Bivvy made by

A good survival kit should include shelter items such as a tube tent (left). If you don't have space for that, consider taking a Heatsheets Emergency Bivvy, which is shaped like a sleeping bag (right). At the very minimum, carry a pocket poncho.

Adventure Medical (www.adventuremedicalkits.com), a pocket poncho, and a tube tent. I also carry a few yards of ⅛-inch nylon rope to help with shelter building. (Review Chapter 2 for a complete discussion of shelter in the backcountry.)

Water

In addition to the water bottles attached to the fanny pack, I take a water filter that is capable of eliminating harmful organisms such as *Giardia* and *Cryptosporidium* and processes water directly into my water bottles. (Review Chapter 4 for a complete discussion of water-finding and purification in the wild.)

Food

I have felt the debilitating effect of "hitting the wall" or "bonking" as it is known among endurance athletes. That's what happens when the body runs out of fuel, and it leaves you pretty helpless. To avoid that, I carry GORP blended with M&Ms in a plastic zip baggie. That's OK to keep me going for a little while, but for long-term survival, I need the ability to catch food, so I have a small spool of monofilament fishing line and an assortment of hooks. The plan is to catch bugs or worms to use as bait, if the need arises. Or, a bit of feather and hair can be fashioned into a "fly" for lure fishing. It doesn't hurt to learn the art of fly tying, so you can build your own in the wilds. (You'll find an overview of food and food safety in Chapter 5.)

Navigation

When I'm exploring the hinterlands, I always carry a good compass and a topographic map of the area. The compass has a lanyard, so it hangs easily around my neck. The map is kept in a zip-up plastic baggie, for protection from the elements.

A GPS is a wonderful navigation tool, so for my outings, I carry my small Garmin Geko in my pocket. Extra batteries are a must.

One reason for the map and compass in addition to the GPS is that I already know what it's like to witness a malfunction of technology that leaves a GPS staring blankly back at me when the batteries bonk. The compass never does that. (Chapter 8 provides detailed instructions for using dead reckoning, the position of the sun, a map and compass, and/or a GPS unit to navigate through the wilderness.)

Flashlight

I carry a small LED flashlight and a set of spare batteries. LEDs draw less power than incandescent bulbs, so this type of flashlight will operate longer on a set of batteries than a conventional flashlight. And there is virtually no worry about the bulb burning out, because LEDs are rated at about 100,000 hours of use. It's a good idea to have a lanyard on the flashlight to prevent accidentally dropping it if you lose your grip.

First Aid

A small first-aid kit is part of the survival kit. In my kit is an assortment of adhesive bandages and sterile compresses, a few antiseptic towelettes, toilet paper,

TO protect your navigation equipment, keep the map in a zip-up baggie and have the compass in the pocket of an article of clothing you never leave behind in camp. A lanyard on the compass allows you to sling it around your neck, where it's always available.

PART of any good survival kit is a compact flashlight and a spare set of batteries. Rotate the batteries periodically, even if they haven't been used, to make sure you're not carrying dead cells.

FIRST-AID supplies should be close at hand, so you can grab them quickly in an emergency. A small kit carried on the belt is convenient. Customize the kit to include any special medical items you need.

sunscreen, and bug repellent. Those who have special medical conditions should include up-to-date medications or other supplies to handle their particular needs. In addition to a larger kit that is used in camp, a small kit can be affixed to your belt, which ensures that you always have it with you. (Review Chapter 7 for field treatment of medical emergencies.)

For the vehicle

You never know when an emergency situation will occur, so it's a good idea to have a basic survival kit that is always carried in the vehicle. Over the decades of wandering some pretty marginal back roads, Becky and I have ended up stranded a few times. Out of those experiences, we have developed a list of items that should always be carried in the vehicle. The list can be expanded, of course, but this covers the basics. We keep our stuff in a small duffel bag and transfer it from one vehicle to another as needed. In our vehicle-based kit we carry the following items that cover all the bases—signaling, water, food, shelter, fire, first aid, sanitation, and general safety:

- ▶ cell phone (Actually, we don't keep the cell phone in the kit, but we always make sure we have it with us when we travel.)
- ▶ personal locator beacon, also transferred to other survival kits as needed
- ▶ drinking water
- ▶ food (jerky, granola bars)
- ▶ fire starters
- ▶ Space Blanket for each of us
- ▶ pocket poncho for each of us
- ▶ multitool/knife
- ▶ camp cup for emergency cooking or boiling water
- ▶ windup flashlight
- ▶ small first-aid kit

- liquid camp soap
- toilet paper
- hand-sanitizer wipes

PROFICIENCY

No matter how complete your survival kit is, the equipment alone is worthless unless you know how to use each piece. It's important that you practice starting fires, go into the outback and do some orienteering with map and compass, and obtain some training in proper emergency medical techniques. Then, after all the training and practice, when you buckle on your fanny pack or load your cargo pants pockets with a well-thought-out and assembled survival kit, you will know you've given yourself a better chance of handling any situation that comes up.

THE SURVIVAL KNIFE

If I had to choose only one piece of gear to take into a survival situation, I would choose a knife. A strong, sharp knife allows me to make just about everything else I need. It can be used to help make a shelter. I can fashion the tools necessary to start a fire and build primitive traps from available resources, dig edible roots, excavate for subsurface groundwater, and assist with other projects. Indeed, the uses to which a proper survival knife can be put are limited only by the ingenuity of the user. The knife must be spared from abuse, such as using the blade to dig in the ground, which subsequently diminishes its cutting ability. For

RATHER than ruining your knife by using it to dig for water or digging roots out of the ground for food, make a digging stick by sharpening one end of a stout stick into a chisel shape that can penetrate the soil.

a job like that, use the knife to construct a digging stick. Don't use the knife as a weapon to be thrown at game, but use it to make a throwing stick for hunting small animals. The same concept carries over to other chores—whenever possible, preserve the knife by making other tools to do the kind of work that might damage the blade.

But what is it about a knife that makes it suitable for the heavy demands of a survival lifestyle? In the next couple of pages, I'll take a stab at answering that question. A survival knife is a piece of equipment in which function definitely takes priority over form. It doesn't matter what the knife looks like; all that matters is what it will do. As I mention the most critical qualities of a survival knife, I am not putting them in any particular order of priority, because they are all important.

Blade Material

As you might expect, the blade is the most important part of a survival knife. The rigors of a survival lifestyle are so demanding that the blade must be tougher than normal. It must have excellent edge-holding ability and be corrosion resistant. Knife metallurgy is a deep and ever-evolving science. The quick and dirty answer to the question about what makes a good knife is that a stainless steel blade manufactured from one of the 440A, 440B, or 440C categories is a good choice.

Blade Geometry

The best knives have a full-length tang that extends all the way to a hefty pommel. In a pinch, a heavy pommel can function as a hammer to crush bone or stone, or to drive home a structural peg in the fabrication of a shelter or primitive tools. The blade of a good knife has aggressive serration for sawing through small limbs. The back of the blade is broad, forming a stout spine that can be hammered upon without suffering damage. Such a knife is the primary tool for splitting firewood or chopping through a tree limb. The blade has a sharp point that can be used as a primitive drill or serve as a spear when lashed to a pole. The body of the blade must offer excellent slicing ability, hold an edge, and be easy to sharpen. Ideally, you should strike a balance in

IN addition to being made of quality steel, a good survival knife should have a combination blade that provides the sharp slicing characteristics of a plain edge and the sawing characteristics of a serrated blade.

THE back of the blade must be strong to withstand the pounding that is sometimes required to chop through limbs or split wood. A full-length tang that goes all the way through the handle is essential.

the amount of blade that is smooth edged and the portion that is serrated. You need both.

Grip

In a survival situation, it is not uncommon to be wet. Using a knife with wet hands and a wet grip can be dangerous. If the grip slips, the knife can instantly turn from tool to weapon, inflicting injury to yourself. For this reason, the grip must be made in such a way that it does not become slippery when wet. Knife manufacturers try to accomplish this by shaping the grip in a certain way, employing contours to fit between fingers, texturing the grip with aggressive cross-checking, and using materials that are particularly "grippy." When looking for a knife with a good grip, first find a knife that feels comfortable and under control in your hand. Next, do a wet test. This might be difficult in the store, but ask the salesclerk if you can soak your hands and then see how the knife grip feels. The grip material must be tough enough to take a beating without falling apart. A good-looking grip that breaks down when the knife is pressed into service as an axe isn't worth having.

Size

If you saw the movie, you know that Crocodile Dundee's knife was overkill. (Apparently, in Hollywood the only thing that matters is size.)

But in reality, size does matter. Your survival knife must be big enough and hefty enough to use as a hatchet, a chisel, a pry bar, a hammer, or a digging tool. To save the blade from the abuse of digging roots out of the ground or slinging it at slow animals, use the knife to carve from wood a few other tools such as a digging stick and a throwing stick. Still, you

THE sheath should be very strong, so the blade cannot penetrate and cause injury to the wearer. Some sheaths feature sharpening stones and small pouches for additional supplies.

never know what's going to happen when you're living a survival lifestyle, so the knife shouldn't be a wimp about it.

Sheath and Accessories

Whether you use a folding or a fixed-blade model, you need a protective sheath that holds the knife fast, so it won't fall out. What I mean by "protective sheath" is one that protects the knife but also protects you from injury. My first fixed-blade knife came with a thin, leather sheath. After several months of daily outdoor use, the blade finally pushed through the leather and jabbed me in the leg. The fixed-blade knives I own now are kept in hard sheaths that have an attached sharpening stone. And speaking of the sheath being a multipurpose accessory, on the sheath of my favorite knife there is a pouch for carrying a disposable lighter.

Keeping Your Knife Sharp

If you're going to have a knife, you should keep it sharp, otherwise the thing is only dead weight, and dangerous dead weight at that. It's a fact that a dull knife is not only next to useless, but it's also more likely to cause an injury than a sharp one. A sharp knife is easier to cut with, requiring less forced and awkward motion that can result in the blade slipping or jumping in an unwanted direction.

At first glance, it may appear utterly simple to sharpen a knife blade—just slide it along a sharpening stone a few times until the edge gets shiny again and you can feel the sharpness as you run your thumb across the edge, right? Well, it's not quite that simple. There are actually a few techniques involved in sharpening a blade to help you get a proper edge on it and help it stay sharp longer.

KEEP your knife sharp with a high-quality sharpening kit that helps maintain the proper edge angle.

First, it's important to have the right equipment. For restoring a blade on an outdoor utility knife, use a selection of sharpening stones of different grits. A coarse stone (300 to 400 grit) removes more metal from the blade and leaves micro-serrations. A fine stone (600 grit or higher) polishes the edge. Depending upon your use of the knife, a coarse edge may be preferable to a highly polished one, as the serrations aid in cutting some materials such as rope and wood. Of course, if you're shaving with your knife like Crocodile Dundee, you want a nice polished edge. A 1,200-grit stone gives an extra fine finish.

Some knife experts argue for, and others argue against, the use of honing oil on the stones. Those in favor say it lubricates during sharpening and holds in suspension the metal residue removed from the blade, preventing it from clogging the stone. Those against say the sharpening process goes faster due to higher abrasion between blade and stone if no oil is used. They also say that an oiled stone actually clogs more easily and that if you never use oil on the stone it won't clog. So, the choice is yours, to oil or not to oil. But if you have ever oiled your stone, you must continue to do so or it will surely clog. If you choose to oil, use the best honing oil you can buy, like Buck or Smith's. Do not use a lesser-grade lubricating oil, because it will damage and clog the stone.

OK, so now you have your knife, your stone(s), and maybe your oil. If you're going to use oil, place a small amount on the stone before you begin the actual sharpening process.

Place the blade edge on the stone and prepare to sharpen. Now comes another controversy—at what angle do you hold the blade in relation to the stone? The folks at Buck say that an angle of 10 to 20 degrees gives you a perfect edge. Another source says the angle must be 23 degrees. Yet another says the angle depends entirely on what you're trying to accomplish, because a thin blade edge created by a low angle is too fragile for heavy work, and a thick edge created by a high angle is too gross for fine cutting. A chisel edge, like a razor blade, has one fine angle of around 12 degrees. A double-grind is typically used for utility knives and has a compound edge with two angles (15 to 18 degrees for the fine angle and 20 to 23 degrees for the grosser angle). As a knife owner, you are perfectly within your rights to alter the factory angle of the blade edge to suit your needs. But regardless of the edge angle you choose, the rest of the sharpening process remains the same.

What you are trying to accomplish with the sharpening process is to remove enough metal, first from one side of the blade and then from the other, to create a burr, sometimes referred to as a *wire*, along the edge of the blade. And this cannot be done by following a five-strokes-on-one-side-then-five-strokes-on-the-other-side routine.

Here's how to get the edge you want. Lay the blade edge on the stone at the angle you decide is right for your purposes. Sharpening kits are available that include aids to help you maintain blade angle. One type of aid is nothing more than a plastic 23-degree wedge that you place on one end of the stone. You lay the blade on the wedge to obtain an initial angle, then you try to maintain that angle during the sharpening process. Another kit utilizes a more elaborate system, with a clamp for the knife blade and angle guides for the stones as they are moved across the blade.

Many experienced knife owners, however, prefer to use nothing but a stone and the blade, feeling the angle in their hands and learning to know when it's right. To help maintain the same angle throughout the sharpening stroke, the pad of the thumb can serve as a spacer between the blade spine and the stone. Move the entire length of the blade over the stone, edge first, as if you were attempting to slice a thin piece of the stone away, always making sure to maintain the same blade angle to the stone. Count your strokes and repeat this shaving action over and over again on the same side of the blade until a burr forms on the side of the edge that is opposite the contact with the stone. It may take twenty strokes, it may take fifty strokes, depending upon the pressure applied—it doesn't matter, keep going until the burr forms. You will be able to feel this burr if you run your thumb crossways over the blade from the side on which the burr is forming. Now, switch sides and repeat the same number of strokes on the opposite edge, still making sure to maintain the same angle to the stone.

Once the burr is created, switch to a finer stone to smooth the edge and remove the burr. Repeatedly slice the full length of the blade along the finer stone, but this time alternate sides with each stroke, maintaining the same stone-to-blade angle throughout the process.

It is sometimes possible to end up with what you believe is an incredibly sharp edge, only to have the blade become dull quite quickly under use. This is probably because the burr was never completely removed and you had what is called a wire edge. The blade may feel razor sharp, but the burr can break off and leave a blunt edge. To prevent that, make sure the burr is totally removed while honing with the fine stone. The final few strokes toward the end of the process should become progressively lighter to avoid raising another burr.

It's easier to keep a knife sharp once the edge is properly honed than it is to bring it from dull to sharp. Don't wait for the edge to become too dull before you resharpen. Look at it this way—keeping your knife sharp is kind of fun and semi-heroic in a Hollywood sort of way. After all, there's nothing like sitting around the campfire with blade and stone in hand, listening to the soft "swick-swick" of steel on stone, working toward the day your knife is sharp enough to do a Croc Dundee impersonation with it.

ROPE AND KNOTS

One day your life might depend on a rope being in good condition and your knowledge of how to use it in the right way. There are only a few rules to follow to make sure your rope is in always in good condition and ready for use.

Five Rules of Rope Care

1. The first rule is to keep your rope clean. Dirt particles, if examined under a microscope, look like jagged rocks. Because these particles are small, they work their way inside, where they come in contact with the individual fibers. When that happens, the jagged edges cut the fibers, weakening the rope from the inside, where you can't see the damage. Keeping the rope clean is more for safety than for tidiness. To clean a rope, place it in a mesh bag (to keep it from tangling with itself in the washing machine) and wash it in warm freshwater. If you do this at home, add a touch of fabric softener. This lifts out the dirt and softens the fibers so the rope is more supple. After washing, rinse twice, then store the rope in loose coils.

2. Never step on a rope. Stepping on a rope spreads some fibers and compresses others. The spreading and compressing action deforms the lay of the strands, allowing dirt to work deep into the structure. Not only that, but the sharp edges of a boot sole or something sharp beneath the rope can cause physical damage to the rope as it is stepped on.

3. Don't allow kinks or tangles in the rope. Kinks, knots, and tangles weaken the fibers, which weakens the overall rope. Before adding a load to a rope, make sure there are no kinks or tangles. Remove knots when they are no longer needed.

4. Guard against chafe. Chafing is a form of exterior wear damage caused by friction of the rope against something hard, sharp, or rough. If a rope must come in contact with a potentially damaging surface, it is important to provide chafe protection. This can be something as low tech as running the rope through a piece of cut-off garden hose that serves as a shield between the rope and the rough surface. Wrappings of leather, cloth, rubber, or other materials also make good chafe protection.

DON'T just throw your valuable rope down in a heap. Coil it properly, and hang it up for storage out of direct sunlight and in a dry place.

5. Stow your ropes properly. Some ropes are very sensitive to direct sunlight and can be damaged by UV rays, which shortens life (the rope's life and perhaps your own, if your life depends on that rope). Coil your ropes, and hang them loosely in a sheltered storage place. Allow air to pass around and between the loops to help keep them dry. Store ropes away from chemicals, which can damage fibers.

If these basic procedures are followed routinely, ropes will last longer and deliver better service throughout their life.

Knots You Can Bet Your Life On

Do you know how to tie a square knot? Would you bet your life on it? Those two questions were among a list of others asked at a recent Eagle Scout board of review. While we personally may not be testing for such a distinguished award, those questions and the demonstration that followed made me think how important it is to be able to tie a secure knot when necessary. It could even be a matter of survival.

Square Knot. Let's take a look at the venerable square knot, as an example. Properly done, this is one of the simplest and most basic methods of tying a knot that won't slip but can be easily untied. It is used to join two pieces of rope that are nearly the same diameter. Let's say, for ease of explanation, that you're joining a red and a blue rope of the same diameter using a square knot. Begin by facing the ends of the two ropes toward each other, then simply tie an overhand in one direction, then turn the short ends back to face each other and tie a mirror-image overhand in the other direction—forming a loop at each side of the knot. (If this sounds too complicated, remember left over right, then right over left.) If done correctly, the blue rope loop at one side passes over two straight lengths of red rope (one of which will be the short "running" end of the red rope and the other will be the long "standing" end of the same rope). At the opposite side of the knot, the red loop passes beneath the two parallel blue ropes (one of which will be the short "running" end of the blue rope and the other will be the long "standing" end of the blue rope).

This knot is supposed to be immediately identifiable simply by looking to see that the loops at each side pass properly over or under the parallel running and standing ends of the respective opposite ropes. Everyone knows that if the loop has one rope running over and one running under, it's an untrustworthy granny knot—not a square knot. However, not everyone is aware that what looks, at first glance, like a perfect square knot may actually be a "fool's" knot—a false square knot

THE square knot has each set of short and long tails exiting on the same side of their respective loops and also on the same side of the knot as their respective twin tail.

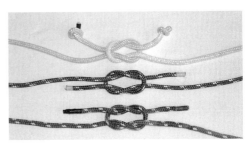

THE square knot (top), the fool's knot (center), and the granny knot (bottom) all have the same basic appearance. But study the knots and see how the short tails exit each knot differently and how the loops are arranged differently in relation to the running (short) and standing (long) tails.

that has a built-in fatal flaw. Fatal flaws are not good, especially when your life depends on a knot holding securely. Here's how to tell the difference between a square knot and a fool's knot.

When the knot is tied, look at it to see if both the running ends (the short tail ends) are exiting their respective loops at the same side of the knot. In other words, if you hold the knot so you can see the loops facing you, both running ends should exit their loops either at the top or the bottom. It doesn't matter which it is, as long as they are both exiting the same. If they aren't, you have a fool's knot, which can slip.

The square knot also goes by the name "reef" knot, dating back to early sailing days when this knot was used by mariners to reef their sails. It was also called the "thief" knot, a name that was applied because as sailors (who did not trust landlubbers) came ashore with all their possessions in a sea bag, they used the "thief" knot to tie things up, because the secret of tying this knot correctly was unknown to non-sailors. If a landlubber broke into the sea bag, the sailor knew, because the knot was probably not re-tied correctly when the thief tried to cover his tracks.

Bowline. Mountain climbers use this knot to secure themselves to a climbing rope for one simple reason—if tied correctly, it will not slip.

But there is a way to make a fatal error in attempting to tie a bowline, guaranteeing that it will slip very easily. First, let's look at how a bowline is tied.

THE bowline, if tied correctly, is a very secure knot that you can trust with your life. But if it's tied wrong, it turns into a slip knot.

An easy explanation of how to tie a bowline involves a little story about a rabbit, a tree, and a rabbit hole. Take the running end (the short tail of the rope) in one hand and the standing end (the long piece) in the other. Near the hand that is holding the standing end, make a simple loop in the rope so the standing end passes beneath the loop. Imagine the loop being a rabbit hole and the standing end of the rope being a tree growing beside the hole. Now, take the running end (the rabbit) and bring it up out of the hole, run it around the tree, and then back down into the hole. This forms a loop around the tree. When the knot is properly cinched down, it will not slip.

Ah, but there's the catch—the bowline must be properly cinched down or you may actually create a very slippery knot. To cinch it down the right way, pull on the standing end (the tree) to tighten things up. If you pull on the running end (the rabbit), it is possible to pull the tree right down the hole with the rabbit, causing the knot to "flip over" and become a slip knot.

The way mountaineers use the bowline is to take the rope around behind their back, holding the running end in one hand (usually the right hand) and the standing end in the other. Then, with the left hand, the loop is made, and the right hand passes the running end up through the loop, around the tree, and down the hole again. By cinching the knot up close to the waist, the rope becomes an effective lifeline.

Two Half Hitches. To make a bowline even more secure, some climbers leave enough running end to allow them to finish the knot by adding two half hitches. This makes it virtually impossible for the rabbit to come back out of the hole (because he's tied up down below).

To attach a rope to a tree, two half hitches are quick and easy to tie. It is sometimes used as a finishing knot when tying a bowline around the waist of mountain climbers, to ensure that the tail of the bowline cannot slip.

Half hitches are made by bringing the running end parallel to the rope the hitch is being tied to (in this case it's the rope that goes around the climber's waist). The running end is then passed under the other rope and brought up over from the backside, and then down the gap formed between the two ropes. That makes one half hitch. To make the second one, simply repeat the process, taking the running end below the rope again, up over, and back through the next gap. When snugged up, this secures the running end very nicely.

Two half hitches can be used to tie a rope to a railing or a tree, etc. It is not a knot to bet your life on, but it is an accessory knot that can make other knots such as the bowline even more secure.

ATTACHING two ropes of the same or different diameter to each other can be done quickly with the sheet bend. This is useful for adding length to a rope by attaching a second piece.

Sheet Bend. For those times when you need to join two pieces of rope of differing diameters, the sheet bend is a favorite. As the working ends of the two lines are placed under load, the loops cinch down on each other and are held secure by the way the smaller-diameter rope crosses over itself. When this knot is formed, care must be taken to avoid tying it improperly. Ideally, you want to end up with the short tail of each rope on the same side of the knot. If it is tied so the loose end of the rope is on the wrong side (with the short tails on opposite sides), you'll have a left-handed sheet bend, which is a weaker knot. However, if the knot is well seized, as shown here, it doesn't matter if it is tied right- or left-handed.

Sheepshank. If a rope is too long and you don't want to cut it to make it shorter, use a sheepshank to take up the slack. This is a very useful knot for everything from tying down a tarp across a truckload of stuff to taking up the slack in a tent guy line. The sheepshank is tied on a pair of bights, with a loop passing over each. This is a knot that can also be useful when you want to protect a weak or damaged section of rope. Just tie it so the damaged

THE sheepshank is a clever knot that is useful for shortening a rope that is too long. It is often used to take up the slack in a tent guy line that is longer than it needs to be.

section of rope is somewhere in the bights between the two loops, and it will be effectively taken out of action.

Clove Hitch. The clove hitch is a great way of temporarily attaching a rope to a tree or post. It works equally well horizontally or vertically. The clove hitch is easily loosened by repeatedly varying the angle of the pull, which should serve as a warning if you use it to secure a boat to a piling. Wave action may rock the boat back and forth, eventually loosening the clove hitch. To avoid having to worry about things like that, add one or two half hitches to make the attachment more secure.

To tie a clove hitch, make a turn with the rope around the object you are tying to, then bring the rope back over the top of itself. Follow with a second turn with the rope around the object. Then pull the end of the rope up under the second turn so it runs between the rope and the object. Tighten by pulling on both ends.

There are hundreds of different knots, but it isn't necessary to know how to tie them all. If you become confident with the knots covered in this chapter, you'll be able to handle most of the chores outdoors that require a knot.

FOR temporary attachment of a rope to a secure point, for example, tying a horse to a tree or a hitch rail, the clove hitch is a preferred method.

Lashing

To build the structure for a shelter, a tripod over a campfire, or camp furniture (such as a sleeping platform), knowing how to lash poles together is an important skill. The poles can be cut from native materials that you find. The lashing can be done with rope that you carry or thin, supple roots that can be twined together to make a primitive rope. There are several styles of lashings, but the one I'll cover here that is most basic to our purposes is the square lashing.

The square lashing is used when you want the lashed members to be at a right angle to each other. This works for attaching crossmembers to uprights when building a lean-to shelter, for example, or for constructing a sleeping platform with upright legs supporting a horizontal platform. To begin binding the pieces together, place the poles on the ground at a right angle to each other, with the crossing point where you want the poles to be joined. Tie a clove hitch around

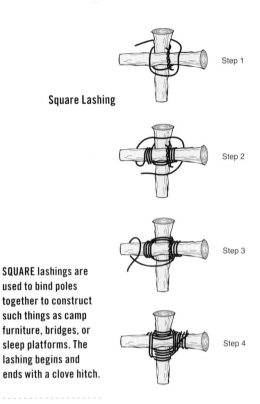

Square Lashing

Step 1

Step 2

Step 3

Step 4

SQUARE lashings are used to bind poles together to construct such things as camp furniture, bridges, or sleep platforms. The lashing begins and ends with a clove hitch.

one of the poles near the crossing point, and tuck the short tail of the rope so it is not in the way. Make three or four wraps, using an over-under wrapping technique to bind the crossed poles together. Take three wraps of the rope tightly over the earlier wrappings, passing the rope over the opposite side of the poles from the former wraps. Complete the lashing by tying the free end of the rope to one of the poles with a clove hitch.

Other lashing techniques, including the diagonal, shear, and tripod, are useful for projects such as lashing poles together to make a raft (shear), making a campfire tripod (tripod), or joining poles at other than a right angle (diagonal). While some outdoor enthusiasts employ slightly different techniques, such as starting with a timber hitch instead of a clove hitch, the general concept of attaching ropes and using them to bind poles together is the same for all these styles, and the biggest change is the juxtaposition of the poles and the direction of the wraps.

Primitive Rope

Some plants have bark, roots, or fibers that can be used to make cordage. Palm tree bark and the husk fibers of coconuts make excellent rope-making material. In the deserts, the fibers from juniper tree bark can be used for the same purpose. And some thin and supple tree roots can be braided into a kind of primitive rope to use in lashings. Because you can't predetermine where your survival situation will occur, it's impossible to know what kinds of plants you'll have available. The best you can do is explore the local plant life wherever you happen to be and see if any of it provides the materials for making rope.

Some of the plants to look for include milkweed, stinging nettle, dogbane, cattail, and bulrushes. The stocks (leaves, in the case of the cattail) of these plants contain long fibers that can be stripped out and twined together to make string. Those strings can then be twined together to make rope.

Long, thin strips of willow bark that has been soaked in water can be used for purposes similar to rope. I once used willow bark to make a pair of primitive sandals, by twisting and weaving the bark as if it were rope. The same material could be used for lashing.

Less tedious is to simply pull up the spidery roots of trees and test them for flexibility and strength. If you're in an area where vines grow among the trees, test them in the same way. To improve flexibility, soak the roots or vines to soften them so they can be bent without breaking. It's possible that you'll find roots or vines that are suitable for use in lashings without having to braid or twine them together. But if you need longer rope, it will be necessary to braid or twine pieces together, so you can keep adding new segments. To make long rope, begin to introduce and overlap new fiber or root materials into the existing materials several inches before reaching the end of the materials that you're already working with.

The art of twining fibers into cordage is not difficult. Begin by laying the long fibers out in either two or three thin bundles—depending upon whether you want a two-strand rope or a three-strand one. If you are right-handed, grip the end of these bundles in your left hand and allow the long fibers to point toward you. Start with the bundle to the left, and use your right hand thumb and forefinger to twist the bundle around itself in a clockwise direction. Now, while holding the already twisted strand with the other fingers of your left hand, and without allowing that bundle to untwist, move to the next one and do the same and then lay it in a counterclockwise direction over the previous bundle. This takes some finger dexterity, but it doesn't take long before you'll get the feel of the technique. If you're making a three-strand rope, do the same thing to the third bundle. By twisting each bundle and then laying the bundles over each other in this twist pattern, the fibers tend to grip each other and form a stranded rope. As you start to run out of fibers, introduce new ones in a couple of inches before reaching the end of the previous bunch of fibers. Try to keep the bundles at uneven lengths, so you aren't splicing new fibers into all of the strands at the same place.

Knowledge of how to make, care for, and use rope for knots and lashings makes life in the outback much easier.

STOVES: A STEP UP FROM CAMPFIRE COOKING

Ah, a hot meal—there's nothing better. Well, all right, Becky, almost nothing.

Campfires are great, when they're allowed, but there are times and places where an open fire is not permitted. Besides that, if you're on the move, hiking from one spot to another, it's tough to stop and build a campfire every time you want something hot to eat or drink. In cases like those, it's far more convenient to use a camp stove.

Camp stoves come in a wide variety of sizes and shapes, ranging from multi-burner giants that are best suited to transport by the family vehicle to fairly compact one-burner units that are lightweight and easy to carry in a backpack. I have both types and juggle them according to the type of outing we've planned.

One of my favorite stoves is the JetBoil. It's an impressive performer—I've used it to bring two cups of cold water to a boil in 2.5 minutes. With the burner's control valve opened halfway, the piezo pushbutton igniter instantly fires up the system, and the control valve makes it easy to dial up the right amount of heat for a cooking range from simmering to full-throttle blowtorch mode. When you need to purify water by boiling, this is the stove to use. It comes with a cooking container that holds a fuel canister and the burner in a most compact manner.

On the extreme lightweight side of compact stoves are the ones I call pocket stoves, because they are almost small enough to fit in one. There are lots of different types of pocket stoves on the market today. One of the major differences between the

JETBOIL stoves are self-contained, with a cooking container that fits on top of the burner unit that is attached to the butane canister. The fuel canister and burner fit inside the cooking vessel, making this stove very compact.

STOVE fuels include liquid white gas (center), pressurized canisters (left, right, and left front), and gels (right front). Liquid fuels require pressurization of the fuel tank, while canisters are already pressurized and ready to use. Gel fuels burn less hot than the others.

THE Sterno stove uses a gel fuel that puts out a modest amount of heat for cooking that doesn't require high temperature. The system is inexpensive, and the convenience is that the stove folds flat.

various stoves is the fuel they burn. Some use liquid fuel such as white gas or Coleman fuel. Others use pressurized canisters of propane, butane, or a combination of the two. Then there's the semisolid fuel (Sterno), and, finally, there's nature's solid fuel (wood). Cost, convenience, safety, and fuel availability are the issues you face when choosing between these systems.

When it comes to convenience, some of the pressurized-fuel and liquid-fuel stoves from Coleman, MSR, Optimus, and Primus are flyweight jobs that can fold down to pocket size. But there is still the issue of carrying enough fuel (read weight and bulk) to see you through. These stoves (and there are dozens of models) range in weight from a few ounces to half a pound. Fuel weight and size depend on canister size and the intended duration of your trek but run from a quarter pound to more than a pound, and from softball size to twice that. Costs for these stoves range from $30 to $130.

The semisolid-fuel Sterno stove folds flat for convenient carrying. It's too big for a pocket (well, maybe it will fit in a cargo pants pocket) but quite compact nonetheless. A seven-ounce can of fuel is about the size of a softball. This is really a low-buck, low-tech way to go, but don't expect it to produce a really hot flame the way a pressurized stove does.

TRAILSTOVE is a stainless steel cylinder with breather holes top and bottom to create a chimney effect that promotes lively burning of small bits of wood that can be easily collected along the trail.

Another alternative is to use natural fuels. We're talking wood. One interesting stove on the market is the Stratus TrailStove. It weighs less than a pound, is about the size of a hiking shoe, costs about $25, and fuel is free. It will burn twigs, small pieces of wood, charcoal, or alcohol when natural fuel is absent. There are no moving parts to break, and the thing is dumb as a tin can, so you can hardly screw it up. Go to www.trailstove.com to learn more about this clever stove.

But, if you don't even want to spend $25 for the commercial version, build your own tin-can stove for next to nothing. Start with a coffee can, cut out the top, dump the coffee into another container, and let the lid fall to the bottom of the can. Turn the can over and, while holding the free lid tight against the bottom inside the can, take a punch-type can opener, the kind that makes triangular-shaped holes, and work it around the outside of the can adjacent to the bottom so you end up with ten or twelve vent holes punched in the side. The metal that is punched into the can by the opener will hold the free lid in place. When the can is turned over, this will be a double top that serves as your cooking surface. The double layer of metal helps distribute the heat a little more evenly and slowly.

At the wide-open end of the can, cut two slits up the side about four inches apart and three inches in length. This allows you to bend the "door" up so you can feed fuel into the stove, and so it can draw air inside.

You can fuel this stove with pinecones, needles, twigs, small bits of wood, or whatever you can find. But you can also fuel it with a home-made "buddy burner" made from a discarded tuna can, a bit of corrugated cardboard, and paraffin wax. Start with a clean, empty tuna can from which the lid has been removed, but save the lid. Cut long strips of corrugated cardboard that measure about an inch in width. Coil the cardboard inside the can so that it is completely stuffed, but not crammed too tightly. Melt paraffin wax into the can until it is full. A wick is useful and can be made from an inch of wax-soaked string.

To use the burner, light the wick and slide the burner through the door of the tin-can stove. It will burn for about two hours before all the wax is consumed. Use the lid that you saved to put the fire out when you're through cooking, and you can use the burner for several meals before it runs out of fuel. Replenish the fuel by melting more wax into the cardboard coil.

Using this type of stove allows you to carry lots of fuel safely in plastic baggies. No worries about explosions or running out of fuel. Do take precautions, however, to ensure that the ground beneath the stove is nothing but mineral soil or rock, so you don't start the forest on fire.

When not in use, the stove is an empty cavity into which you can stuff whatever will fit.

Fuels

So let's talk about fuel for a minute. It's heat you need when you're trying to cook something or boil water, whether for purification or for preparing a warm drink. And the amount of heat you get from burning different fuels varies tremendously. If you're burning wood, the thermal output depends on the quality of the fuel. Damp or punky wood isn't going to produce much really usable heat, while snapping-dry wood with some pitch in it burns very hot. It's difficult to predict and control the amount of heat wood will give you, if you're depending on wood that you find lying beside the trail.

Sterno burns at a fairly low heat, so although you won't have to worry about charring your dinner if you turn your back for a minute, you will have to be patient while everything cooks. The flame is easy to ignite, easy to use, and easy to extinguish—just slide the lid back over the can and the flame goes out.

Pressurized fuels, such as butane and propane, burn fairly hot. But in high elevations and at cold temperatures, the pressurized canisters lose efficiency.

Liquid-fuel stoves are also pressurized, but the pressure isn't something that is built in at the factory. It's the person operating the stove who is responsible for keeping the pressure up by pumping air into the fuel tank. You can increase flame intensity by adding more pressure, thereby creating a hotter blaze.

Liquid- and Pressurized-Fuel Safety

Every year people are injured or killed by liquid- and pressurized-fuel stoves. It isn't just novice campers who are involved in these tragedies. I've got stories that range all the way from the professionals at Mt. Everest base camp to the newest tenderfoot at the local Boy Scout camp. The best way to prevent accidents is to rigorously observe a simple set of rules:

▶ Don't take shortcuts; follow manufacturer's directions.
▶ Keep fuel containers a safe distance away from heat sources.
▶ Make sure connections are tight.
▶ Check for leaks by using soapy water on the connection.
▶ Don't refuel a hot stove.
▶ Use a funnel to avoid spills.
▶ Wipe up spills before reigniting.

Solid-Fuel Safety

Accidents also occur when using a solid-fuel stove, and there's a separate set of rules for using that type of stove.

▶ Don't use the stove while it's sitting on combustible material.
▶ Store the extra fuel a safe distance away from the fire.
▶ Keep tools handy for extinguishing a fire (shovel, water, dirt).
▶ Make sure there are no errant sparks getting away from you.

All types of stoves require certain safety precautions that are not related to the type of fuel they burn.

▶ Keep small children away from a hot stove.
▶ Allow the stove to thoroughly cool down before packing it away.
▶ Make sure the stove is on steady ground, so it won't capsize.

Wildlife

Every year visitors to the backcountry are injured by wild animals that are, for one reason or another, put in a situation that leads to dangerously close contact with humans. Most of the time, it isn't the animal that chooses to have such close contact. I know a guy who rode his snowmobile under a moose one time, an incident that I guarantee was not the moose's idea. While on cross-country skis, I have suddenly skied around a tree and come face to face with a moose that I had no clue was there. Hikers in certain areas also run the risk of encountering bears or cougars.

This leads to a question: what is appropriate behavior when we are in the vicinity of wildlife? I'm not talking about times when we're hunting. I'm talking about those times when we're just out enjoying the wilderness and suddenly come face to face with wildlife. What do we do in those instances? The answer isn't always simple, because some wild animals are small and seemingly harmless, while other species are carnivorous predators that can become very aggressive. And we have to admit that part of the fun of being outdoors is seeing the wildlife. But even if we aren't intentionally seeking encounters, sometimes we run into wildlife by accident. What then?

There are some rules to follow to make our experiences with wild animals less stressful for them and less dangerous for us. The first rule is to check your warm, fuzzy feelings at the door, because these aren't Disney characters. They're wild animals that are in a constant life-and-death struggle, sometimes against each other—every one of them is looking for its next meal, and every one is looking over its shoulder to try to avoid being somebody else's next meal. They're skittish, often shy of people, unpredictable, and will rise to defensive behavior if they feel threatened. And some animals are downright aggressive. We need to understand how to behave when we encounter animals in the wild so we can minimize the danger.

Rules Regarding Baby Animals

▶ From time to time, young animals, such as fawns, will be temporarily left alone by their mothers. Do not intervene, because it will only cause problems. If you approach closely or handle a young animal, a lingering human scent may lead to total abandonment by the mother.

▶ If the mother catches you messing with her young, she may perceive it as a threat and attack you.

▶ Never get between a mother and her baby.

RULES REGARDING SMALL ANIMALS

▶ Don't feed them—even if they come into camp looking hungry. It's a temptation to feed seemingly friendly wildlife, but that accomplishes two negative ends: it makes them dependent, and it encourages them to hang around a human camp, which is dangerous for the little critters.

▶ Don't try to touch. A startled or sick animal may scratch or bite you, which can transmit disease. A fifteen-year-old Wisconsin girl picked up a bat that was infected with the rabies virus, and the bat bit her. Normally, without traditional rabies treatment that consists of six injections taken over the course of a month, people die within ten days after contracting the disease, as the virus attacks the brain. The lesson for us is that touching wild animals is a serious matter that can be life threatening, even if the animal is small.

RULES REGARDING BIG ANIMALS

The #1 rule for all wildlife is to keep your distance. The best thing you can do if you want close-up photos is to buy a telephoto lens so you don't have to crowd the animal. Now, here are some specific recommendations.

Bear

The two situations that cause the biggest problems between humans and bears are the attraction to food and surprise encounters. Black bears are opportunistic foragers, always looking for a free meal, so it is important to keep a clean camp because they will walk

PAY attention to posted warning signs where you hike or camp. Before your trip to the area, contact the local authorities to find out if there have been any recent incidents related to predatory animals.

right into camp and take what they want. They are generally regarded as less dangerous than the grizzly, but people have been injured and killed by black bears, so don't take any chances. Mother bears are very protective of their cubs and do not hesitate to charge intruders. Some bears just seem to have a bad attitude and will charge into camp and rip things apart without provocation. The things to remember about all bears are that they are unpredictable, they are large and powerful, they can outrun you, and they can injure or kill you.

The grizzly bear is a powerful predator, capable of outsprinting a horse, and you are its prey. There is absolutely nothing about a wild grizzly that is compatible with man. Ah yes, there have been stories and films that attempt to demonstrate peaceful coexistence between man and this beast. But perhaps the most telling story of all is the one about the "Grizzly Man," Timothy Treadwell, quintessential bear enthusiast and environmentalist. Treadwell spent many years of his life working in close proximity to grizzly bears in the Katmai National Park and Preserve in Alaska, filming them and believing that he had become accepted by them and that they had come to trust him. He reportedly approached the bears close enough to even touch them, and filmed his adventures for the purpose of raising public awareness about the bears, even though park officials repeatedly warned Treadwell that his interaction with the bears was dangerous, both to him and to the bears. And it served as a bad example for other people who saw his films or read of his exploits and might be led to believe the bears are not dangerous. Then it happened—during his thirteenth expedition to the grizzlies in 2003, Timothy Treadwell and his girlfriend Amie Huguenard were killed and eaten by a bear. Naturally, the offending bear ended up getting shot by officials, because they don't permit man-eaters to live. Treadwell's severed arm was found, with the wristwatch still ticking.

Here are some rules to live by when you're in bear country.

▶ Don't leave food in your vehicle. Bears break into vehicles if they see or smell food.

▶ In the backcountry, hang food high in a tree. Sleep at least 100 yards from where you hang the food, cook, and eat. Toiletries also attract bears, so store them as you would food.

▶ Don't sleep in the same clothes you wore while cooking and eating. In fact, don't even take those clothes into the tent. Hang that clothing in plastic bags away from camp, exactly as you do with food and garbage. Make sure to hang these bags high enough that a bear cannot reach them—at least 15 feet in the air.

▶ At campsites that do not have bear-proof garbage cans, treat garbage and leftovers the same as food. When leaving camp, pack out all food scraps and garbage. Place food and garbage in tightly sealed plastic bags. Double-bag to prevent the odor from escaping.

▶ Wash dishes immediately; clean up any spilled food.

▶ If a bear comes into camp during the day, bang pots and pans together to make noise. After the bear leaves, check around to find and eliminate food or garbage that attracted the bear.

A clue that there are bears in the area is a sign that points to a bear wire for suspending food and garbage high off the ground. Camp some distance away from the bear wire, so animals that are attracted to the food or garbage won't come right into camp.

▶ If a bear gets into your food or garbage, you are responsible for cleaning up the mess and packing out all debris. Report the incident to the nearest ranger.

▶ Don't confront a bear to protect your property. In the case of repeated encounters, leave the area, with or without your stuff.

▶ Hike in groups and in the open when possible. Never hike at night. Wear a bear bell or make noise when visibility is limited, so bears know you're coming.

▶ If you meet a bear on the trail, don't run. Running may trigger an attack response. If the bear is unaware of you, detour away and take another route. If the bear is aware of you but has not acted aggressively, wave your arms overhead, speak in a firm voice, and slowly back away. If the bear charges, hold your ground and speak firmly to the bear—pray it is only a bluff charge. But if the bear makes physical contact with you, take a fetal position face down on the ground, keeping your backpack (if you are wearing one) between the bear and yourself. Cover your head with your arms and hands. Then play dead (as hard as that may be).

▶ If a bear comes into camp at night, it is hunting food and will not hesitate to attack you. This scenario is different from a chance encounter with a bear on a trail. At night, the bear is after prey, and you are on the menu. You must fight back or die.

▶ Never get between a mother bear and her cubs.

Bison

An adult bull bison grows to be six feet tall at the shoulder and weigh 2,000 pounds. Bison appear big and slow, but they can run up to 30 miles per hour. Just about the only place you will encounter a bison is in Yellowstone National Park. Although the bison are accustomed to people, visitors to the park are gored every year because they get too close while trying to take photos.

Keep your distance, and don't press your luck.

Cougar

Cougars, also known as mountain lions and pumas, are large animals, often weighing over a hundred pounds, and they are potentially dangerous. It seems that every year I hear stories of cougar attacks against humans. One of the disturbing things about cougar habits is that, unlike other predators, this big cat will actually stalk its human prey, silently sneaking closer and closer until it can spring into an attack. On July 16, 2001, a lady who lives in British Columbia looked out her window and saw a cougar closing the distance on two men who were working in her backyard. In California from 1992 through 1995, there were cougar attacks every year on victims—men, women, and children ranging in age from six to fifty-six. In 2004, a thirty-year-old California woman riding a bicycle with her friend was attacked and dragged 100 yards while the friend tried desperately to fight the animal and cause it to release its grip on the victim's head and neck. Becky and I had our own close encounter with a mountain lion, as we hiked less than a mile from our home. That day, we were lucky. Cougars are nothing to mess with.

To prevent an encounter:

▶ Hike in small groups rather than alone.

▶ Move slowly—running may trigger an attack.

▶ Make noise to avoid surprising a cougar.

▶ Carry a sturdy walking stick that could be used to fend off a charging animal.

▶ Keep children under close control.

▶ Be alert, especially in dense cover and when sitting, crouching, or lying down.

▶ Watch for tracks and other animal signs.

▶ Avoid dead animals.

▶ Reduce odor by storing food and garbage in double plastic bags.

▶ Maintain a clean camp.

▶ Pets attract cougars. Don't leave a pet tied up in camp.

Here are the rules to follow if you happen upon a cougar:

▶ Stop, stand upright, and *do not* run.

▶ Face the animal, talk to it calmly, and slowly back away. Leave the cougar an escape route.

▶ Try to appear larger. Wave your arms, raise your jacket over your head, and stay higher than the animal.

▶ Most cougars will retreat. If the cougar becomes aggressive, shout, wave your arms, and throw things at the animal. Stay on your feet. Don't turn your back or take your eyes off the cougar. Try to convince the animal that you are a danger to it.

COUGARS are becoming an increasingly common threat to hikers and campers in the backcountry. These big cats will stalk and attack lone hikers, so the rule in cougar country is to never go it alone.

Deer and Elk

These animals are generally unapproachable because they flee at the first hint of human presence. However, when the animal is cornered or protecting its young, it might become aggressive. During the rut season (late summer and early fall of the year), buck deer and bull elk lose their minds and become more aggressive. Hunters love this season because it's easier to coax an animal into range. But this is also the time of year when the males will do whatever it takes to prove their manhood, which can be dangerous if you get between the male and his harem.

Unless you're hunting them, keep your distance. Don't harass or follow the animals closely.

Moose

Mature bulls weigh more than a thousand pounds. Their size and demeanor may fool you into thinking they are slow, but they are very fast on their feet, and they come at you like a runaway locomotive. Calves are born in the spring and remain with their mother for a year. A cow aggressively protects her young from any perceived threat. There is a story about an eighteen-wheel truck that was attacked by a moose in the Island Park area of Idaho. As the story goes, the driver stopped the truck because a big bull moose was standing in the road. The moose and the truck stared each other down quietly for a while, but then the driver honked his air horns to try to scare the moose off the highway. Local legend has it that the moose turned to face the truck, raked the radiator with his antlers, and then walked away, leaving the trucker stranded with a dead truck and a puddle of antifreeze on the ground. I can't verify that story, but old-timers, even in grizzly country, say the most dangerous animal in the forest is a moose.

▶ Observe only from a distance.
▶ While hiking in moose country, keep a watchful eye so you spot them well in advance.
▶ If you see a moose, alter your route away from the animal.
▶ Don't get between a cow and her calf.

Wolves

It's rare to see a wolf in the wild, but with the government's reintroduction program, a confrontation is more likely to happen. Lest you believe the Hollywood version of the gentle wolf that hunts only field mice for dinner, consider the experience of a twelve-year-old boy who was dragged from his sleeping bag by a wild wolf. He ended up with eighty stitches, a broken nose, a severed piece of ear, and numerous injuries. In January 2006 there was an attack on a twenty-two-year-old geology student who was killed by wolves while hiking in northern

Saskatchewan, Canada. There is no reason to doubt that wolves are predators that must be regarded with due respect for the potential danger they pose.

▶ Avoid eye contact.

▶ Face the animal but don't smile or bare your teeth.

▶ Slowly back away.

▶ Don't run; running may trigger an attack.

VENOMOUS CRITTERS

It was one of those ideal full-moon nights where we camped along the edge of Lake Powell. As I looked at the scene, I wanted to shoot that perfect photograph of the moon rising over the black water and scarlet cliffs. Then I made a decision that easily could have had fatal, or at least very damaging, results.

With camera in hand, I walked away from camp through the brush along a sandy trail that led around the tiny inlet where we had set our tents. The shot I wanted was from across the inlet, with water in the foreground and the vast body of lake in the background. Our camp, positioned on a finger of sand, glowed in the moonlight. Perfect.

Less than 20 yards from camp, something moved across the trail directly where my next step was about to land. Recognition was immediate—a rattlesnake, about two feet in length. It was too late to pull my foot back—my weight was committed to the next step already—and I mentally prepared myself to pay the price for foolish nocturnal wandering in a known rattler domain.

As my foot hit the ground, my eyes were riveted on the spot where the snake had been, but by some miracle he was gone. Not far, mind you, but gone from the danger zone and coiled nicely in the sage next to the trail, buzzing softly. What followed would have been hilarious had it not been so serious. It was a ballet act, leaping and flapping my wings, singing lyrics about pending injury and death in perfect falsetto while heading full tilt in reverse down the trail back toward camp. Fear does that to a guy.

It was not my first nor my last encounter with rattlesnakes, but this one was a very close call. Had the snake decided to do so, he could easily have struck me. And I would have earned it as a consequence for my lack of attention to the rules of snake country.

Snakes

Anyone who ventures into the outdoors needs to know the rules of survival in snake country. Rattlesnakes are found in all but a few isolated pockets of terrain, and chances are high that if you trek around the backcountry long enough, you'll see a few of them in your lifetime.

Contrary to the fears of some, rattlesnakes are not out to get you. You don't need to worry about an offended buzztail hunting you down to get revenge for nearly running over him. In fact, the opposite is the case; generally, the snake tries to avoid people unless molested, cornered, or feeling otherwise threatened. There are, of course, accidents where man and snake encounter each other with unfortunate results.

Rattlers have a hard time with public relations. Their very appearance has a lot to do with this. A flickering forked tongue, intense yellow eyes with vertical slit pupils, a triangle-shaped head, pits on the face, fangs, raspy skin, and rattles do nothing to endear these snakes to people, even those people who otherwise enjoy the company of animals. The whole package looks wicked, making rattlers fairly despised members of the wild kingdom.

Actually, these animals are fascinating. The flickering tongue is a tool used by the snake to locate and identify food in the dark. Particles of scent are caught by the tongue, which is then drawn into the mouth and stuck into holes in the roof of the mouth where scent glands are located. Another mechanism employed by the snake for locating prey (or a possible enemy) are the heat-sensing pockets on the face, which tell the snake about the size, distance, and direction of a heat-producing source such as an animal or a human. These pockets are what give the pit viper its name. If you encounter a rattlesnake and it flicks its tongue in and out of its mouth while swinging its head back and forth in your direction, it is using both scent- and heat-sensing mechanisms in an effort to identify you and determine the distance between itself and you.

If you come across a rattlesnake, rule number one is to keep your distance and warn others in the group about the snake's presence. A rattlesnake does not have to coil before striking. It can strike from any position. The snake cannot "jump" or strike a greater distance than the length of its own body (unless it is striking downhill). But it is pure foolishness to underestimate the rattler's strike zone. The decision to strike or not to strike belongs to the snake, and one can never predict what that decision will be.

When a snake sheds its skin (which may be one to several times per year, depending upon available food supply and speed of growth), the eyes temporarily glaze over, reducing the snake's vision, which is none too sharp anyway. This makes the snake especially nervous, and during this period the snake is more likely to strike.

If the snake strikes, it decides how much (if any) venom to inject. Snakebite does not always involve injection of venom, and this is for a number of reasons. Perhaps the snake recently caught and killed some prey and is low on venom. Perhaps the snake's venom glands don't produce very much. Perhaps the snake decides to reserve its venom supply for food and is striking only as a warning. Whatever the reason, you cannot know in advance if a strike will occur, and if it does, you cannot know in advance how much venom will be injected.

While death by snakebite in the United States is fairly rare, the resulting injury can be absolutely devastating among survivors. You rarely hear about victims of snakebite who don't die. But those who are bitten and injected with venom and manage to live through the experience frequently suffer loss of a limb. Rattlesnake venom attacks the circulatory system and actually digests the flesh surrounding the wound. The outcome may be a severely deformed limb or even amputation. And even a bite by a so-called harmless snake can lead to dangerous infection or allergic reaction.

According to the University of Florida, there are around 7,000 reported venomous snakebites in the United States each year. The

University of Maryland Medical Center has the number pegged at roughly 8,000. Fatalities number around 15 per year. People are obviously not paying close enough attention to what's going on around them when they're in snake country. Either that or they're acting irresponsibly, a conclusion that is easy to reach, given that approximately 3,000 of the bites are classed as "illegitimate," indicating that they occur when people are handling or harassing the snakes—either trying to pick them up or to kill them.

University of Florida statistics say that 85 percent of venomous snakebites are below the knee, indicating that stepping on a snake is probably a common cause. Other bites occur when the person steps over a log or beside a boulder beneath which a snake is hiding. Deep grass and brushy country are also prime snake habitats that contribute to the snakebite statistics each year. Bites that are not below the knee happen because the person is trying to handle or kill the snake, or they are bitten when picking up logs or rocks or placing hands in dangerous spots while climbing or scrambling along a slope using both hands and feet.

With that bit of information, we can formulate an avoidance plan to help keep us safe when we're in snake country. There are times when people are more likely to encounter venomous snakes—generally between late spring and early fall, especially during the months of March and October, in most of the country. Of course, this varies with geography, based on local climate, so it is necessary to determine prime snake season for your own region. That doesn't mean you can ignore the danger other than during that season, but it means that you should be especially vigilant when the snakes are in season.

A snake safety plan should include the following:

▶ If you come across a snake, point it out to others in your group and then give it wide berth and leave it alone.
▶ If you know that you will be camping and hiking in snake country during snake season, wear high leather boots or snake gaiters and remain on clearly visible trails as much as possible.

▶ Stay out of tall grass and dense brush.

▶ Be very careful where you place your feet and hands, especially when climbing on rocks, around ledges, or crossing logs.

▶ Carry a long stick so you can probe the area ahead of you as you travel. But don't use the stick to tease the snake or try to kill it.

IN snake country, use a stick to rattle the bushes and probe beneath logs and rocks before you approach.

The types of snakes that merit the greatest concern in the United States include rattlesnakes, copperheads, cottonmouth water moccasins, and coral snakes. Each has its own kind of venom—some are hemotoxins that attack the circulatory system and everything it leads to, and some are neurotoxins that attack the central nervous system and everything connected to it. Either way, a bite can be extremely serious, even if death is not the result.

The medical industry has developed antivenin (a.k.a. antivenom) to help counter the effects of the different types of venom, but knowing which type of snake inflicted the bite is critical to selecting the correct antivenin after the victim arrives at the medical treatment facility. Because it is important to be able to correctly identify the offending snake, bring the dead remains of the snake to the hospital or give it to the medical response team that comes to your aid. But don't get yourself bitten again or cause someone else to be injured trying to capture or kill the snake. After the snake is killed, remove the head and bury it or cremate it in a fire, because the fangs can still inflict a bite even if the snake is dead.

Treatment. The current doctrine regarding field first-aid treatment of snakebite is:

▶ Calm the victim and have him relax as much as possible to slow the transport of venom through the body.

▶ Immediately call for medical assistance. Time is of the essence.

▶ While waiting for help to arrive, remove rings, watches, or anything else that may restrict circulation when the affected limb swells.

▶ Wash the wound with soap and water. Don't worry about becoming poisoned yourself while treating someone else, because the toxin doesn't transfer that way.

▶ Use a splint to immobilize the limb, but keep it loose enough that it does not restrict blood flow. Periodically check fingers or toes, depending upon which limb is affected, to make sure they are still pink and warm, indicating good circulation.

▶ Keep the affected limb lower than the heart.

▶ Monitor vital signs so you can tell the medical team what's been happening.

If it is going to be more than thirty minutes before the victim can be transported to a medical facility, do the following:

▶ Apply a wide, constricting band around the limb two to four inches above the bite to help slow the spread of venom. This is not a tourniquet, and it should not restrict the flow of arterial or venous blood. It operates at the capillary level of blood flow. Keep the band loose enough that you can easily slip a finger or two under it. Keep this in place until the victim reaches the hospital.

▶ Within five minutes of the bite, apply a suction device over the fang marks and leave it in place for thirty minutes, but do not slit the skin to open the wound before applying suction.

A little preparation, common sense, and caution go a long way toward avoiding problems in snake country.

Scorpions

Of the ninety varieties of scorpions in the United States, all but four make their home west of the Mississippi River. These venomous critters can be found in forest, mountain, and desert terrain, although they are most common in the southwestern desert areas. As with all venomous creatures, the toxin is intended to be used to kill its prey and to defend itself against predators. Scorpion venom is a neurotoxin. Only one species of scorpion in the United States is known to have powerful enough venom to be harmful to humans. The habitat of this one, *Centruroides exilicauda*, a.k.a. the Arizona bark scorpion, covers much of Arizona and Mexico, although small numbers of them have also been found in parts of Nevada, New Mexico, Texas, southeastern California, and southern Utah.

The venom is delivered through a stinger on the tail, and a victim of a scorpion sting may experience symptoms that include severe pain and swelling at the location of the sting, numbness, muscle twitch, convulsions, frothing of the mouth, blurry vision, and difficulty breathing. Death is rare, but the venom is more dangerous to infants and the elderly or infirm.

Treatment. Wash the site of the sting with soap and water, then apply a cool compress (ice wrapped in cloth) to the area for ten minutes. Remove the compress for ten minutes, and then reapply it. Repeat this cycle until there is relief from the symptoms. Even though death is not expected, transport the victim to a medical facility for further treatment.

Venomous Spiders

Black widow and brown recluse spiders are the two common venomous spiders in North America. Of the two, the brown recluse is the most dangerous to humans because the effect of the venom is worse. Bites can take several months to heal and result in horrible necrosis (tissue death) that leaves the affected area black, swollen, split open, and ugly. As if that weren't bad enough, other symptoms include burning pain, headache, body aches, rash, fever, and nausea.

Black widow venom is highly toxic and can result in symptoms that include severe muscle spasm, burning, swelling, headache, dizziness, nausea, weakness, paralysis, and high fever and may require hospitalization. Children and the elderly are most at risk of adverse symptoms.

Treatment.   For the bites of both of these spiders, the field treatment is to wash the area with soap and water, apply a cold pack, protect against infection by applying an antibiotic cream, and give acetaminophen to help relieve pain. In the case of the brown recluse bite, treatment also includes elevation of the affected area to help reduce swelling.

Both of these spiders inject venom that can have extremely serious consequences, so as soon as possible the victim should be transported to a medical facility for further treatment that doctors might deem necessary.

YOUR ANIMAL ATTITUDE

This chapter is not intended to scare you. Wildlife attacks on humans are rare. When they do occur, there are often extenuating circumstances in which people actually contribute in some way to the incident, either by getting too close to the animal or encouraging the proximity through poor food- or garbage-handling habits. Yes, there are unexplainable attacks in which nobody is to blame, but you are more likely to be struck by lightning than assaulted by an animal. There is no need for irrational fear of these creatures, but there is every reason to take precautions. Wild animals are part of the great outdoors that we all enjoy so much, and the only intent of what has been presented here is to give you an understanding of how to minimize the risks of a too-close encounter of the animal kind.

Weather

11

Forecasting the weather is a combination of art, science, and luck—which is why weather reporters always deal in percentages rather than absolutes. This is a concept that left an indelible impression on me years ago while boating on Lake Powell. Before setting out, I listened to a weather report that said there was a 20 percent chance of a storm. I turned to Becky and said, "That means there's an 80 percent chance that the weather will be fine." She pointed at the black clouds on the horizon and said, "I'm not so sure." I, much to my eternal chagrin, discounted her concern and proclaimed my undying faith in the weather report. We sailed out onto the lake, and within half an hour we were pummeled by what felt like the mother of all storms with lightning, thunder, high winds, and heavy rain. So now when I hear weather forecasts in terms of percentages, I understand that the weather guy has no idea what's actually happening where I am unless I'm standing next to him. I confess that the incident left me a weather-report cynic.

Even though the process isn't perfect, it's a good idea to monitor the broadcasts. Just don't stop there. Turn your face to the sky and pay attention to the clues about what's coming. For your own safety, you must keep your own "weather eye" on the sky, looking for local atmospheric activity that the distant forecasters might not be aware of. After all, the rain in your face is a more reliable indication of the weather than a report coming from someplace else.

I know weather forecasts are not infallible, but I still monitor them with great respect. After completing the National Weather Service weather spotter course and also the U.S. Coast Guard Auxiliary weather specialty course, I have a greater understanding that the professional weather forecasters do the best they can, but that they operate in a very broad-brush manner. Atmospheric conditions that create the weather are extremely variable. Things can change unexpectedly in a heartbeat, sending weather systems off in another direction or stalling them so they can do more damage than previously anticipated. Local squalls can seemingly leap up out of nowhere, sending wind speed from zero to sixty in a flash, and sometimes the best the forecasters are able to do is report on the incident after the fact.

Even though it's near impossible to precisely forecast local conditions from a weather station many miles away, that doesn't mean the forecast information is worthless. Getting a big-picture view of where the high- and low-pressure systems are, how the jet stream is behaving, and what frontal systems are forming can give important clues about what's coming and when. Your job is to take that information, combine it with what you're actually seeing in your location, and come up with your own local forecast. Then you have to decide what to do about it.

Keeping track of what's happening with the weather is especially important during the trip-planning phase. Without knowing what the short-term and long-term trends are, you might inadvertently travel into the path of storms that are taking aim at your intended campsite. So along with packing the hot dogs, pop, and ice in the cooler, filling the vehicle with fuel, and making sure the sleeping bags and tent are aboard, one other vital item on the pre-trip checklist should be tapping into weather information sources.

Thanks to modern technology, obtaining weather information is easier today than ever before. For $30 to $80, you can buy a compact, battery-powered (good for when the power goes out) weather radio from Radio Shack that continuously broadcasts NOAA (National Oceanic and Atmospheric Administration) weather reports all across the country. The National Weather Service, a nationwide network of radio stations operating on seven frequencies, broadcasts reports of severe weather emergencies such as tornados, hurricanes, floods, blizzards, earthquakes, wildfires, avalanches, and other hazard information 24/7. As you travel from one area to another, you simply shift from one of the seven channels to another to pick up the nearest station and continue getting current conditions and forecasts.

A portable, battery-powered weather radio can keep you informed of severe weather coming your way in the backcountry.

THE Stormtracker is a weather radio on steroids, incorporating an AM/FM radio, TV, lantern, and flashlight all in a single unit. Multiple power sources include C-cell batteries, 12-volt vehicle battery, 120-volt AC, and a hand-crank generator.

In addition to a small weather radio, we own a Weather Channel Stormtracker that we bought at Costco. This unit combines a five-inch black-and-white TV, AM/FM radio, NOAA Weather Radio, cell phone charger (with universal adapter set), three-LED lantern, and six-LED emergency flashlight. All this comes in a single, compact, lightweight unit with a built-in handle and a removable nylon shoulder strap for easy carrying. Power is provided by regular or rechargeable batteries, 12-volt DC vehicle power, or 120-volt AC household power. The hand crank can be used to recharge a built-in 600-mAh Ni-MH rechargeable backup battery, a secondary power source for emergency use when the main power is not available.

If you have Internet access, you can visit NOAA at www.noaa.gov and then follow the prompts to search for weather information on whatever part of the country you are interested in. The Weather Channel is another favorite, at www.weather.com; it allows you to input the city and state or simply the zip code of the area you're concerned about. Not only can you obtain a relatively long-term forecast, but you can also tap into such tools as satellite images that show the movement of clouds and storm systems. And don't overlook the evening news broadcast on TV or weather forecast in local newspapers.

Accessing all these sources of weather information gives you a better chance of planning your trip around the weather and of preparing for what is coming. Make no mistake about it. Severe weather can kill you, so don't be shy about altering your plans until a better weather window opens up.

The weather can also take a sudden and unexpected change for the worse. So once you're out there having a good time, it's important to keep a weather eye on what's happening. You might detect significant local atmospheric activity that eluded the forecasters. In fact, the National Weather Service depends on trained volunteer weather spotters all over the country to tell the professionals what is happening by reporting it. So being able to recognize the weather signs can be a lifesaver.

As you watch for signs of bad weather, what you are looking for are cloud patterns and movement. The atmosphere is made up of gigantic air masses that differ from one another in temperature, pressure, and humidity. Interaction between these air masses results in changing weather conditions such as cloud formation, precipitation, and wind. Clouds are the biggest clue to the type of weather that is coming. The three primary types of clouds that we will discuss are cumulus, stratus, and cirrus. Watching the progression of cloud evolution tells the story.

Cumulus clouds are the puffy ones. They are the most unstable type of clouds and are often associated with cold fronts or air rising over mountains. The puffiness indicates that there is some degree of upward movement, a rising air mass, causing air to climb to a colder altitude where the water vapor in the air condenses and "grows" the cloud at the top. A bunch of little cumulus clouds scattered in the sky like so many sheep on a pasture don't pose a threat. But when cumulus clouds bunch together into a huge mass or grow into towering monsters, a thunderstorm (or worse) is possible. Cumulus giants can spawn sudden downpours, lightning and thunder, violent wind, flash floods, hail, and tornadoes. This is especially true when warm, moist air collides with cooler, drier air along a frontal boundary.

Stratus clouds form shapeless solid layers of overcast, leaving a gray, dreary sky. If there is a lot of light penetrating the stratus layer, it probably isn't dense enough to produce much precipitation. It takes a cloud thickness of 4,000 feet or more to produce steady rain. But if the clouds become dark and low, expect showers or drizzle. Stratus clouds don't result in sudden and violent downpours the way cumulus clouds do, but the rain can continue steadily for hours or even a couple of days, so there is still a danger of flooding.

But there is the potential for a hidden danger with stratus clouds, because you can't see what is happening above them when you're standing on the ground. It is possible that a giant cumulus formation is above the stratus layer, so be alert to the possibility of violent weather, even if things look pretty benign from below the cloud deck.

Cirrus clouds form so high in the atmosphere that they are made of ice crystals instead of water vapor. These wispy clouds (sometimes called mares' tails because of their shape) don't cause rain, but they can foretell the coming of a warm front that brings precipitation. If stratus follows cirrus, and if that stratus evolves into a thicker and darker layer, expect rain. How quickly the rain comes depends on the speed that the front is moving.

Clear, blue sky doesn't necessarily mean everything is hunky-dory. If a high-pressure system moves in and pushes a low-pressure system out of the way, it brings clearing skies—but it might also bring strong and gusty wind as the pressure between the two systems attempts to equalize. Trees can be knocked down and tents blown away under clear, blue sky.

By tapping into the available weather information and keeping an eye on the sky, you can make better judgments about what kind of weather to expect. And hopefully, that helps you enjoy your outdoor experiences all the more.

LIGHTNING SAFETY

Late summer and early fall are prime times for campers to be caught in thunderstorms. If thunder were the only element in these storms, there would be nothing to worry about. But the reality is that there can't be thunder without lightning first. And lightning is a very serious problem.

Before we even discuss the hazards posed by an actual lightning strike, let's deal with another danger—the myths and misconceptions surrounding this electrostatic light show. The common acceptance of unreliable information is dangerous because it leads people to do the wrong things at the wrong times.

Among the most popular myths is the assertion that lightning never strikes twice in the same place. Evidence to the contrary is seen in the fact that the Empire State Building takes a direct hit twenty-two to twenty-five times per year. OK, but you're not the Empire State Building, so you're safe, right? Wrong. There are many people who have been hit more than once by lightning strike—like former park ranger Roy C. "Dooms" Sullivan, for example, who owns the *Guinness Book of World Records* title as the most lightning-struck man, with a record seven hits.

Another dangerous myth is that rubber tires or a foam sleeping pad insulates you against a strike. The problem with that one is that it takes only about 10,000 volts for a spark to jump a one-inch gap, and lightning is loaded with millions of volts, so it can easily jump several feet! Rubber tires or a sleeping pad won't stop a strike, and there is no evidence that these things help avoid the strike.

Some people believe that a cave is a safe place in a lightning storm. But if the cave is shallow or if you're taking refuge in a mine shaft with metal nearby, it can actually be a hazardous location.

Fortunately, modern science and technology are at work studying the realities of lightning strike. There is even a National Lightning Safety Institute (NLSI) that disseminates information dealing with everything from how to protect your home or office from lightning to how to be safe while enjoying outdoor activities. It is this last aspect that we are most interested in.

Statistically, you are not very likely to be hit by lightning while working inside a building or driving your vehicle. Civilization appears to be a fairly safe environment when it comes to being struck down by a bolt from the blue. A sturdy building or the "steel cage" effect provided by a vehicle are very protective. But once you step outside, whether it's to play golf, go camping, or to backpack your favorite trail, the statistics are no longer so firmly in your favor.

According to the NLSI, at any moment around the globe there are approximately 2,000 active thunderstorms, and lightning strikes the earth about 100 times per second. Due to atmospheric conditions, lightning is more abundant in the lower latitudes (closer to the equator) and in the higher altitudes (mountainous terrain).

In the United States, Florida is the lightning capital, averaging more than fifteen strikes per square mile per year. In the high elevations of the Rocky Mountain West, there are about ten strikes per square mile per year on average.

The mechanism of a lightning strike is fascinating. Scientists have determined that lightning "leaders" from thunderclouds progress in steps. These leaders electrify objects on the ground as they approach the earth. In response, objects on the ground may launch lightning "streamers" to reach up and meet the leaders. Some who have witnessed this event up close report that streamers sound like bacon frying. In the presence of these steamers, your hair may stand on end.

A friend of mine who is a knowledgeable outdoorsman was hiking in Colorado one summer. After the trip, he told me that as he reached a ridge during the early stages of a storm, he felt his hair stand on end and heard a crackling sound. Although he did not suffer a lighting strike, he could literally feel the electricity in the air. He immediately got off the ridge—which was the right move!

Obviously the risks rise when you're camping and hiking, but there are ways to minimize the danger of being a victim of lightning strike.

Among the published safety tips from the National Lightning Safety Institute are these:

AVOID

- ▶ water
- ▶ metallic objects
- ▶ high ground
- ▶ solitary tall trees
- ▶ close contact with others (If you're in a group, spread out 15 to 20 feet apart.)
- ▶ contact with dissimilar objects (water and land; boat and land; rock and ground; tree and ground)
- ▶ open spaces

SEEK

▶ clumps of shrubs or trees of uniform height

▶ ditches, trenches, or the low ground

▶ a low, crouching position, feet together with hands on ears

KEEP

▶ a high level of safety awareness for thirty minutes after the last observed lightning or thunder

NOTE: If you are on the water in a boat, immediately get off the water and take shelter in a low area among bushes or small trees of similar size.

Flash, Bang

As a storm approaches, it's fairly easy to determine the distance from your position to that of a lightning strike. The sound of thunder trails behind the flash of lightning by approximately five seconds for each mile of distance. For example, if you see lightning, and the sound of thunder doesn't reach you for ten seconds, the strike was about two miles away. If the thunder is fifteen seconds behind the flash of lightning, you can assume the distance was three miles.

That may sound comforting at first, but new research indicates that successive, sequential lightning strikes (the distances from one strike to another and then to yet another) can be six to eight miles apart. Take immediate precautionary actions when lightning is striking within six to eight miles. With successive strikes, the next one could be close enough to pose an immediate and severe threat. At the first sign of lightning or thunder, put off any further activities and seek shelter.

Don't rely on small shelters, such as camp tents, to protect you against lightning strike during thunderstorms, especially if they are positioned on high ground or near a tree or a small group of trees that dominate the area. For campers whose only shelter is a tent, the tent should be located in a relatively low area, preferably surrounded by a large number of trees of approximately the same height.

After taking shelter, kick back and wait for the storm to pass. Then wait an additional thirty minutes after the last lightning or thunder before heading outside to continue with your activities.

These precautions sound like an overprotective nuisance. But the reality is that lightning is a totally capricious and random event. On more than one occasion, I personally witnessed it in the middle of a Teton Mountain blizzard in the dead of winter.

You cannot predict lightning strike with any degree of accuracy or reliability. There is absolutely nothing you can do to prevent a strike. All you are left with is a set of safety rules that offer the best defense for maximum safety.

And at the end of the day, I'd rather live by a bunch of nuisance rules than look down and see my boots smoking.

Flash flood

Becky and I were hiking near our camp late one summer evening, enjoying the sunset, when the distant growl caught our attention. It was a rumbling roar, and it was getting louder. A few seconds later we saw it coming—a wall of muddy water swept around the bend in the canyon and rushed toward us like a hundred bulls in the streets of Pamplona.

"Flash flood," I yelled, grabbing Becky by the hand and running for high ground. Lucky for us this was a small flood. An hour later, the water was gone, and our camp was untouched. But along with the debris that was swept into the canyon, the flood left the memory of our experience with one of nature's most deadly forces.

According to national statistics, flooding is the leading cause of weather-related deaths in the United States, killing, on average, about 200 people each year. This statistic includes all types of flooding. Two hundred deaths per year might not sound like a lot, until you compare that number with the statistics for other potentially dangerous weather phenomena: hurricanes kill 24 people, on average, per year, tornadoes kill 69, and lightning strikes kill 81.

One of the deadliest flash floods in U.S. history swept down Colorado's Big Thompson Canyon during the height of the 1976 summer tourist season. People were trying to escape Denver's city heat by going to a popular camping area, where the temperatures were cooler and the day was perfect.

As it turned out, the day was perfect for an unusual combination of atmospheric conditions to join forces, with deadly results. Afternoon heat created powerful updrafts that carried moist air aloft, and when that air reached the cooler upper atmosphere, it didn't take long for a thunderstorm to form.

Heavy rain began to fall in the mountains above Big Thompson Canyon. Normally, thunderstorms move fairly rapidly across the landscape, pushed across the countryside by strong winds. But this one didn't. It just sat there and dumped. Three hours later, more than a foot of rain had fallen, with eight inches falling during one intense hour-long cloudburst.

The canyon's stream began to swell, and soon it grew from its normally placid two-foot-deep trickle to a violent killer that was 19 feet high and raging through the canyon, wickedly propelling 10-foot boulders and broken trees that had been ripped out of the ground. In a heartbeat, everything was gone—vehicles, buildings, and people. The crushing flood swept through the canyon with such speed and violence that it was impossible to outrun. Buildings and vehicles instantly became death traps, and there was no possible avenue of escape except straight up the canyon walls. Two hours later, the death toll was 145, including six people who were never found.

The trouble with flash floods is that they arrive unannounced, often coming from many miles away. It might not even be raining where you are, but 20 miles away a cloudburst can set things in motion, and a few hours later a raging torrent sweeps you and your camp away.

Flash floods feed on three things: heavy rainfall or perhaps sudden snowmelt, a system of drainages or lowlands where the water collects and then funnels downstream, and time. A ten-minute monsoon isn't going to create much of a flood, but one that lasts an hour and dumps several inches of water will.

Soil that doesn't absorb moisture easily is a huge contributor. And if the area is denuded of vegetation by fire, timber harvest, or other land-clearing operations, the problem is made worse. There is literally no region that is safe from the possibility of flash flood—deserts, mountains, and plains are all vulnerable areas.

Flash floods are sneaky—they seem to come out of nowhere. There could be a violent thunderstorm taking place farther back in the mountains or on a distant desert plateau—a downpour might be hitting the rocky ground and funneling runoff into a drainage that eventually leads to your location. You might have no clue a deadly flash flood is roaring toward you like a liquid freight train until you hear the approaching rumble, feel the ground tremble, and suddenly see a wall of water carrying trees and boulders through your camp.

So you need to have a survival plan, just in case you find yourself in a place like Big Thompson Canyon on the wrong day.

Prevention

▶ Listen to the weather forecast before heading out. If the forecast talks about unstable air, thunderstorms, or other violent weather, don't go into places where a flash flood might catch you.

▶ Periodically monitor the NOAA Weather Radio station in your area to learn if there are weather events taking place that will affect you. You can buy a fairly inexpensive and compact, battery-operated weather radio at places like Radio Shack.

▶ If flood advisories, warnings, or watches are issued, heed them.

▶ When you arrive in camp, look the situation over and imagine what the place would look like if it were suddenly swept by a 30-foot wall of water (yes, they get that big). Choose a campsite that is above the danger zone. Don't camp in lowlands or even in a minor drainage.

Surviving a Flash Flood

▶ Get to higher ground immediately. The water level might rise incredibly fast.

▶ Don't stop to gather up your equipment. Saving your life (and the lives of others) is more important than saving your vehicle or other gear.

▶ If you are trapped by floodwaters that are surrounding your vehicle, get out immediately and make your way to higher ground. It takes only two feet of water to sweep away a vehicle, and it will roll and tumble and smash as it is swept downstream. A vehicle is not a safe place to be. Approximately half of flood-related drownings are vehicle related.

▶ Do not attempt to drive across a flooded road. What you can't see is that the roadway might have been ripped up by the rushing water, leaving a hole that will swallow your vehicle.

If you recognize the potential danger of a flash flood, take steps to keep yourself, your friends, and loved ones safe during your travels and camping trips.

Epilogue

SITUATIONAL AWARENESS

A guy steps out of his tent, yawns, and stretches into the pink dawn, watching his breath form a small cloud as he exhales. Suddenly, a bear rises from the bushes and charges across the clearing, tearing our camper right out of his pajamas. At first glance, that sounds like a mishap that was unavoidable. It certainly wasn't caused by anything the camper did—right?

But accidents don't just happen. Survival situations don't just happen. There is always a root cause for every outcome. In many instances, some decision, somewhere along the line, leads to a set of circumstances that eventually evolves into the consequences (either good or bad) related to the situation.

I am not saying that people intentionally get themselves into hot water, nor that they deserve what happens when problems arise. I've seen my own share of uncomfortable consequences that could have been prevented, had I (or someone else) made different decisions. Stuff happens. But lots of that kind of stuff can be prevented, if we learn to pay attention to what's going on around us.

Let's have a look at the unfortunate situation above, to see if we can identify some root causes and decisions that led to these unpleasant consequences.

- The man chose to go camping. Hey, good decision, but a decision none-theless, so we can't say this was inconsequential.
- The man chose where to camp, perhaps understanding that this was bear country. But then maybe not. Decisions based on ignorance or incomplete understanding might be deemed innocent, but they can still lead to unfortunate consequences.
- After last night's supper, the unburnables were gathered and stuffed in a plastic trash bag, ready to be hauled out and disposed of later. This was a decision about food/trash etiquette. A scrap of tinfoil with the hint of last night's supper on it is all it takes to invite unwelcome company into camp.
- It was his decision, although probably not consciously made, to exit the tent with less than complete awareness of what was going on outside.

We could go on, but hopefully you see the pattern. Decisions, even those we aren't intending to make, contribute to final outcomes. Nothing just happens. Again, this is not an attempt to fix blame. You step left instead of right and—Wham!—a rattlesnake strikes your calf from behind a log. Who is to blame? Well, blame isn't the name of this game—the name of this game is *situational awareness*, a technique that is valuable in the prevention of mishaps.

Situational awareness is nothing more than being aware of what's going on around you all the time. If you're aware that rattlesnakes like to hide in the shade where they feel safe, and if you are aware that you are in rattlesnake country, then you can make decisions to avoid "snaky" places and take other measures to reduce the chances of a nasty encounter.

But it isn't just about bears and rattlesnakes. It might be running out of gas, food, propane, or firewood. It might be about a lost child, or getting lost yourself, or getting sick from drinking foul water, or a family mutiny caused by failure to plan camp duties in advance. It's about a lot of things, all of which involve decisions that lead to consequences of one nature or another.

In order to put situational awareness to work, it's necessary to gather a lot of pertinent information and be able to answer some fundamental questions. Here's a bit of a checklist to get you started. It is by no means complete, because you will need to customize your own checklist to fit your situation.

WHERE ARE WE GOING?

▶ Are there natural predators in the area? If so, what are their habits? What is proper behavior to avoid confrontations?

▶ Are there seasonal hazards? (extreme heat, cold, flood, avalanche, etc.)

▶ Are there other dangers? (tides, waves, poisonous spiders, snakes, disease-bearing insects, killer bees, fire ants, etc.)

▶ Will we need passports or photo IDs and birth certificates?

▶ Do we need special permits?

▶ Are inoculations required?

▶ Is it recommended that we take precautions for water purification or that we avoid certain foods?

WHEN ARE WE GOING?

▶ Is it hunting season?

▶ Is it tornado season?

▶ Is it hurricane season?

▶ Is this the season and region that baby rattlesnakes are born?

▶ Do we have to travel through rush-hour traffic?

▶ What is the long-term weather forecast?

WHAT ARE WE GOING TO BE DOING?

▶ Are we adequately trained and equipped for special activities?

▶ Have we personally inspected and tested the equipment?

▶ If we get separated, can we maintain voice contact?

▶ Are we prepared to handle medical emergencies?

▶ Are we prepared to handle evacuation?

▶ Are we prepared to fight a vehicle fire or a runaway campfire?

WHO IS GOING?

▶ Does anyone have special medical or nutritional needs?

▶ Are there children who will require constant supervision?

▶ Is there a detailed plan about camp duties?

- How will we be traveling?
- Are we prepared to handle vehicle-related emergencies?
- Do we have maps for the route?
- Have we made reservations, where necessary?
- Do we have enough food and water for the trip?
- Do we have a cell phone so we can call for assistance?
- Do we have a PLB to summon search and rescue?
- Do we have enough money (are you kidding!)?
- Have we left a "flight plan" with relatives or friends?

HOW DOES EVERYBODY FEEL?

- Is anyone ill, or does anyone feel something coming on?
- Is anyone apprehensive about the trip?
- Is everyone well rested?
- Is anyone nursing an injury?

These questions might seem tedious and trivial, but answering them will lead to decisions that will, in turn, lead to consequences. Being aware of what is going on around you and the way the situation is evolving will help you identify and trap potential problems before they can become mishaps.

There is almost no place I would rather be than outdoors, but I have to admit that there have been times when I wanted to be anywhere other than the place outdoors where I was. Life in the wilds can be fantastic, or it can be miserable and frightening. Fortunately, the misery and fear can both be tempered through preparation and experience. The more wilderness miles you have under your belt, the easier it is for you to become physically, mentally, and emotionally strong enough to survive the challenges. Armed with sound survival knowledge and a modicum of good equipment, you have a greater chance of coming home alive and well.

Index

Page numbers followed by *f* indicate a figure.